# COTTAGES :
## THEIR PLANNING, DESIGN
## AND MATERIALS

A GROUP OF SIX COTTAGES AT ASHBY ST. LEDGERS. DESIGNED BY SIR EDWIN LUTYENS.

# COTTAGES:

## THEIR PLANNING, DESIGN
## AND MATERIALS

## By SIR LAWRENCE WEAVER
### K.B.E., F.S.A., Hon. A.R.I.B.A.

1926
LONDON:
COUNTRY LIFE,
20 TAVISTOCK STREET, COVENT GARDEN, W.C.2
NEW YORK: CHARLES SCRIBNER'S SONS

*First printed in 1926, being a third edition of the "'Country Life'
Book of Cottages," so greatly revised that a new title has been
given to it, in order to indicate the enlargement in the treatment
of the subject*

PRINTED IN GREAT BRITAIN

# PREFACE

WHEN the "'Country Life' Book of Cottages" was first published in March, 1913, I made some apology for adding to the already large literature on the subject, but claimed that there was room for a review of what has been done to produce types of true cottages, excluding the country houses costing thousands which masquerade under the name of cottages. With one or two exceptions, therefore, the cottages shown included none of more than eight rooms. At and below that limit most country types were shown, whether built for the rural labourer, the small holder, the estate servant, the clerk who lives outside the town, the "week-ender" or the people of moderate means and refined taste whose permanent home must be built with severe regard to economy.

The large new edition issued in 1919 included much new subject-matter, but in this, the third, edition, I have been drastic in cutting out much pre-war work in favour of the cottages which the post-war period has produced. I have also so expanded my references to suburban cottages and town planning in relation to them, and have introduced so large an amount of matter on the new materials and methods of construction now in use, that the title of the book has been altered also.

Less emphasis has been laid on details of building costs, because they cannot yet be said to be stabilized, and none can prophesy what will be their ultimate level when the shortage and consequent high cost of bricks have given place to normal supply, and when bricklayers and plasterers are to be secured in normal numbers (if ever). But without prophesying, I would counsel those intending to build not to multiply pre-war prices by less than $2\frac{1}{2}$ for some time to come. Even that may be optimistic. I have quoted from a few of the many reports of committees on housing, and I give their full names below should readers wish

vii

to seek for fuller details than can be included in a short review of a very large subject.

Report of the Departmental Committee of the Board of Agriculture on Buildings for Small Holdings : chairman, Mr. Christopher Turnor, 1913 [Cd. 6708] (The Turnor Small Holdings Report).

Report of the Advisory Committee of the Board of Agriculture on Rural Cottages : chairman, Mr. Christopher Turnor [1915, 1s. 6d.].

Report of the Committee of the Local Government Board to consider questions of building construction in connection with the provision of dwellings for the working classes : chairman, Sir Tudor Walters, 1918 [Cd. 9191] (The Tudor Walters Report).

First report of Women's Housing Sub-Committee of Advisory Council, Ministry of Reconstruction [Cd. 9166, 1s.] (Women's Committee).

Report of Departmental Committee on Building By-laws : chairman, Mr. Stephen Walsh, M.P. [Cd. 9213, 6d.].

Board of Agriculture Manual on the Equipment of Small Holdings.

I have to acknowledge the courteous help of scores of architect friends in supplying me with photographs and preparing plans for reproduction, and also of the Ministry of Agriculture and Fisheries in placing at my disposal a mass of material relating to the cottages built under the Land Settlement (Facilities) Act.

LAWRENCE WEAVER.

*March*, 1926.

# CONTENTS

## Chapter I

### INTRODUCTORY

## Chapter II

### THE PRE-WAR SEARCH FOR THE CHEAP COTTAGE

## Chapter III

### ACCOMMODATION AND PLANNING OF THE WORKMAN'S HOUSE

## Chapter IV

### CHOICE AND RIGHT USE OF MATERIALS

## Chapter V

### NOVEL METHODS OF CONSTRUCTING "SUBSIDY COTTAGES," 1925

# CHAPTER I

## INTRODUCTORY

IT is desirable to put in the forefront of this book the exact purpose of its compiling. A treatise on cottage building which sought to deal efficiently with all the problems of construction, and to give specifications and working drawings for all, or even for a few, of the manifold types of cottage illustrated in the following pages, would make a ponderous and costly volume. No attempt is made to give the reader that amount of information which would enable him to build a cottage with this book in his hand. The fact that cottages are among the smallest of buildings does not reduce the complexity of the architectural problems they raise ; it rather increases it. The designer who is bound by narrow limits of cost has to consider, not what elements of accommodation and features of equipment he can well provide, but what he can safely omit without falling below a reasonable standard of efficiency. The questions bound up in the successful design of cottages are different in character from those which belong to, say, the building of a big town house, but the skill and experience necessary are equal in degree though different in kind. The amateur is likely to be no more successful with the cottage than the town house when it comes to the actual facts of building. The present aim, therefore, is to set out some of these problems, and to show how various architects have succeeded in planning convenient and successful cottages, and how a number of methods of construction, alternative to brick, have been lately brought to a practical stage. It will be shown that cheap cottages do not mean ugly cottages ; that architectural amenity is, in fact, the outcome of skill rather than of money. This book will serve its purpose if it emphasizes the need to provide cottages of a sort that shall not disfigure the existing beauties of the countryside, and to

1

create a positive seemliness in all villages and suburbs, and if
it shows how that need can be met.

Thus far I have reprinted, with a few additional words,
what I wrote in the 1919 edition, but the situation of cottage-
building has changed very much for the worse since then, in
the matter of amenity.  Whatever may be said of the Addison
programme of cottage-building on which the Government was
embarking in that year, as to the financial burden it laid
upon the State, no one can quarrel with the town-planning and
architectural aspects of the scheme.  I am persuaded that the
housing student of the future will look back on the Addison
period with satisfaction and regret—satisfaction at the high
standard of design achieved, and regret that financial exigencies
compelled the authorities to slacken their control of housing
schemes launched under the Chamberlain and Wheatley Acts.

Still more depressing are the results which have followed the
complete lack of control of design in the case of private building.
In pre-war days the chief lament of the housing enthusiast was
concerned with the operation of building by-laws which controlled
the sizes of rooms, and forbade the use of various cheap materials.
Inevitably, no doubt, this control disappeared with the overwhelming pressure of the need for more houses of any sort, but
the housing enthusiast of to-day begins to sigh for its restoration.
Every one who loves the character of the English countryside
must be appalled by the rash of squalid little bungalows which
disfigures even remote beauty spots.  It is impossible to with-
hold sympathy from those people who must have a roof over
their heads and are driven to resort to all manner of cheap and
mean materials, in order that they may secure it at a cost within
their means.  It is difficult to imagine that public opinion will
ever allow the appointment of a body of ædiles furnished with
powers to forbid designs or materials which offend against a
reasonable standard of taste to be set up by some official body.
The only way of salvation is by educating public opinion, and
by drawing attention to inexpensive types of cottages which
are seemly.  That is the main function of this book.

I know there are still people who think that beauty lurks in
barge boards and little oriel windows and the quirks and tricks
of the pre-war speculative builder which can be catalogued as
" quaint," but their number is growing less.  The attempt at
prettiness has too long been the curse of architecture, the attempt
to capture the elusive beauty of the craftsmanship of past centuries in our day, when the men and the social organism of which
they were a part have passed into the limbo of history.

But the public taste has happily set steadily in a return to
eighteenth-century traditions, and we have the right to be

Georgian in our houses as in our loyalties. For the eighteenth century was the Age of Reason, and to that our architecture is returning.

With the Gothic Revival of the nineteenth century common sense departed. People wanted their houses served up like little abbeys on toast, and enthusiasts feared for their salvation if their kitchen windows lacked a pointed head. There is, perhaps, something inspiring about the very words "half-timber work" that gave to this way of building a peculiar sanctity even when half-timber meant a good deal less than half, for inch boards were often gravely nailed to nine-inch brick walls.

It was bad enough when these solemn follies were the religion of the architect more or less trained, but when they became the stock-in-trade of the imperfectly-informed jerry-builder, the disaster to the art of house design was complete.

Happily a new generation of architects had arisen when the garden city and garden suburb movement set alight the imagination of the large public which had hitherto regarded architecture as belonging only to the large houses of wealthy folk. At first Letchworth and Bournville, Port Sunlight and Hampstead clung to the mediæval notion of a village with the goose on the green, but that is passing.

The tragic cost of post-war building has had one supremely good result : it has driven architects to express the people's need for homes in the simplest terms. At the worst this has produced dullness—the spirit of Gower Street. At the best it has driven the designer to make his work succeed by qualities of sheer design, right proportion, good grouping, rhythm, and other intangibles which critics try to describe for the confusion of plain men.

Economy has brought us back, by the elimination of inessentials, to an art of common sense. At the same time the best of our architects have put the best of their skill into planning for comfort and health and not for appearances. They have taken counsel with the makers of grates and baths and sanitary dodges, so that economy and efficiency might be allied with seemly forms.

That is not to say that simple houses are easy to do. The plainer the house, the more need for those subtle differences which give a plain building that elusive quality that we call style for want of a better word. The public will get what it ought to want, when it has the wit to go to the architects who can give it.

Architecture is everybody's business because it is the one Art which affects everyone's eye and everyone's comfort. Carlyle said after passing Chelsea Hospital again and again that he

perceived it to be the work of a gentleman, and a better thing
was never said about Sir Christopher Wren.

It is that quality, compounded of dignity, modesty, urbanity,
and orderliness, that we want to see created in greater measure
in our domestic architecture.   We are on the way to it.   There
are architects in plenty who can give form to the conception.
It is for the public to see that they get the chance.

In order to make the information given as practical as possible,
the majority of the illustrations are photographs of actual buildings.   Cunningly-drawn perspective views of labourers' cottages
may make attractive pictures, but they are not so helpful as
plans and elevations.   What seems wanted in the case of the
smaller types of cottage is a record of fact, made up of plans,
photographs and (where they are available and informing)
ascertained costs of building.   To such a record the following
pages are devoted, but it is important to make one point clear
as to the prices which are given.   Since some of the examples
illustrated were built the cost of building has risen to an enormous
extent.   Cottages which are stated here to have been built for,
say, £150, a few years before the war, might have cost £180 or
£200 in the first half of 1914.   The present level of building
prices (I write in 1926) is likely to be maintained until the scarcity
of materials and of bricklayers and plasterers has been over-
taken, and not to fall materially even when that happy time
comes, if ever.   I am therefore leaving the prices of the pre-war
cottages as they were in the first edition published in 1913.   To
estimate the present cost of similar cottages it would be wise to
multiply by not less than $2\frac{1}{2}$.

My readers must make their own additions in accordance with
future fluctuations as well as they may.   All the figures quoted
in the following chapters must be considered in the light of this
fact, which must be squarely faced by those intending to build,
or the information given in the following chapters will be gravely
misleading.   The principal usefulness of the figures is in the
comparisons they afford as between different types of cottages.

In some cases the cost per cubic foot has been given in addition to the total cost.   This method of calculation has its good
points, but it is not safe as a basis of comparison.   Such comparisons are futile and misleading, the more so because a " cubic
foot cost " does not take into account the expenditure on foundations and interior fittings, which have no relation to the cubic
content of the house, and are the outcome of conditions over
which the designer has often little or no control.

No attempt is made to lay down detailed rules for the
planning of cottages, but I have quoted from the reports of
various Government Committees in support of general prin-

ciples and have given some examples of bad plans, so that the more obvious faults may be readily recognized. The reader is assumed to know what type of cottage most interests him, and to be able to pick it out from the many examples illustrated. The factors that determine what is the best plan for a cottage are so many and so various that anything like a code of rules is impossible. Success will come only from an independent examination of the conditions arising out of each site and the requirements of the people who will live in the cottage. It is sometimes supposed that money can be saved by going direct to a builder and asking him to prepare plans and an estimate for a cottage with the desired accommodation. No greater mistake can be made. Every one who has to do with cottages knows that only by severe economies have they ever been made to pay a moderate return, but a cheeseparing policy in the matter of professional advice is not likely to be successful. If the builder is also the designer, the thought and labour that have gone into the preparation of plans have to be paid for in the cost of the building. Though there may be in the accounts no separate item for designing, it is obvious that the charge will be there, wrapped up in something else. The standard remuneration payable to the architect is six per cent. on the cost of a building, but when this is less than £1,000 he is entitled to charge more. If we assume, however, that in consideration of doing other and larger work for the same client he will accept the six per cent. basis for, say, a £500 cottage, his fees will amount to £30, plus his travelling expenses in visiting the work in progress. Half of this six per cent. is for preparing plans and half for superintending the work. Unless the cottage is close by the architect's office or home, or, indeed, in any case, £30 is not an adequate remuneration for the time and trouble he will expend on it from first to last. When, however, two cottages or more are being built at the same time on neighbouring sites, the work falling on the architect is not increased in the same proportion, and is, therefore, not so unremunerative. When many cottages are to be built for a housing scheme reduced fees are payable in accordance with a special scale issued by the R.I.B.A. It must be remembered that half the architect's work, and the more tedious and exacting half, is to superintend the builder in his carrying out of the building contract. If, *but only if,* the builder is known to the owner as a man who will faithfully carry out his contract and supply all materials and labour in the letter and spirit of the drawings and specifications, superintendence by the architect can be dispensed with and half his charges saved. In the case of estate cottages, where the owner himself builds with the aid of a competent foreman, or has an estate agent with a practical knowledge of building, who can superintend a contractor, the architect need only be called in to prepare plans and specifications. The point to be emphasized is, that the building owner must first be satisfied that his plans and specifications are the work of a competent architect, who is both practical and artistic, who knows the needs and habits of cottage-folk, and yet has an eye for the unpretentious, gracious qualities that make an old cottage a delight to the eye. Very often the estate agent of a landowner has large experience as to the accommodation wanted in his district and as to the materials which can be most economically obtained, but lacks the power of design, by which alone his ideas can be shaped in a satisfactory way. In such cases it should always be possible for him to submit his preliminary drawings to a skilful architect for such amendment as may be necessary to give good architectural form to the scheme. This can generally be done without undue cost to the building owner. In the case of buildings of more importance than cottages, any such arrangement is greatly to be deprecated. The complete work should be put into the hands of an architect of experience and taste, and he should be left to carry out the scheme from start to finish. In the case of cottage work, some modification of approved practice is sometimes inevitable, owing to the small sums of money involved, and the possible remoteness of the cottage site, which may involve great waste of the architect's time in visiting it.

A word may be said about specifications, etc., though the manner of preparing these is for the decision of the architect employed. I mention them only because some building owners are anxious to have their contracts prepared in a very complete and businesslike manner, and this sometimes works out to their disadvantage.

It is not generally realized how frightened are some small country builders of giving a tender on a " bill of quantities " for small work such as cottages. This method is normal in town building, and contractors who do town work know what it means. Country builders, however, confronted with the formidable document setting out with full technical descriptions the details of the work, will sometimes quote as much as 40 per cent. more for some unimportant piece of work than they would do if they only had a drawing and a short specification before them. An apposite example may be taken from the Essex practice of pargetting. I once had occasion to ask a local bricklayer to estimate for the building of a small outhouse with brick walls plastered, and received his quotation. I had said nothing about treating the surface with the attractive " comb-work " enclosed in panels by flush beads on the face of the walls, which I wanted done. When I asked how much more this would be, my bricklayer friend replied, " Nothing ; that is all in with the plastering." I might, however, have given him a bill of quantities to price, which would have included items somewhat as follows :

    200 ft. run 1 in. quirk beading .   .   .   .   .   .
    2,400 ft. super zigzag surface ornament executed with iron comb

This would have been a faithful description of the work required, and such as a conscientious quantity surveyor might have used, but I am satisfied that the result would have been an extra item of at least £5. The moral of it is that the papers on which builders are asked to prepare their estimates should be as short and informal as is consistent with due security that the contract will be properly carried out. There is another and cognate difficulty which may be mentioned here. If a country builder is asked to tender for two pairs of cottages, one of the ugly, thoughtless and ill-planned type to which he is accustomed, and another involving not a pennyworth more of materials or labour, but modified to make it an attractive design, he is quite likely to quote a larger price for the more seemly cottage. This is due to sheer lethargy of mind. He does not examine the drawings with a view to seeing whether the more unusual plan involves any more actual cost, but makes the offhand assumption that what is novel must necessarily be difficult and expensive. In such cases the zealous architect, by painstaking explanations, may often convince him that his fears are groundless, but such explanations have to be made. The failure to make them will often lead to the new and better design being abandoned in favour of the old and bad one, a circumstance which simply drives good housing into a hopeless backwater and perpetuates ugliness and incompetence. The experience of those who are concerned to restore the vitality of local building traditions goes to show that the country builder, when invited to quote for cottages, however simple in design and construction, must be handled carefully to prevent him taking fright at a simple artistic quality which, unhappily, appeals to him as a mysterious novelty.

Most of the available space in this book is given to new cottages ; but the right reparation of old ones is so important that it is made the subject of a separate chapter.

It is important because the saving of an old building is like the preservation of an historical document. The social history of our land is written as clearly in its ancient humble dwellings, as is its political history in keep and city wall.

At this crisis of the housing of the people it is important because intelligent repair, instead of careless demolition, conserves the materials of which there is so serious a shortage.  But the preservation of precious little bits of our building history must not be the excuse for stereotyping unhealthy or cramped accommodation.  Very often a pair of old cottages provides no more floor space and cubic space than is proper for a single cottage, and should be converted into one.  Many a single cottage can be made a decent habitation by tacking on a little wing or even a single storey back addition, but it is very desirable that even such small works shall be supervised by architects who have a feeling for the old craftsmanship and judgment in devising additions in the same spirit.

Since the day when Coleridge wrote rather bitterly of the " cottage of gentility " with its double coach-house, the word " cottage " has been widely used to embrace houses of affectedly small pretension but often costing thousands.  Throughout this book " cottage " retains its plain meaning of " a dwelling house of small size and humble character."

In order to simplify references in the text, the name of the architect is given under each illustration.

# CHAPTER II

## THE PRE-WAR SEARCH FOR THE CHEAP COTTAGE

THE LETCHWORTH EXHIBITION—MR. ST. LOE STRACHEY'S ATTEMPTS—
AND MR. ARNOLD MITCHELL'S—" COUNTRY LIFE "COMPETITION FOR
RURAL COTTAGES—STANDARDS OF ACCOMMODATION—MR. HARVEY'S
SOLUTION FOR MR CHRISTOPHER TURNOR

FOR many years before the war the cheap cottage was the
" King Charles' head " of everyday architecture, and
during the first fourteen years of the century there were many
spirited and well-organized efforts to prove that a reasonable
habitation could be built for £150, exclusive of site. Such a
cost enabled the cottage to be let at between 3s. 6d. and 4s.,
gave a reasonable return on the money invested, and allowed
a small sum annually for repairs.

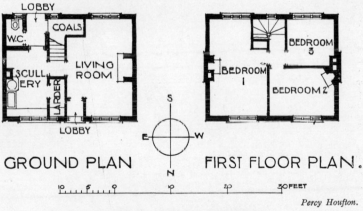

*Percy Houfton.*

I.—PRIZE COTTAGE, LETCHWORTH.

The establishment of a garden city at Letchworth gave opportunity for a largely supported competition on practical lines, and
if the result was to gather a considerable number of cottages
which were freakish or unsatisfactory in design or material, it
nevertheless did much to clear the air.

9

The first prize was awarded to Mr. Percy Houfton, and while his cottage technically fulfilled the conditions of the competition, none knew better than both the judges and Mr. Houfton that the conditions were abnormal and could not be repeated in any ordinary locality. Under ordinary commercial conditions Mr. Houfton did not produce the same cottage before the war for

Percy Houfton.

2.—PRIZE COTTAGE, LETCHWORTH.

less than £250 singly or £400 for a pair. The plans and a photograph of Mr. Houfton's cottage are reproduced in Figs. 1 and 2. The accommodation provided was a living-room, a working kitchen, and three bedrooms. The walls were of brick rough-cast and the woodwork of deal.

Another interesting contribution to the problem was made by Mr. St. Loe Strachey, of the *Spectator*, to whom a debt of gratitude is due for his persistent efforts in the cause of rural housing.

His builder did not use bricks for the walls for the pair of cottages he built on Merrow Down, but concrete blocks, 18 in. by 9 in. by 9 in. As these have a cubic content equivalent to about twelve ordinary bricks, Mr. Strachey claimed that they could be laid more rapidly, and probably he was correct, but the saving in labour is insignificant. Concrete blocks are certainly cheaper as material, where gravel is available on the site or near by and only the Portland cement needs to be hauled from the nearest station. The actual making of the blocks is an easy matter. There are plenty of simple and inexpensive hand-machines on the market which can be operated by wholly unskilled labour. The partition walls are built of thinner blocks, and only the living-rooms need to be plastered, for the surface of the blocks themselves is reasonably smooth.

As will be seen from Fig. 3, the roofs are pantiled, and the cottages, though not beautiful, are not unpleasant in appearance.

Mr. Strachey built his pair of cottages for £300 ; but even at a time of low costs, pre-war, he scarcely proved his claim that £300 was a possible price for a pair of cottages, built in solid fireproof materials. Some time later, he succeeded in putting up for £150 a single weather-boarded cottage, shown in Fig. 51.

Mr. Strachey's next move towards an inexpensive solution of the rural housing problem was to issue a challenge to architects which was taken up by Mr. Arnold Mitchell, who in October, 1913, published in *The Times* and the *Spectator* particulars of a pair of cottages built at Merrow for £220. The sum of £110 for a

3.—MR. ST. LOE STRACHEY'S COTTAGES.

cottage (even if it were trebled to £330 by war increases in cost) is so challenging, that it is desirable to examine closely the planning, construction and equipment of the cottage as built (Figs. 4 to 6). The plans were made from a survey of the cottage as built and may be inaccurate in one or two trivial details, but for the purposes of this discussion they can be regarded as correct.

The following criticisms are based mainly on the point that the accommodation is below what is necessary for health and comfort.

The entrance door on the west side opens directly into the living-room, and the fireplace is between this door and the doors to the scullery and staircase. The cottager sitting by his fireside would therefore always be in a draught. The size of this room is 140 square feet. It is 7 ft. 5 in. in height to the under side of the joists and 8 ft. to the floors boards above. This gives a cubic content of 1,112 cubic feet, after deducting space occupied by joists, as against 1,440 cubic feet, which should be the minimum. A door in the south-east corner of the room leads to the scullery, which contains a fireplace, a copper, a sink, and, under the stairs, a tiny coal-cellar which can scarcely house more than 2 cwt. There is an outer door to the scullery, giving access to the earth closet. This has a separate door to the outside. It is unpleasantly close to the larder window, and there is only a very thin partition between the two. Returning to the living-room, we find at the north-west corner a door to a little room 9 ft. 2 in. by 8 ft. 1½ in., which has a fireplace. This is available as a small parlour, but would be more often used as a third

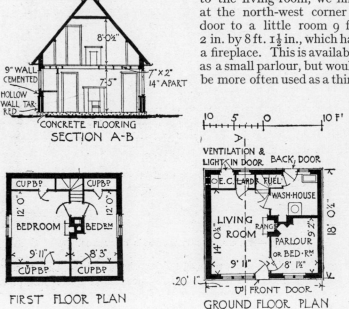

4.—PLANS AND SECTION OF THE MITCHELL COTTAGE.

bedroom. Its floor space contains 67 square feet, and its cubic content is 530 cubic feet. Upstairs are two bedrooms. In the larger the slope of the roof begins 4 ft. 6 in. from the floor level. Its cubic content is 832 ft., which is quite insufficient for two adults, say husband and wife, but enough for one adult and one child under ten. The second bedroom has a floor area of

77 square feet and a cubic content of 550 cubic feet, which is only suitable for one adult or two children under ten. The dimensions of the best bedroom are much below what is known as the Letchworth standard of 1,070 cubic feet, which is itself too low. Twelve hundred cubic feet should be regarded as the irreducible minimum for the health of a married couple and infant.

5.—MR. ARNOLD MITCHELL'S PRE-WAR £110 COTTAGE : FRONT VIEW.

The foundation is a layer of cement concrete, which, with a rendering of cement, forms the floor surface downstairs. The walls are 11 in. with cavity, and tarred for a height of 2 ft. 6 in., and 9 in. solid above, cemented and whitewashed. The roof begins at the first floor level and is covered with pantiles. The first floor consists of flooring boards laid direct on the joists, with no ceiling beneath. The fireplaces in such cottages must necessarily be cheap, but a 2 ft. closed range in the kitchen would be " gey ill " to live with and cook by.

*The Times* article stated that the cottage, excluding land, cost £110. Its total cubic content (measured outside the walls and from below the 6 in. of concrete on the ground to half-way up the roof) works out at 5,315 cubic feet, which made the cubic foot price a shade under fivepence. This was, after all,

6.—THE £110 COTTAGE : BACK VIEW.

in no way a remarkable figure for pre-war cottages, and it meant that the low price of £110 had been achieved by the simple process of cutting down accommodation and equipment. The facts are shown by printing in parallel columns the floor areas and cubic contents of the Merrow cottage and the cottage recommended by the Turnor Small Holdings Committee which became Schedule I, given on page 17.

| | Mr. Mitchell's Cottage at Merrow. | | Minimum accommodation recommended by Small Holdings Committee. | |
|---|---|---|---|---|
| | Superficial Area. | Cubic Content. | Superficial Area. | Cubic Content. |
| Living-room . . . . | 135 | 1,112 | 180 | 1,440 |
| Scullery . . . . . | 56 | 448 | 80 | 640 |
| Larder . . . . . . | 8 | 64 | 24 | 192 |
| Bedroom—1 . . . . | 125 | 832 | 150 | 1,200 |
| Do. 2 . . . . | 77 | 550 | 100 | 800 |
| Do. 3 . . . . | 67 | 530 | 65 | 520 |
| Total . . . | 468 | 3,536 | 599 | 4,792 |

But Mr. St. Loe Strachey went farther and asked for another cottage to cost £110 only—to be met by Mr. Clough Williams-Ellis with a cottage on Merrow Common, which cost a hundred guineas. The accommodation as shown by the plans (Figs. 7 and 8) is rather in excess of Schedule I (page 17), and the planning is very compact without being ideal: The low cost is due to the nature of the structure, which is lath and plaster, with slated roof.

Fig. 8 shows that the cottage is of a seemly appearance, and after five years' occupation by a small-holder, his wife and six children, it needed no repairs except the replacement of a broken slate.

Mr. Williams-Ellis answered the challenge cleverly, but he does not himself claim lath and plaster as a solution of the housing problem, and I have observed that on his own estate he builds cottages of extreme solidity at a high first cost, well knowing that course to be the most economical in the long run.

With the present shortage of plasterers a lath-and-plaster cottage has ceased to be practical politics, except for a big housing scheme which justifies the use of a cement-gun for the plastering.

The most comprehensive effort to secure a better standard of cottage design with regard alike to economic value, seemliness and good planning, was the *Country Life* National Competition held in 1914. The immediate cause of this enterprise was a considerable measure of public indignation in 1913 arising out of the destruction by a famous College of a beautiful cottage and its replacement by a building of unusual ugliness. This came at a time when rural housing was being widely discussed and there were many advocates of the building of cheap standardized cottages, unregardful of the destruction of England's beauty that would follow their scattering over the country-side. A leader in *Country Life* was followed by a vigorous correspondence, contributed by many well-known public men. The general view was summed up in a letter by the late Lord Curzon, which ran:

" It would be a national tragedy if these old buildings were to be replaced by a new type of standardized cottage, dumped down either singly or—still worse—in rows like a lot of band-boxes, or canisters, or dog-kennels. *The best way to prevent such a catastrophe seems to me to lie in the preparation of plans, sketches and models of cottages of different materials and styles, suitable to differences of locality, climate and surroundings, which could be erected at moderate prices.*"

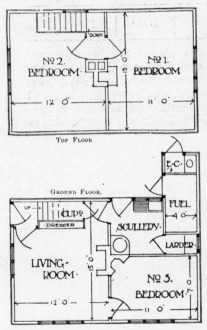

Top Floor

Ground Floor.

7.—PRE-WAR HUNDRED GUINEAS COTTAGE.

Lord Curzon's suggestion that *Country Life* should undertake this important work was justified by the results of the Competition which grew out of it.

The conditions were drawn with a view to bringing out the traditional differences of design which exist in different counties, due to local variations in the materials available, and to the influence of local habits of life, climate, and that impalpable but real factor, *genius loci*.

Eighteen representative landowners in Great Britain agreed to build a pair of cottages from the design awarded first prize for their local type. Unhappily the outbreak of war caused the construction of many of them to be postponed, but those that were built are illustrated in later pages, and justify the effort that was made to establish not only local character in cottage-building but also a high standard in planning and accommodation.

In 1914, as well as since, economic considerations were arrayed in battle against the comfort of the rural labourer. Mr. Christopher Turnor's Small Holdings Committee had laid down two minimum standards of accommodation, one for the small-holder's cottage, a reasonable minimum, and another, more restricted,

*Clough Williams-Ellis.*

8.—PRE-WAR HUNDRED GUINEAS COTTAGE : MERROW.

for the rural labourer, which may be called the irreducible minimum. These are given in the table below.

It was left to each landowner who agreed to build his local type to choose whether Schedule I or Schedule II should be set

| | SCHEDULE I. | | SCHEDULE II. | |
|---|---|---|---|---|
| | Dimensions recommended as a minimum (from Section 17 of Small Holdings Committee Report). | | Dimensions to be regarded as the irreducible minimum (from Section 175 of Small Holdings Committee Report). | |
| | Floor Areas. | Cubic Contents. | Floor Areas. | Cubic Contents. |
| Living-room or kitchen . | 180 | 1,440 | 165 | 1,320 |
| Scullery . . . . . | 80 | 640 | 65 | 520 |
| Larder or pantry . . . | 24 | | 18 | |
| Bedroom—1 . . . | 150 | 1,200 | 144 | 1,152 |
| Do.   2   . . . | 100 | 800 | 100 | 800 |
| Do.   3   . . . | 65 | 520 | 65 | 520 |

C

to the competitors.  Mr. Christopher Turnor asked that competitors should endeavour to achieve Schedule II within the cost of £250 the pair.  In this chapter I deal only with the last example. Fig. 9 shows the drawings by Mr. W. Alex. Harvey and Mr.

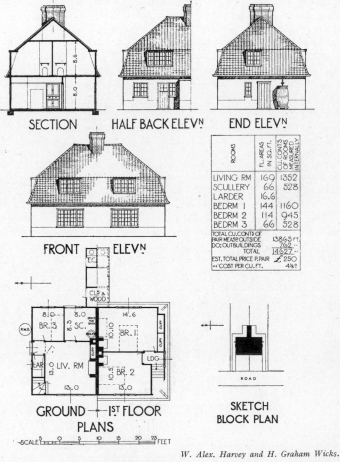

SECTION      HALF BACK ELEV.ᴺ      END ELEV.ᴺ

FRONT      ELEV.ᴺ

| ROOMS | FL. AREAS IN SQ. FT. | CU. CONTS OF ROOMS MEASURED INTERNALLY |
|---|---|---|
| LIVING RM | 169 | 1352 |
| SCULLERY | 66 | 528 |
| LARDER | 16.6 | |
| BEDRM 1 | 144 | 1160 |
| BEDRM 2 | 114 | 945 |
| BEDRM 3 | 66 | 528 |
| TOTAL CU. CONTS OF PAIR MEAS.ᴰ OUTSIDE | | 13865 FT. |
| DO. OUTBUILDINGS | | 762 ·· |
| TOTAL | | 14627 ·· |
| EST. TOTAL PRICE P. PAIR | | £250 |
| ·· COST PER CU. FT. | | 4½ᴰ |

GROUND ─┬─ 1ˢᵀ FLOOR
PLANS

SCALE ⊢⊣⊢⊣⊢⊣ FEET

SKETCH
BLOCK PLAN

*W. Alex. Harvey and H. Graham Wicks.*

9.—MR. CHRISTOPHER TURNOR'S PAIR.

H. Graham Wicks, which secured the first prize, and Fig. 10 illustrates the pair of cottages as built near Grantham, South Lincolnshire.  Some of the larger cottages are described in later pages.

A glance at the accompanying plan shows that extreme simplification in the disposition of the rooms has been secured without loss of comfort. The scullery is conveniently placed with reference to a kitchen-living-room of good size and convenient proportions. The third bedroom is downstairs, as is inevitable in the smallest type of cottage, but it opens from an entrance lobby inside the front door. The staircase rises from the corner of the living-room and not from a separate lobby, and although this is not ideal, it means a saving of cost. Both the upstairs bedrooms are of good size, and indeed No. 2 is 14 ft. larger in floor area than Schedule II demands. Coals, wood and the E.C. are provided in a back addition, so arranged that the E.C. is 10 ft. from the main block. The walls are carried up to the sill level of the first-floor windows, and almost the whole of the first-floor rooms is consequently in the roof. There are six dormer windows, but of very inexpensive construction, and a single chimney-stack serves all the rooms in the pair except the downstairs bedroom. The appearance is thoroughly satisfactory, and the cottages would look well in any district where pantiles are employed, which means a considerable proportion of England and Scotland. We come now to the question of construction. Mr. Harvey proposed to build the walls and the floor of reinforced concrete. The thin walls that would have been obtained on this system would have reduced the total content of the pair of cottages with their outbuildings to the low total of 14,627 cubic feet, which, at 4½d. per cubic foot, represents £250. It was, however, thought wiser to build in ordinary brickwork, and this added 1,800 cubic feet to the pair of cottages, which, at the same price per cubic foot, meant an extra of £31, making £281 per pair in all.

It remains only to give Mr. Christopher Turnor's own opinion on the pair as built and on their cost, given to me in September, 1916.

" When I asked you to set down so low a sum as £250 the pair in the conditions of the competition, it was not with any very strong hope that a pair of thoroughly sound cottages could be done at the price. That I actually paid £350 16s. 7d. is partly my own fault ; £30 17s. 11d. was absorbed by the use of very attractive buff bricks and hand-made tiles, which add much to the architectural charm of the cottages, but nothing to their efficiency as homes. One has to suffer in pocket sometimes for the determination to preserve local colour. I have not got my cottages at £125 each, but they are well planned and built, very popular with their tenants. and an ornament rather than an eyesore."

If it should be said that I have filled unnecessary pages with records of pre-war experimental cottages, of which some are already out of date, my reply would be that it is important to lay stress on the recent sudden rise in the standard of comfort, and on the probability that it will rise still more rapidly during the next fifty years. Cottages should be financed and built

10.—MR. CHRISTOPHER TURNOR'S " COUNTRY LIFE " COTTAGES

to last eighty years at least, and we need to look at the problem with some sense of its history as well as of its future development.

At the beginning of the last century landowners were content to provide, for their labourers, homes, which we now think incredibly bad, but they satisfied them. In 1805 one Joseph Gandy, an architect sufficiently distinguished in his day to become an Associate of the Royal Academy, published a volume of designs called *The Rural Architect*, and this book illuminates the ideas of his day. A gardener's cottage is illustrated estimated to cost £90, and containing two rooms only, a kitchen-living-room, 9 ft. 9 in. by 14 ft., and a bedroom 9 ft. 9 in. by 8 ft., both only 7 ft. high. A double cottage for a labourer, who also was to work indoors (presumably at some rural handicraft, like basket-making), contains a kitchen 10 ft. 3 in. by 13 ft., a workroom 13 ft. by 16 ft., and a bedroom 8 ft. by 16 ft., and was estimated to cost £150, the rooms being 9 ft. high.

If we compare these roughly with Mr. Harvey's cottages on the basis of superficial area of rooms provided, we find that Gandy, despite his distinctions, provided in 1805 only about 470 superficial feet of floor space for £150, whereas in 1916 Mr. Harvey could have provided the grandson of Gandy's client with 725 superficial feet at the same cost. The advocate of "the good old times" and all that was done in them cannot therefore say that modern architectural skill has fallen behind that of our forefathers, and it is a fortunate thing in the interests of a general decency of life that nobody now proposes to build cottages with a single bedroom to take the labourer and his family.

By the same token, let us beware of regarding the five-roomed cottage of to-day as the last word in the problem of housing the working man. A writer of cottage literature in 2026 may refer to this book as an amazing record of the five-roomed squalor with which England was satisfied a hundred years before.

# CHAPTER III

## ACCOMMODATION AND PLANNING OF THE WORKMAN'S HOUSE

The Parlour Question—Kitchen and Scullery—The Downstairs
Bedroom—Women's Views on Bedrooms—The Bath—Common
Defects in Planning—Bungalows *v.* Two-Storey Cottages

ON page 17 are given two schedules of accommodation with
sizes of rooms, which have been accepted during the last
few years as reasonable minimum standards, but neither includes
a parlour, and the most debatable question is whether this should
be regarded as an essential feature of all new cottages. Until
the war I had regarded it as extremely desirable, but generally
unattainable on the score of cost. It is still unattainable, but
no Housing Policy can be regarded as ideal unless a parlour
is provided in all new cottages, not because all cottages need
one, but because so few existing dwellings have them that it
is only by building none but parlour cottages that a reasonable
average will be secured. The Tudor Walters Committee have no
doubts on the point, and I am in full agreement with their view
(expressed in paragraph 86 of their report).

" The desire for the parlour or third room is remarkably widespread
both among urban and rural workers. The provision of a living-room of
sufficient size, and of a scullery so equipped as to relieve the living-room of
cooking and other such work goes some way to meet the wishes of many
of the tenants, particularly in view of the extra rent which the provision
of a parlour must involve ; nevertheless it is the parlour which the majority
desire. Numbers of individual tenants would undoubtedly be willing to
sacrifice the size of the living-room and scullery in order to secure the
parlour ; some would even be willing to adopt the old type of house with
combined living-room and scullery, in order that the second room might
be retained as a parlour. We were struck by the fact that none of those
who spoke on behalf of either working men or women regarded such alternatives as desirable ; and while they were emphatic as to the need of the
addition of a small parlour, they were equally emphatic that the parlour
should not be given at the expense of the necessary accommodation and
area of the living-room and scullery, but should either be given in addition
to these or omitted altogether.

" Such witnesses state that the parlour is needed to enable the older
members of the family to hold social intercourse with their friends without
interruption from the children, that it is required in cases of sickness in

22

the house, as a quiet room for convalescent members of the family, or for any who may be suffering from a long-continued illness or weakness ; that it is needed for the youth of the family in order that they may meet their friends ; that it is generally required for home lessons by the children of school age, or for similar work of study, serious reading, or writing, on the part of any member of the family ; that it is also needed for occasional visitors whom it may not be convenient to interview in the living-room in the presence of the whole family.  It will be seen from these instances that considerable importance is attached to the provision of a parlour, and that the difficulties arising from the absence of one are only partially met by transferring cooking and other similar work from the living-room to the scullery, and by increasing the size of the scullery so that it may occasionally be used as a second room.

" We consider, therefore, that whenever possible a parlour should be provided and that, in all schemes, a large proportion of houses having parlours should be included.  In view of the higher standard of accommodation likely to be demanded, and having regard to the fact that well-built houses may last far beyond the building loan period of sixty years, we are convinced that the provision of a parlour will in the long run prove to be conducive to economy.  We do not, however, consider that the parlour should be secured by cutting down the desirable minimum sizes of the living-room, scullery, or other essential parts of the house, and, where it is not possible to provide it except in this way, we recommend that it be omitted."

Our desperate desire in 1926 to get any sort of cottage makes this 1918 Report read very optimistically, but I am thankful that the Addison policy was based on it, for it at least produced a considerable number of parlour cottages and raised the average.

It may be added that although the Fisher Education Act, with its provision of continuation schools which young people were to attend up to the age of eighteen, has been put into abeyance in the interests of economy, it will come into force some day, and will then create a new and urgent need for parlours.  How can serious study be done in a common living-room where the rest of the family are talking or busy with domestic duties ?

Nor must it be forgotten that working people are increasingly taking part in social and political activities, and that they need a room in which they can confer with their friends on such matters.  It is true that the provision of a fire in the parlour is a difficulty, both on account of the extra labour involved and the cost of coal, but with a proper standard of wages this will be overcome, sooner or later, and I refuse to take a pessimistic view of the long future, however great our employment difficulties to-day.  In all such questions " sooner or later " counts, because we are now going to provide houses to last a century, and the new buildings ought, where possible, to be in advance of present needs rather than behind them or just level with them.

The old argument that parlours are a needless expense because cottagers use them only as a museum for useless furniture, wax flowers and wool mats may surely now be given decent burial, but even if it were true, the instinct is not unsound. The desire for wool mats is an embryonic appreciation of a higher standard of living and of the place of art in the home. Given the means of gratifying those instincts, their fit exercise will follow with education. Without the means, and the parlour with its possibilities provides the means, there can be small development in the right direction.

If then the parlour be accepted as a normal feature of the working-class home, how are the kitchen living-room and scullery to be equipped and used ? The Tudor Walters Committee lay stress on the desire of working class occupants to banish from the kitchen the dirty work, and especially the cooking of meals. The Report goes on as follows :

" For this reason the plan of house which has been so common in the past in many parts of the country, having downstairs a front parlour and a back kitchen and living-room combined, in which are situated the cooking-range, the sink, and often the copper, is now out of date. The tendency is to require a scullery in which cooking, washing up and all other similar work is carried on. The kitchen becomes the living-room in the ordinary sense, which may be kept for use as a sitting-room, as a meal-room, and for the cleaner activities of the family. The older plan of arranging the living-room to serve also as a cooking-room simplified matters ; one fire served all purposes, thus saving labour and cost of fuel. In many districts this custom is still common and will continue for some time to be followed, particularly in rural areas and in houses where, in addition to the scullery, a parlour is provided. It is evident, however, that a steady tendency is at work to eliminate the cooking from the living-room. Looking to the future, this should be taken into account in planning and equipping new houses. The difficulty of the two fires is partially overcome, in districts where gas for cooking is available at reasonable cost, by placing a gas cooker in the scullery. In that case a modified form of fire is sometimes used in the living-room, the grate having an open fire, but at the same time having a little oven and a small hob with which minor cooking operations can be carried out ; such types of stoves are very popular and are made in different forms. Where gas is not available, it is a common custom to have a cooking-range in the scullery ; the fire in the living-room is still used for part of the cooking, but this arrangement involves the use of two fires on most days during the winter months.

" There can be no doubt that in houses having no third room or parlour the enlargement of the scullery is somewhat dangerous, as many tenants would live mainly in the scullery and keep the large living-room as a parlour. This danger was pointed out by some of the working-class witnesses, although they quite realized the full convenience of the extra space to those who would use the rooms properly. Perhaps too much weight should not be given to the danger of improper use of the rooms, in view of the strongly-marked tendency of working-class families to live in the living-room and to confine the cooking, etc., to the scullery."

The Women's Housing Committee also claimed that the scullery should be the working centre of the house. They demanded a " regular and efficient hot-water supply as a *sine qua non*," but this will generally be impracticable in rural cottages and certainly costly in all cottages. What is reasonable is that the bath should have hot water laid on from the range, to prevent the need of carrying it from copper or side boiler.

The tendency to use the scullery as a living-room can partly be overcome by skill of planning. The aim should be to make the scullery a workroom pure and simple, and so to dispose the working fixtures and also the doors that it becomes impracticable to provide a table at which the household can sit.

In writing so far of a parlour I have referred to a third room on the ground floor in cottages which provide three bedrooms upstairs.

In the cheapest form of cottage, e.g. Mr. Christopher Turnor's shown in Figs. 9 and 10, there is a third ground-floor room with two upstairs bedrooms, but in this case the third room is theoretically intended for use as a bedroom. It has, however, rarely been so employed in the past.

The especial objection to a downstairs bedroom is that the temptation to the cottager to use it as a parlour, and to crowd his whole family into the two upstairs bedrooms, is rarely resisted. A well-known landowner who has given particular attention to rural housing on his estates made a census of the habits of twenty-five families living in cottages with a downstairs " bedroom." In only four cases did he find that this room was used as a bedroom. In one the occupant was a cripple who was unable to get upstairs ; in a second there was a parlour in addition to the bedroom ; in only two, therefore, out of twenty-three did the family use the accommodation provided in the way it was intended. Another landowner with whom I have discussed this question was on the side of the downstairs bedroom, on the ground that there is often a bed-ridden person who cannot get upstairs, and would be cut off from the family life if there were no ground-floor bedroom.

With regard to the total number of bedrooms in new cottages, it is most desirable to regard three as the minimum. There are already two-bedroom cottages in excess, and none should be provided except in new districts. At the other end of the scale it is important to provide some cottages for large families with four bedrooms. The fourth can be an attic room above the first floor, or be arranged on the first floor if the downstairs rooms are a good size and if the bathroom is downstairs. In blocks of four with a central archway through to the back gardens, the space above the arch provides for a fourth room in one or two cottages.

The Women's Housing Committee asked that " no bedroom should be too small to contain two adults, children over ten

being counted as adults." This is the sort of demand that makes
the practical man despair, as it would mean no bedroom with a
floor area of less than 125 super feet. The Tudor Walters
Committee approved of one bedroom out of three being of 65
super feet, i.e. for one person, and that seems common sense.
To maintain a minimum area of 125 feet would defeat all efforts
at economy, would often give more bedroom space than is
necessary, and would drive the architect either to make the living-
rooms downstairs unduly large, or to omit the third bedroom
altogether.

As to the bath, it is no longer necessary to argue the need of
one. No one believes now that the working classes prefer to
keep coal or potatoes in it. As to the placing of it, I quote
again from the Tudor Walters Report (paragraphs 118–19) :

" When the bath was first introduced into the smaller types of cottages,
reasons of economy suggested that it might be placed in the scullery.
Water and drainage were both available there at the minimum cost ; and
the copper could be used to provide hot water without the introduction
of any circulating system. Baths so placed have proved to be a very
great boon, and many tenants who have had experience of the bath in
the scullery have little fault to find with the arrangement. Nevertheless,
there are obvious drawbacks, and these have been increased where the
custom of cooking in the scullery instead of the living-room has grown.
In such cases the difficulty of keeping the scullery shut whenever any
member of the family wants to bathe is much greater. With many types
of plan the closing of the scullery involves cutting off the living-room
from access to the larder, coal-store and back door. Working-class witnesses, both men and women, and those who spoke for them, were vigorous
in their objection to the arrangement, and we consider that it can no
longer be regarded as entirely satisfactory : it should particularly be avoided
where the scullery is used for the preparation and cooking of meals, or
where the closing of the scullery would practically arrest all the ordinary
work of the house. When the scullery alone is interfered with the inconvenience is much less. Where either the probable class of tenant, the
limitation of water supply, or the necessity of reducing the cost, precludes
the possibility of providing any form of hot-water supply from the range
boiler, and where, therefore, the copper must be used to heat the bath
water, the bathroom may be placed adjacent to the scullery and entered
from it, or, better still, from the lobby at the foot of the stairs. It should
in that case be so placed that the hot water can be run directly from the
copper to the bath ; this involves either lowering the bathroom floor or
raising the copper, and in the latter case a broad raised step against the
copper is necessary.
" An alternative plan is to enlarge the bathroom, place the copper in
it, and use the bathroom as a wash-house also."

The Women's Committee demanded a separate bathroom, and
makes no reference to the last alternative, which in the case of
rural cottages seems a good compromise. I later illustrate
some plans of Ministry of Agriculture cottages in which the separate bathroom downstairs was practically and economically
planned. The cost of a separate upstairs bathroom with a cold-

water service and with hot-water supply from the range puts this method out of court, though it is very desirable in districts where there is a public water supply laid on.

" Where the bath must be placed in the scullery it should be fitted with a hinged table-top as cover, and this may serve as one of the ledges adjacent to the sink, and thus the foot of the bath can occupy some of the frontage desirable for sink and draining-boards."

There are scores of other points on accommodation, such as the placing of larders, earth closets, etc., but I have attempted to deal only with the major issues which are so often discussed. As to the disposition of the rooms in the general plan of the cottage, and their relation to staircase, etc., it is impossible to lay down rules, especially as there are local variations in habits of living which govern the matter. In Yorkshire, for example, a separate washhouse in a back addition is generally liked : elsewhere back additions are deprecated. I have tried to exclude illustrations of cottages the plans of which are generally agreed to be unsatisfactory, but it is impossible to secure unanimity on such matters. Moreover, some unusual point in a plan, even if it looks bad, is often the result, not of ignorance or carelessness, but of some determining condition of site, level, aspect or prospect. It may be useful, however, to illustrate some common faults which should be avoided.

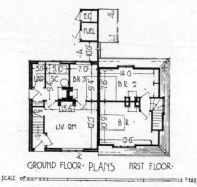

GROUND FLOOR· PLANS FIRST FLOOR·

SCALE OF [scale] FEET.

11.—FIRE, WINDOW AND DOORS
BADLY PLACED.

I deal first with some typical plans which show defects in the placing of the kitchen fireplace. Fig. 11 shows all the faults. The kitchen range is placed so that anyone working at it must be in her own light, and there is a door immediately adjoining it on each side, so that it would be impossible to place a chair alongside it with any promise of comfort to its occupant. It is true that the door leading to the bedroom would not be opened often, but cottage joinery being what it usually is, there would certainly be an uncomfortable draught.

Fig. 12 is a better plan, but the external and internal doors of the scullery are so placed that there is a through draught from the outside driving straight at the fireplace of the living-room. The internal door of the scullery would stand open more

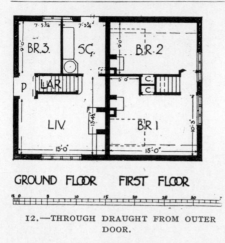

GROUND FLOOR    FIRST FLOOR

12.—THROUGH DRAUGHT FROM OUTER DOOR.

often than not, so that there would only be the outside door to keep out the wind.

Fig. 13 shows a variation upon the same air. There is a door on either side of the fireplace.

Fig. 14 is, if anything, rather worse. The outside door of the scullery almost touches the door to the living-room, and would make an easy way in for draughts. The occupant, if he sat on the far side of the fireplace, would have to get up when the housewife went to the larder, or when the children went to bed in the downstairs room.

In Fig. 15 the same defect is much magnified by the fact that the scullery has three doors, one from the back lobby, one from the front lobby, and one leading into the living-room. Children might play a variation of the game of " Round the Mulberry Bush " very successfully, using the central chimney-stack as the bush ; but it would be at some inconvenience to their elders.

Fig. 16 reveals a defect of another sort, namely, the interposition of two doors between the living-room and the scullery, and a long distance from the fire in the former to the sink in the latter. This defect is not so serious as the faults in the other plans already discussed, but it is sufficiently tiresome to be worth avoiding. This plan, it may be added, also has the serious defect of providing the coal cellar opening from the front entrance lobby of the cottage.

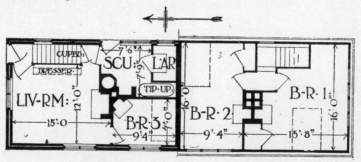

13.—DOORS ON BOTH SIDES OF FIREPLACE.

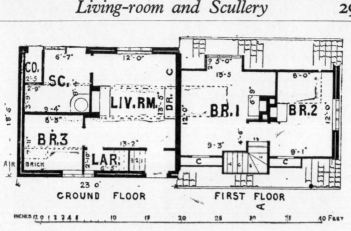

14.—DOORS BY FIREPLACE.

Fig. 17 shows a defect which is comparative rather than actual. The living-room has an area of 180 square feet, and the scullery of 108 square feet. The latter is much too large in proportion, and would tempt the occupants to use it as a living-room and to keep the living-room proper as a parlour. That is a point always to be borne in mind. I strongly press the view that it is ideal to have a parlour, but if limitation of cost prevents the provision of one, it is very undesirable that a spacious living-room shall be kept as a museum for household gods, while the family lives in dirt and discomfort in a little scullery.

There are other defects of planning which come from the

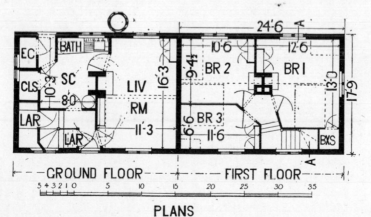

PLANS

15.—FIREPLACE SURROUNDED BY DOORS.

attempt to simplify the disposition of rooms excessively in the pursuit of cheapness at all costs.

Some consideration must be given to bungalows or single-storey

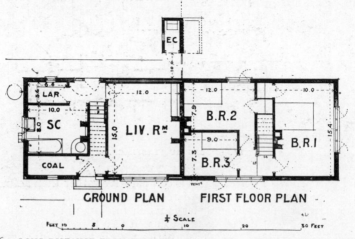

CROUND PLAN     FIRST FLOOR PLAN

16.—LONG DISTANCE FROM KITCHEN FIRE TO SINK, AND BAD COAL SPACE.

cottages, because they have many advocates on the ground of an alleged cheapness as compared with the ordinary two-storey building, but my inquiries do not support that view. It appears that generally they have been more costly per cubic foot. Mr. Raymond Unwin produced a very interesting thatched bungalow of charming appearance at Hollesley Bay at a pre-war cost of £220 (Fig. 18). If one takes the cottages by Mr. Clough as being typical of as good value as could be got for money in two-storey cottages and compares them in the matter of available floor area with the thatched bungalow, the result is, roughly, as follows : For £150 Mr. Clough provided about 616 superficial feet, whereas at Hollesley Bay about 750 ft. cost £220. This means that the single-storey bungalow worked out pre-war at about £50 more than the two-storey cottage, if the comparative areas

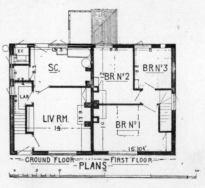

17.—SCULLERY TOO BIG IN PROPORTION.

Raymond Unwin.

18.—SINGLE-STOREY COTTAGE.

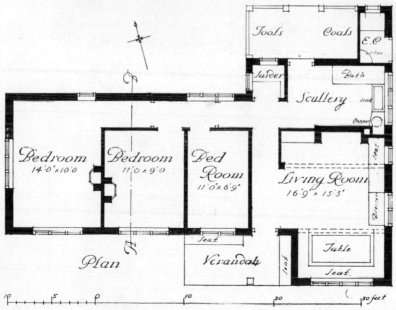

19.—SINGLE-STOREY COTTAGE.

Raymond Unwin.

M. *Maberly Smith.*

20.—CONCRETE BUNGALOW AT HENLEY-ON-THAMES.

are taken into account, though in this computation nothing is allowed for the boxroom space in the loft of the bungalow. The latter has a very interesting plan (Fig. 19), the dinner-table being set in a little bay at the south side of the living-room, which contains the cooking range. The scullery contains a bath, and there are three bedrooms of good size, all well lit.

Fig. 20 shows a concrete bungalow built to the design of Mr. Maberly Smith, without any passage-way. The plan is seen very well in the photograph of a model of the bungalow (Fig. 21). The front door opens into a vestibule from which there are doors to one bedroom, larder, coals, bathroom with W.C., kitchen and living-room. That leaves one bedroom entered from living-room and one from the kitchen. There is, of course, something to be said against the principal bedroom opening off the living-room, but the objection is hardly serious enough to outweigh the advantage of saving passage space. All the rooms have fireplaces, except one bedroom, although there is only a single chimney stack. It is altogether an ingeniously contrived little house.

The high cost of timber for floor joists and boarding suggests

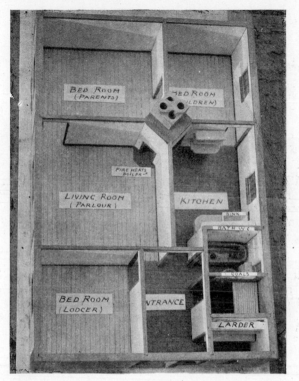

BED ROOM
(PARENTS)

BED ROOM
(CHILDREN)

FIRE HEATS
BOILER

LIVING ROOM
(PARLOUR)

KITCHEN

SINK

BATH W.C.

BED ROOM
(LODGER)

ENTRANCE

COALS

LARDER

21.—MODEL OF MR. MABERLY SMITH'S BUNGALOW, SHOWING
ARRANGEMENT OF ROOMS.

a bias in favour of one-storey building, but by the same token
more timber is wanted for the roof.

There is in some people's minds a real feeling for the word
" bungalow " and all it means, even when they are not quite
clear what it does mean. Ordinarily understood as a single-
storey house, it has come to include houses with one storey
above the ground floor, but that storey wholly in the roof. The
enthusiast for bungalows must be referred to " The Book of
Bungalows," by R. Randal Phillips.

This chapter has dealt only with the home of the working
man, with its limitations of size. In cottages for people of
larger means there is freedom to attempt a greater variety and
to consider effect as well as mere hygiene, and the architect's
hands are less tied. What use the architect can make of his
freedom can best be seen in later chapters.

D

# CHAPTER IV

## CHOICE AND RIGHT USE OF MATERIALS

Cob and *Pisé*—Clay Lump—Welsh Slates—Other Slates—Pantiles —Weather-boarding—Timber—Concrete—Stone

MATERIALS are always the key of building, because æsthetic success and economic success alike are dependent on their right use. The partial paralysis of the building trade in 1919, when I also dealt with materials alternative to brick and concrete blocks, was due to the immediate results of the war, but the lapse of six years has rather crystallized those difficulties than removed them. In 1919, however, transport was a special difficulty that has passed as to the shortage of means, though it has remained as to high cost. That year therefore saw a revival of interest in the possibilities of substituting for brick, which in some areas needs to be brought from afar, such methods of wall-building as enable materials on or close to the building site to be utilized to the full. Where gravel and sand exist, concrete is indicated, but in a clay or chalk district the only available way of dealing with the soil of the site is by cob or *pisé*, and from 1919 onwards there have been many efforts towards devising methods for grafting on to these traditional ways such improvements as scientific ingenuity was able to suggest.

The early stages of cob building were not everything that we might desire to-day, though many of these buildings have stood since the days of Elizabeth. The later building in *pisé* which was much employed about a hundred years ago may give a useful lead. What is *pisé* construction? There remain examples to-day of efficient cottage and farm buildings erected on this system. It must not be confused with cob, which is composed of wet mixtures as compared with the *pisé* method of a dry mixture of material well rammed and consolidated. Can we improve on either method? Why improve? From the stability point of view it may not be necessary; from the hygienic side, yes. Precautions must be introduced against the intrusion of rats by providing proper foundations of stone, bricks, or concrete. A sanitary dwelling needs to be protected against damp by proper damp-proof courses. To prevent decay to either system of

34

*Clough Williams-Ellis.*

22.—P.I.S.E. BUNGALOW FOR SMALL-HOLDER AT NEWLANDS CORNER.

building it is necessary to provide the wall with efficient shoes and hats, that is, good foundations and good roofs, which to-day can be provided if proper skill be brought to bear on the problem.

Though the total cost of a *pisé*-built cottage in any average English district is unlikely to be markedly, if at all, lower than that of the same cottage built in brick, the continued shortage of both bricks and bricklayers makes *pisé* worth considering where, but only where, the conditions are favourable.

As Mr. Clough Williams-Ellis has written a book [1] dealing fully with the subject, I will do little more than quote his caveat regarding soils :—

"Were it not for the fact (often somewhat embarrassing) that soil quite incapable of making good *pisé* will none the less produce enthusiastic *pisé*-builders, a warning as to the vital importance of the earth being really suitable might seem superfluous.

"The author has found some of the staunchest champions of *pisé* building living on and valiantly struggling with stiff glutinous clay and almost pure sand. Even the most vigorous optimism can achieve little under such adverse conditions, unless soil-blending be resorted to, and, even so, *pisé* building begins to lose points in the matter of economy directly complications of this sort are introduced.

"Fortunately, however, England is well off in the matter of *pisé* soils, the red marls being amongst the best.

"A study of the country, or failing that, of the geological maps, will reveal a great tract of this earth extending diagonally right across England, from Yorkshire down into Devonshire, where it ends conspicuously in the beautiful red cliffs about Torquay.

"There is a large area of the stuff in the Midlands, notably in Warwickshire, with lesser patches here and there about the country.

"Second only to the red marls come the brick earths, which, fortunately, are also widely distributed. 'Brick earth' is merely clay that has been well weathered and disintegrated under the action of wind, rain and frost, and organic agents, the sulphides having become oxides, and what was a cold intractable slithery mass having become merely a 'strong' and binding earth.

"It is probable that even stiff clay, if dug in the summer or autumn, and left exposed for a winter, would prove sufficiently reformed to be quite amenable for *pisé* building in the spring.

"After the marls and brick earths, there is an endless variety of soils that will serve well for *pisé*-building—some of course better than others, but all, save the extremes (the excessively light and excessively clayey), capable of giving good results under proper treatment.

"Before putting *pisé* construction actually in hand, however, the intending builder will do well to submit samples of his earth to some competent authority, that they may receive his blessing.

"A fistful taken from a depth of 9 in. and another from, say, 2 ft. below the surface, should give sufficient evidence as to the soil's suitability or the reverse."

Figs. 22 to 26 show a *pisé* bungalow built at Newlands Corner, Guildford, to the designs of Mr. Clough Williams-Ellis. It was

[1] "Cottage Building in Cob, Pisé, Chalk, and Clay," by Clough Williams-Ellis, *Country Life*, 7s. 6d.

a pioneer building, and the accommodation was that laid down for small-holders' cottages at the Ministry of Agriculture, where I was then serving as Director-General of the Land Department and so responsible for the administration of the Land Settlement Act of 1919. Then, as on many occasions before and since, Mr. Williams-Ellis was a delightful collaborator, for he was, for all too short a period, one of the superintending architects on my staff. The Newlands Corner cottage was practically and æsthetically successful, but from the point of view of cost, as compared with brick, it wrought no deliverance. The overhanging eaves necessary to protect the walls from the dripping of wet, which mean more timber and more tiles, and the wider concrete foundations required because the walls were 18 in. thick, involved the use of extra material that must be set against the saving effected by the omission of bricks. But Mr. Williams-Ellis' experiment did not stand alone. In December, 1918, I approached the Department of Scientific and Industrial Research with a view to their co-operating with the Ministry of Agriculture in erecting some experimental cottages to test various methods of building with local materials and so forth. That Department agreed, and the *venue* chosen was the Ministry's Farm Settlement estate at Amesbury, Wilts. The Ministry built a total of thirty-two cottages, some singles, some in pairs, of which five were supervised

23.—*PISÉ* BUNGALOW IN COURSE OF BUILDING.

24.—ANOTHER VIEW OF NEWLANDS CORNER *PISÉ* BUNGALOW.

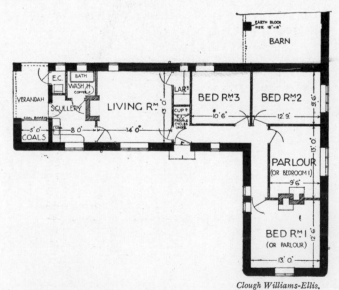

*Clough Williams-Ellis.*

25.—PLAN OF *PISÉ* BUNGALOW, NEWLANDS CORNER.

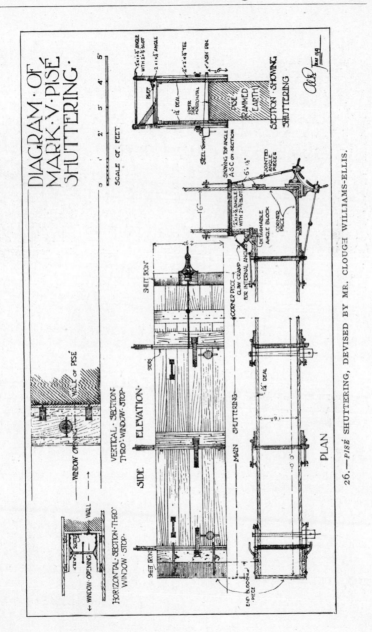

26.—*PISÉ* SHUTTERING, DEVISED BY MR. CLOUGH WILLIAMS-ELLIS.

by the Research Department and the rest by the Ministry's architectural staff. Some of the cottages were of brick to act as " controls " on the cost of the more novel constructions, which included traditional cob, a special rammed cob, *pisé*, concrete blocks, monolithic concrete, chalk concrete blocks, monolithic chalk and cement, timber, and converted Army huts. The conditions of building presented every sort of difficulty of labour and transport, and the cottages cost very much more than had been anticipated. A report on the Research Department's work, entitled " Experimental Cottages," by Mr. W. R. Jaggard, was published for the Research Department by the Stationery Office in 1921, and I refer the reader to that detailed review of the work for further information. But the broad result of the experiments was to show that none of the methods showed any real saving as compared with brick. Perhaps the most successful were those which utilized, in one way or another, the chalk which was dug on the site. I prefer *pisé de craie*, i.e. *pisé* of chalk to *pisé de terre*, in which marl or clay are used, but I feel that *pisé* generally is wholly dependent for its success on the close supervision which can be given by an enthusiast who is determined to make a job of it. It depends too much on local factors, which must vary greatly, for it to be safely employed in the ordinary way by an ordinary builder. The Amesbury experiments covered a good many points. Fig. 30 shows a pair of normal brick cottages which enabled sound comparisons to be made. Fig. 28 illustrates the shuttering used in building walls of chalk *pisé*. Figs. 31 to 33 show plans and photographs of what was possibly the first two-storey *pisé* cottage built in England. Cob has often been used for two-storey buildings, but it is believed that when *pisé* proper was introduced early in the nineteenth century it was thought safe to keep to a single storey. But *pisé* in two storeys at Amesbury proved quite satisfactory. Fig. 33 shows, however, that *pisé* demands a very simple and straightforward type of building. Breaks in the planning of walls add to difficulties and bring no countervailing advantages. Where shuttering is used, whether for *pisé* or concrete, the simpler the plan the cheaper and the better. Fig. 35 shows a method of getting a two-storey cottage without carrying the *pisé* wall any higher than is needed for a bungalow. This cottage at Amesbury was very satisfactory, but the same plan, with the break on one front straightened out, proved better and cheaper in later cottages built to otherwise the same plan in concrete, where the shuttering problem is much the same as with *pisé*. The timber-framed cottages with elm-boarding (Fig. 38) were very handsome, but more costly than brick. I think, moreover, it is a mistake to carry down any wall sheathing material, whether boarding like this or tiling

27.—GROUP OF EXPERIMENTAL COTTAGES AT AMESBURY: TRADITIONAL COB ON THE RIGHT.

28.—SHUTTERING FOR *PISÉ*: MINISTRY OF AGRI-
CULTURE PATTERN.

29.—COB WALLS BEING BUILT AT AMESBURY.

41

30.—MINISTRY OF AGRICULTURE'S PAIR OF NORMAL BRICK COTTAGES
AT AMESBURY.

or slating, so close to the ground. A base of brick or concrete should rise 2 feet before the sheathing begins.

The true and traditional cob cottage seen in Figs. 27 and 29 was built by an old hand at the job, and a very fine cottage he produced, very comfortable within by reason of the deep "reveals"

31.—BUILDING WITH CHALK *PISÉ* AT AMESBURY.

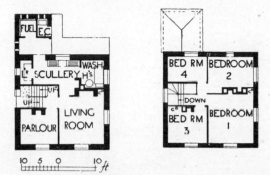

32.—GROUND AND FIRST FLOOR PLANS': *PISÉ* SINGLE COTTAGE : AMESBURY.

33.—*PISÉ* COTTAGE AT AMESBURY.

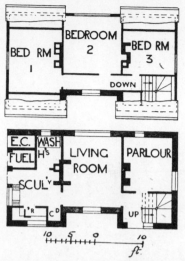

34.—GROUND AND FIRST FLOOR PLANS SHOWING *PISÉ* WALLS, CARRIED UP TO FIRST FLOOR LEVEL, GABLES BEING ELM-BOARDED.

35.—*PISÉ* TO EAVES AND ELM-WEATHER-BOARDED GABLES : AT AMESBURY. PLANS ABOVE.

of the windows. But here again the thick walls lead to an abnormally big and costly roof. A practical trouble is that young men do not like to go into cob-building as a trade. It is a very messy task treading the chopped straw into the wet clay or chalk, and a fairly arduous one to pass up from the ground to the builder on the wall the pats of cob which he lays in place. I am clear that cob has gone out because it is not a feasible way to build except in special circumstances.

The cottage of chalk concrete blocks, made of twelve parts of crushed chalk to one of cement, shaped into blocks by a Dricrete machine and built as a normal cavity wall, was a success and represents one of the practical gains of the Amesbury experiments (Figs. 36 and 37).

Akin to *pisé de terre*, but quite distinct from it, is the East Anglian method of building with clay lump, which has been employed in Norfolk with great skill by Mr. George J. Skipper. In the first edition of this book I illustrated a clay-lump cottage built by Mr. Morley Horder at Garboldisham, at what was even then the fantastically low cost of 2½d. a foot cube. But it was only a four-roomed bungalow and not therefore the best of examples. At Elsenham the late Sir Walter Gilbey built several cottages in the same way, but when I visited them I found the outer face had so far perished as to call for a protective coat of weather-boarding. Mr. Skipper had a good example before him in the old clay-lump cottages at Kenninghall, illustrated in Fig. 41. The method is to dig the clay, remove any stones larger than a walnut, water it, and spread over it short straw or coarse grass, which is trodden in by a horse. The straw is used to bind the material, and explains the unreasonableness of the Egyptians when they required the Israelites to make bricks without straw ; they were making clay lumps, not bricks. The prepared clay is thrown into a four-sided wooden mould and the block is formed 18 in. long, 9 in. wide and 6 in. deep for outside walls, and of the same dimensions but only 6 in. wide for inside walls. They are left a month or more, according to the weather, to dry. The lumps are built with clay mortar or lime mortar on a brick or concrete plinth rising 18 in. out of the ground. By way of outer coat, clay " slurry " used to be washed on, or a coating of tar sanded and colour-washed. To-day a coat of cement plaster is put on and keyed to the clay by a covering of wire netting. As with *pisé* and cob, broad projecting eaves are necessary to protect from rain. Mr. Skipper claimed in 1922, truly I doubt not, that a clay-lump house was about £60 cheaper than one of brick. But with bricks at a normal price I doubt if there would be an advantage any more than is obtained from cob or *pisé*. The common sense of the matter is that mankind in most quarters

36.—BUILDING WITH CHALK AND CEMENT BLOCKS.

37.—COTTAGE AT AMESBURY OF CHALK AND CEMENT BLOCKS.

38.—TIMBER-FRAMED COTTAGES AT AMESBURY WITH ELM-BOARDED
WALLS AND TILED ROOFS.

of the globe came to the conclusion some thousands of years
ago that clay was a better building material if burnt than if
raw. Given normal conditions that is likely to remain true.
Those more or less tropical localities that still use *adobe* and
such-like have probably no coal to turn the clay into brick, and
I cling to the belief that hard brick will always be better than
soft clay in our English climate. But a clay-lump cottage can
be a warm and comfortable home for all that. Of the plans of
Mr. Skipper's cottages I need only say that I miss the provision
of bathrooms, being persuaded that the dwellers in rural Norfolk
need and like facilities for washing themselves as much as folk
in other counties. The large larder is good, but has led to the
planning of a rather wasteful passage (Fig. 43).

I now return to the consideration of more normal materials,
lest the examination of novel or resuscitated traditional methods
should seem to bulk too largely in a general review of cottage-
building. It will be found generally true that materials always
look well in the place where they are naturally found.

We speak roughly of " a brick country," " a stone country,"

39.—CLAY-LUMP COTTAGES IN COURSE OF BUILDING : A LUMP
MOULD IS SEEN IN THE FOREGROUND.

*George J. Skipper.*

40.—A FINISHED CLAY-LUMP PAIR OF COTTAGES.

or " a flint country," and given the traditional use of a material, it will always look well in its own country and frequently look most unpleasant out of it.  Perhaps the best example of the unhappy effect of misplaced material is the Welsh slate.

41.—OLD CLAY-LUMP COTTAGES AT KENNINGHALL, NORFOLK.

Abusive things have often been written, and with justice, about the blots which roofs of purple Welsh slates make on so many landscapes.  One had come to think, in fact, that there

E

George J. *Skipper.*

42.—A PICTURESQUE GROUP OF THATCHED CLAY-LUMP COTTAGES AT
KEEDISTON.

is something intrinsically evil about them, and that they should
be for ever ruled out of the catalogue of building materials.
This was due to three things—the unpleasant colour effect of
a purple crown to red-brick walls, the meagre surface regularity
of the slates, and perhaps, most of all, their association with
cheap and ill-designed dwellings.

There is therefore a particular interest attaching to the Welsh
cottages designed by
Mr. Herbert North, for
it must be admitted
that domestic architec-
ture in the " Celtic
fringes " has failed to
develop as quickly or
as well as in England.
In North Wales it has
certainly remained at
a low ebb, and Mr.
North's work is the
more welcome because
it sets a standard of
what is feasible on a
beautiful coast too
long blemished by un-
sightly dwellings.

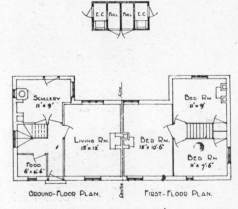

43.—PLANS OF MR. SKIPPER'S CLAY-LUMP
COTTAGES.

Bolnhurst (Fig. 45) groups very attractively, with its slating swept to a pleasant curve over the dormer window.

The success of this cottage and others built by Mr. North at Llanfairfechan is due mainly to his careful study of the factors which make the charm of the old cottages of Snowdonia. The elements of design were extremely simple to the point of baldness, but the instinct of the builders was essentially right. In that country of torrent and craggy upland, solitary and large, the

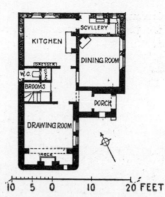

10   5   0     10      20 FEET

44.—PLAN OF BOLNHURST.

engaging qualities of English rural architecture, the varied textures and colours of brick, tile and weather-boarding, dappled with lichen, would have been hopelessly defeated. In such

*H. I. North.*

45.—BOLNHURST, LLANFAIRFECHAN, STONE WALLS AND SLATE ROOF.

surroundings architecture needs to be in a minor key, to recognize its limitations and take its place modestly.

*The late Ernest Gimson.*

46.—ROCKYFIELD, CHARNWOOD FOREST.

The materials of which Bolnhurst is built have a certain dourness, grey stone and purple slate, and their hard surfaces are very slow to take on an air of maturity. The greyness of the stone, however, is generally covered in house walls by a coat of whitewash, and the purple roofs look well above it. Even purple, however, is avoidable, if you will. Some old quarries have been reopened which yield slates of greenish grey shot with yellow stains. Mr. North is careful not to have them cut thin and

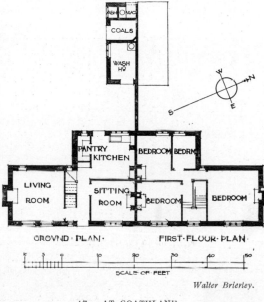

*Walter Brierley.*

47.—AT GOATHLAND.

smooth, or chosen because of their evenness of colour, but thick and rough and mixed in tint, so that the light may make some play and change upon their surface.

*Walter Brierley.*

48.—PAIR OF COTTAGES AT GOATHLAND.

For the West of England the Cornish Delabole slate has many merits, and it is much to be hoped that the old Swithland slate quarries (Fig. 46) of Leicestershire will some day be re-

*H. S. Goodhart-Rendel.*

49.—PAIR OF COTTAGES, WONERSH.

opened. It can hardly be said that slates are a more fitting roof covering for stone cottages than tiles, but it is certainly true of many districts which yield both stone for walls and slate for roofs.

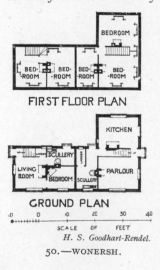

FIRST FLOOR PLAN

GROUND PLAN

SCALE OF FEET
*H. S. Goodhart-Rendel.*

50.—WONERSH.

The Cotswold stone tile is always delightful in conjunction with the masonry of the district. (Figs. 78 and 79.) So is the green Cumberland slate with the whitewashed walls or the grey dry-walling of Lake District buildings.

In localities where slates are not produced, the best crown for a stone wall is the pantile (Fig. 48). Happily the grey pantile which used to be made largely in the Eastern counties has been reintroduced in recent years from Holland, and is now made once more in East Anglia. It gives a cool-coloured roof of delightful texture. The red pantile is traditional in many parts of the country and always looks well.

The pair of long-fronted cottages at Goathland, Yorkshire, built to the designs of Mr. Walter Brierley, give an admirable example of its use (Fig. 48). Plain as they are, their stout masonry walls and pantiled roofs strike exactly the right note in a Yorkshire village. Their cost (pre-war) was £600 the pair, and it will be observed that they each have two sitting-rooms, as well as kitchen and four bedrooms, with an outlying block containing washhouse, etc., so that they fill a comparatively exalted place in the social scale. They deserve study as showing the satisfactory results to be got from straightforward, solid

51.—MR. ST. LOE STRACHEY'S BLACK WEATHER-BOARDED COTTAGE, COSTING £150 (PRE-WAR).

building without any reaching after ingenious features or adventitious prettiness.

Pantiles have the disadvantage that they are difficult and rather costly to use on dormers, and they are unsuitable for tile-hanging on wall surfaces. The ordinary flat tile is more flexible of application and will always be the most usual roof covering for a red-brick building. The pantile can, however, be used well on a Mansard roof as is seen by the pair of cottages at Wonersh, illustrated both by plan and photograph in Figs. 49 and 50. These were built from the designs of Mr. H. S. Goodhart-

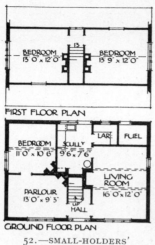

FIRST FLOOR PLAN

BEDROOM
13'0" x 12'0"

BEDROOM
13'9" x 12'0"

BEDROOM
11'0" x 10'6"

SCULLY
9'6" x 7'6"

LAR:

FUEL

PARLOUR
13'0" x 9'3"

LIVING
ROOM
16'0" x 12'0"

UP
HALL

GROUND FLOOR PLAN

52.—SMALL-HOLDERS'
COTTAGES, BEAUMONT, ESSEX.

Rendel, and are a good general example of simple brick and tile cottages. At Wonersh the bricks are ordinary Guildford stocks of a very beautiful true purple colour, and the pleasant feeling of the cottages is enhanced by the red pantile roof, the dark green trellis porches and by white woodwork and gates. The general lines of these cottages are practically the same as of those made familiar by Mr. A. H. Clough, and described in a later chapter.

The use of timber for the walls of a cottage as well as its floors and roof and for joinery was claimed by some before the war as the specific for cheap building, and much venom was expended on the by-laws which forbade it in most districts. To-day the question has a new interest, because of the shortage of brick. Timber cottages are not especially sightly if their design is as bald as in the case of the example shown in Fig. 51, which, however, fulfilled requirements as to standard accommodation (see also page 11).

*John Stuart.*

53.—ELM-BOARDING AND TILES AT BEAUMONT.

Amongst six-roomed cottages those built by the Essex County Council at Beaumont for small-holders are notable for simplicity (Figs. 52 to 54). They were roofed in two ways, thatch or tiling, the construction being wholly of timber except for the brick chimneys.

These chimneys needed only a scaffolding of four poles, and the call on bricklayers' labour was trifling. In 1920 the cottages were thought very cheap at £600 each. They should cost considerably less to-day. The elm-boarding was a local product.

*John Stuart.*

54.—ELM-BOARDING AND THATCH AT BEAUMONT, ESSEX.

" Half-timber " for wall-building is possible in districts where there remain trees to be felled, and desirable where distance from a railway station and the absence of other local materials, e.g. bricks or gravel for concrete, make reliance on timber the obvious course.

Only in especial cases, however, and in large quantities is it possible to use half-timber construction, which even before the war was always hopelessly expensive for labourers' cottages. This question is dealt with comparatively in the next chapter, dealing with the new methods made widely known at Wembley in 1925. Fig. 56 shows, for example, a timber cottage at Yalding,

Kent, designed by Mr. Alan F. Royds. It is a pleasant design, and the plan shows the large parlour provided. The pre-war cost worked out at 7d. a cubic foot, which was little enough for the quality of the work, but markedly more than could then be expended on cottage-building if an economic rent was expected.

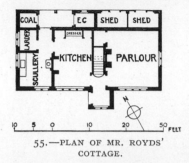

55.—PLAN OF MR. ROYDS' COTTAGE.

A charming example of traditional building in half-timber and thatch is the cottage at Old Buckhurst (Fig. 57) designed by Mr. Dunbar Smith.

Concrete has been so widely suggested as the solution of the cheap cottage question that it needs to be discussed at some length, but first of all it must be made clear what is meant by a concrete cottage. Concrete is in the nature of an artificial stone made by mixing an "aggregate" with Portland cement. This aggregate can be a combination of sand and gravel, or broken stone, or slag, or even, if care be taken, coke breeze or destructor clinker.

*Alan F. Royds.*

56.—HALF-TIMBER COTTAGE AT YALDING.

If the concrete be made into blocks, solid or hollow, for which various machines are available, the blocks will be used for outside walls or partitions like bricks, except that concrete blocks are always made larger. There is little to distinguish concrete blocks from other wall materials in their effect on the essential elements of design. Sometimes blocks are made with a face

*Dunbar Smith.*

57.—COTTAGE OF HALF-TIMBER AND THATCH AT OLD BUCKHURST.

imitating rusticated stonework, but the imitation is both clumsy
and undesirable.  Concrete is a reasonable and proper material
which does not need to masquerade as natural stone.  Blocks
are also made with a " drifted " face which gives a pleasant
texture, and laid with an ordinary cement joint, but more often
the wall when built is covered with a coat of cement plaster and
lime-washed.   The trouble about the latter method is that not
only are bricklayers needed for laying the blocks, but plasterers
for giving the external coat.  With most aggregates, concrete
is an unpleasant cold grey colour, but such materials as pink
granite chippings have a colour sufficiently distinctive to give
an attractive warm colour to the concrete and to obviate the need
of an added colour wash.

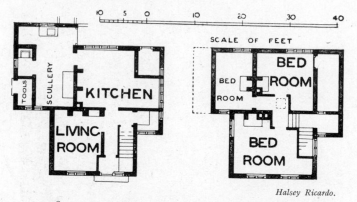

*Halsey Ricardo.*

58.—PLANS OF THE DORSET CONCRETE COTTAGE.

The field in which most scope lies open to the inventor, however, is in the use of concrete for monolithic building, i.e. by
casting large parts of a wall, a side of a house, or even a whole
house in one piece.   Mr. Edison made a great stir some years ago
by claiming to have solved the whole problem of cheap housing.
An examination of the merits of the idea made me hesitate
then to accept them at the inventor's own valuation.  The scheme,
shortly, was to make cast-iron moulds for a complete house.
Into these moulds was to be poured semi-liquid cement concrete.
It was claimed that if the materials were bought in large quantities, a house of two main storeys and basement and attic could
be built for £240 (pre-war prices).  As such a house would be
more than twice as big as the ordinary workman's cottage, it
meant normal cottages at £120 each (pre-war).  The moulds
were to cost £8,000, which meant a vast number of dwellings in

a row identical in pattern.   Little has been heard of any great achievements along these lines.

*Halsey Ricardo.*

59.—CONCRETE AND THATCH IN DORSET.

   Modifications of the idea are to be studied in the descriptions of the Easiform steel shuttering and the casting of whole walls in "aerated" concrete, given in the next chapter.

There are many practical objections to the pure Edison doctrine. The thin walls proposed would be cold and the walls would " sweat," not being made with a continuous cavity as in the best English practice of building with concrete blocks. For rural housing the moving about of heavy steel moulds would kill any economy that might be inherent in the " poured house."

Whether concrete is cheaper than brick for walls depends almost wholly on what materials are available on the spot. If there is sand and gravel, and if there is no brickyard near,

*Arthur E. Collins, City Engineer.*

60.—CONCRETE COTTAGES AT NORWICH, WITH BRICK QUOINS.

concrete is indicated. A real advantage of a concrete system, which does not need the bricklayer, is that, given a supply of suitable aggregate, building can go forward, whereas the supply of bricklayers must continue inadequate for some years.

A warning may be added against building with solid concrete blocks. Concrete is a very porous material and tends to let the rain through readily. There are machines which make blocks with large cavities and these minimize the evil, but it can be avoided entirely by building the wall with a continuous cavity, like an ordinary brick cavity wall, the inner and outer parts being tied together at suitable intervals. Figs. 58 and 59 show a six-roomed thatched cottage in Dorset, built of cavity blocks. It is inevitable, however, that between the cavities are webs of concrete running from the outer to the inner face of the wall, and damp is apt to work through by that way. It was therefore found necessary to give the finished wall a layer of cement plaster on the outside in order to exclude damp. Fig. 59 shows the cottage, which was photographed before the plastering was finished, and so indicates the size of the blocks used.

There is, however, the possibility that with quite perfect aggregate, a solid concrete wall may be made impervious. The later chapter on Welwyn Garden City cottages deals further with this point.

Some variety was given to concrete-block walls at Norwich by Mr. Arthur E. Collins, who used brick quoins. But the effort scarcely seemed worth making, as the variety arose out of no structural necessity (Fig. 60).

61.—GALWAY SHUTTERING FOR CAVITY CONCRETE WALL.

Porous as concrete is when it has to face driving rain, it is not ordinarily porous enough to prevent condensation on the inner face of the wall. The best compromise is to build the outer half of the cavity wall of blocks made of " wet " concrete, which is dense and non-porous, and the inner half of " dry " concrete, which is more porous, and to plaster the latter with ordinary slow-setting lime plaster instead of with the more popular quick-setting varieties, if the better alternative of doing without plaster altogether cannot be devised.

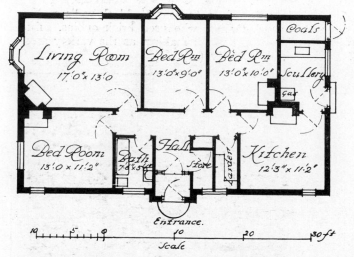

62.—PLAN OF CLINKER-CONCRETE BUNGALOW.

Among the many systems of concrete construction is the Calway, which was tried on a large scale in 1915 by Mr. C. D. Leng, of the *Sheffield Daily Telegraph*, on his estate at Sandygate, Sheffield. There are in the neighbourhood huge spoil heaps of clinker ash, no new material for concrete, but one that has often given bad results because the sulphur in the ash is apt to " kill " the cement and bring about blow-holes in the concrete and subsequent disintegration. He used one part of sand and one of cement to six of clinker, and the cottages remain sound and dry to-day. The Calway system of shuttering provides a cavity wall of monolithic character, and Fig. 61 shows the shuttering employed. Unskilled labour only is needed for the wall-building, but cement or rough-cast is needed on the outside face to ensure a weatherproof job, and plaster within, as the shuttering does not leave a smooth enough face. Mr. Leng thought the rate of building such walls equivalent to brick walls with bricks laid at the rate of 1,200 a day.    The roofs at Sandygate were of tiles or slates laid on laths below which was two-ply " Rok " felting stuck down

*Arthur Nunweek.*

63.—BUNGALOW OF CLINKER-CONCRETE AT SHEFFIELD.

with hot tar.    This was of course cheaper than boarding and felting.

F

The accommodation was good, with a big living-room in addition to kitchen and scullery (Fig. 62).

The methods of concrete cottage-building can be divided into three main classes :  (a) Concrete blocks instead of bricks, which demand the mason or bricklayer to lay them.  (b) Monolithic walls, i.e. concrete poured into shuttering, whether of wood or steel or other materials.  (c) Post-and-panel building, or post-and-slab.  Classes (a) and (b) have been long employed and under many systems, which are described *passim* in these pages.  Post-and-slab is a more difficult proposition, and is suitable only when undertaken on a large scale.  Amongst its varieties the " duo-slab " looms large.  In 1920–22 H.M. Office

*Sir Frank Baines (Office of Works).*

64.—PAIR OF CONCRETE HOUSES (DUO-SLAB SYSTEM), BEDFORD
HOUSING SCHEME.

of Works carried out a large housing scheme at Bedford for the municipality, partly of brick, partly of monolithic concrete, both solid walls and cavity walls, and one experimental pair of " duo-slab " concrete illustrated in Fig. 64.  Some of the brick houses, with 9-in. solid walls and without a coat of plaster outside, showed signs of damp, and the same complaint was made of some of the monolithic " poured " concrete walls, though it is always difficult to say whether internal damp in a concrete house is due to wet passing through, or internal condensation.  But in the " duo-slab " pair there was no sign of damp, and they are, moreover, of seemly appearance.  The " duo-slab " system is the invention of Sir Edwin Airey, of Messrs. William Airey & Sons, contractors, of Leeds, who carried out the Meanwood Housing Scheme

65.—MEANWOOD HOUSING SCHEME, LEEDS: GENERAL VIEW OF SCHEME.

66.—MEANWOOD: SOME OF THE PAIRS OF HOUSES BUILT ON DUO-SLAB SYSTEM.

*H. S. Chorley.*

(Figs. 65 and 66). The claim for duo-slab is that it is efficient, employs unskilled labour for more than half the number of men needed, and is twice as fast as brick building. The method is simple. The main part of the wall consists of concrete slabs 3 ft. 8 in. by 8 in. by 3 in. thick, cast on the site in frames. For the posts, wooden shuttering is set up (after the foundations are in) at 4-foot centres and the slabs are dropped in dry within the post-shuttering, leaving a 4-inch cavity between them. When the slabs have been inserted up to first floor level, concrete is poured into the post-shuttering, and the slabs are thus made homogeneous with the posts. A concrete beam is then carried round the house at first-floor level and the same process is repeated for the upper storey. An exterior face is given by rough cast applied with a cement gun, which fills the joints between the slabs and gives a uniform surface.

This duo-slab system has been employed for 2,000 houses at

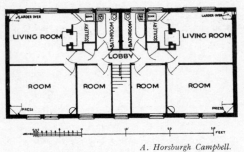

*A. Horsburgh Campbell.*

67.—LOCHEND HOUSING SCHEME : FIRST-FLOOR PLAN OF TENEMENT.

Leeds on the Meanwood Estate, and blocks of some hundreds of working-class flats at Edinburgh, on the Lochend Estate, for which Mr. A. Horsburgh Campbell was the architect. Plan showing two flats of three rooms is reproduced in Fig. 67. It has to be admitted that the duo-slab method is somewhat limiting to the architect in the character of his design, but not enough to drive him into anything like ugliness of elevation. It does not, however, lend itself to so much variety of treatment as the concrete block, well seen in another Edinburgh scheme (Fig. 69) designed by Messrs. Robertson & Swan.

On the grounds of cost, speed, weather-tightness and availability of labour the duo-slab system seems to beat the concrete block, at all events in the present abnormal situation.

The concrete system represented in Messrs. Henry Boot & Sons' exhibit at Wembley by one side of a cottage will be more appropriately described here than in the " Wembley " chapter, because it is an efficient example of " Duo-slab " or " Post-and-

(*a*) Making slabs with unskilled labour.

(*b*) Applying the cement facing with a " gun."

*A. Horsburgh Campbell.*

(*c*) Showing, on the right, shuttering for posts, and slabs in position, and, on the left, the shuttering removed and the concrete cast.

68.—LOCHEND HOUSING SCHEME, EDINBURGH : DUO-SLAB SYSTEM.

Robertson & Swan.

69.—CONCRETE BLOCK HOUSES, WARDIE ESTATE, EDINBURGH.

70

70.—BOOTS' POST-AND-PANEL CONCRETE COTTAGES BEFORE
PLASTERING.

*E. W. Edward.*

71.—BOOTS' POST-AND-PANEL CONCRETE COTTAGES AT SHEFFIELD
AFTER PLASTERING.

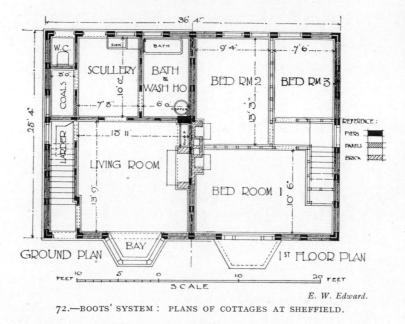

*E. W. Edward.*

72.—BOOTS' SYSTEM : PLANS OF COTTAGES AT SHEFFIELD.

panel.'' The method differs from the Airey Duo-slab in the erection of concrete piers which have previously been cast, to the full height of the house, at the corners and at the sides of door and window openings, and also as necessary at suitable intervals. The intervening spaces between the uprights are then filled in with pre-cast concrete slabs, made by the semi-dry process, usually in a standard 9-inch Winget machine. These slabs are in effect concrete planks 9 in. by about $2\frac{7}{8}$ in., cast of the appropriate length to fit between the posts ; the mixture being seven parts of aggregate to one of cement. The concrete posts or piers are first erected and held in position by wall plates running along the top, and the slabs, as they are put in, are bedded in liquid mortar. The total thickness of the wall is 8 in., made up of two 3-inch slabs and of a 2-inch cavity. A straight joint between the piers and the slabs is avoided by the provision of a nosing which fits into a groove. Fig. 70 shows the house as built before it is covered all over with a coat of rough-cast which can be applied with a cement gun, and Fig. 71 when thus finished. The chimney-stacks are of ordinary brick.

A report, dated November 15, 1924, of the Housing Committee of the Dundee Corporation sets out the results of a careful examination of all concrete systems as they were to be seen in housing schemes at Leicester, Birmingham, Liverpool, Wakefield, and Leeds, as a result of which the deputation recommended that Dundee should adopt the Boot system. It need scarcely be said that this system is applicable only to large housing schemes. The cost of the house varies with local conditions from £450 to £480 each. The value of the system is based upon standardization and mass production, but it is not so inelastic as to prevent a considerable variety of design in any one scheme. The architect is, of course, limited in the placing of doors and windows by the necessity of arranging them to go between the concrete piers ; they cannot be dotted on to the elevation just where he may

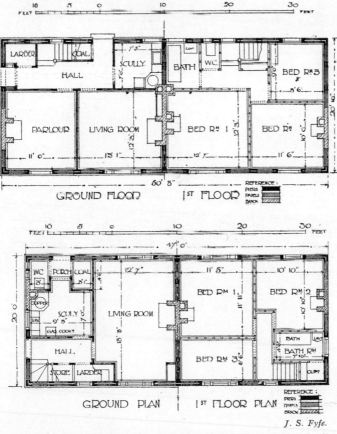

*J. S. Fyfe.*

73.—PLAN OF PARLOUR AND NON-PARLOUR COTTAGES BUILT AT LEICESTER ON BOOTS' POST-AND-PANEL SYSTEM.

*J. S. Fyfe.*

74.—BOOTS' SYSTEM : POST-AND-PANEL NON-PARLOUR PAIR AT
LEICESTER.

*J. S. Fyfe.*

75.—BOOTS' SYSTEM : POST-AND-PANEL PARLOUR PAIR AT LEICESTER.

please. There seems no reason why houses of this type should
not be practically indestructible, and as there is no brickwork (save
in chimneys) to be repointed, the cost of maintenance should be
low. It can at least be said that Messrs. Boots, who are building
these houses literally by the thousand, have a long experience

in concrete building, and must know all the troubles which are to be avoided.

*Sir Edwin Lutyens.*

76.—COTTAGE AT GREY WALLS, GULLANE: STONE WALLS, GREY PANTILED ROOF.

It may be hoped that economic necessity will not forbid altogether the building of stone cottages, for they give in many parts of the country the most perfect opportunity to maintain the traditions of design and workmanship which have grown out of the very character of the material.

77.—ROCKYFIELD, CHARNWOOD FOREST : STONE WALLS AND SWAITHLAND SLATE ROOF.

*Ernest Gimson.*

Whether in Scotland (Fig. 76), in Leicestershire (Fig. 77), or the Cotswolds (Figs. 78 and 79), the skill of architects swift to understand the qualities of the local stone results in buildings no less beautiful and characteristic than those of bygone days.

*Sydney Barnsley.*

78.—TYPICAL COTSWOLD MASONRY AND STONE TILES : GYDE ALMSHOUSES.

The great step forward in the introduction of new materials and methods made in 1925 raises so many important questions that I deal with them in a separate chapter.

*Sydney Barnsley.*

79.—A TYPICAL COTSWOLD CHIMNEY : GYDE ALMSHOUSES.

# CHAPTER V

## NOVEL METHODS OF CONSTRUCTING " SUBSIDY COTTAGES," 1925

The Housing Problem, Technical rather than Political—The Flight from Brickwork—" Steel " Cottages—Alternative Methods exhibited at Wembley—Timber—Slate—New Sorts of Concrete—Shuttering—Cork

THE three post-war Housing Acts which are conveniently recognized by the names of their political parents—the Addison Act, the Neville Chamberlain Act, and the Wheatley Act—contributed to the Housing Problem all the administrative and financial wisdom of Liberal, Conservative, and Labour policies. When Mr. Ramsay Macdonald's Government fell and the election battle which carried Mr. Baldwin a second time into power was set, no party seriously put forward any new financial policy with regard to housing with a promise that its adoption would solve the problem. It seemed to be generally agreed that salvation could be found only in the technical field. The problem had come to be the discovery of materials or methods of construction which would avoid drawing on the small and diminishing strength of bricklayers and plasterers. The factors of inadequate men and materials dominate the situation. The " steel house " with the manufacture of which Lord Weir associated himself, and others with which the Duke of Atholl and Messrs. Braithwaite are concerned, were acclaimed as the solution of rapid housing. The two latter perhaps more justly deserved the title of " steel house " because the bones of the house were of metal as well as the skin, but the " Weir house " is essentially a timber house with a steel skin. Sir Ernest Moir's Committee, set up to report on the housing materials and methods which offered a sound alternative to brick, does not seem to have been enthusiastic about steel houses, but very wisely abstained from rejecting any feasible method that showed a way of catching up the shortage. The Government made it financially easy for Housing Authorities to build specimen houses of the Weir and other experimental types, in order that they might

be able to judge of their merits.   Lord Weir contemplated that
his steel cottages would be made and put up by engineering,
not by building, labour, and would thus serve to relieve a trade
suffering from abnormal unemployment.   This led to a loud
controversy and the setting up of an official inquiry into rates
of wages, Trade Union rules, and so forth, resulting in a Report
which left matters much as they were.

While this rather arid and obscure discussion of Trade Union
difficulties continued, there was provided in the Palace of Housing
and Transport at the British Empire Exhibition of 1925 an in-
tensely practical commentary, in a group of complete cottages
built in various novel ways.   None of the steel houses was among
them, and, because it prevented effective comparison, their
absence was a loss.   But the English building public seemed
to have come broadly to the conclusion that a wooden-framed

*Stanley Hamp.*

80.—THE TIBBENHAM COTTAGE (PLANS OPPOSITE).

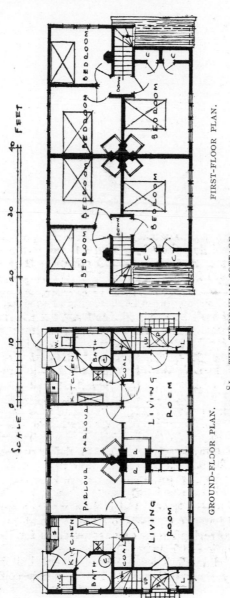

FIRST-FLOOR PLAN.

GROUND-FLOOR PLAN.

81.—THE TIBBENHAM COTTAGE.

G

*Clough Williams-Ellis.*

82.—THE ALL-SLATE COTTAGE.

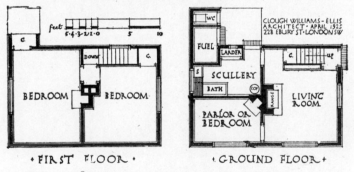

• FIRST FLOOR •          • GROUND FLOOR •

83.—PLANS OF THE ALL-SLATE COTTAGE.

house with an ungalvanized steel skin was too much like the Army hut of familiar memory to capture the affections, and too likely to involve high recurring repair costs for it to yield an economic solution of housing difficulties.

The main characteristics of the different building methods illustrated by these cottages, and such simple comparisons as may fairly be made, are the subject of this chapter. The order in which they are described has no significance, but it may be convenient to begin with the pair of cottages which presents the most traditional appearance. I have added also at the end of the chapter particulars of other 1925 developments not seen at Wembley.

There is no more historical method of building a wall than in " half-timber." The Tibbenham Construction Company produced from the designs of Mr. Stanley Hamp a pair of cottages which would look normal in any English village. Moreover, the construction is genuinely " half-timber," for the framework is entirely of oak. The modern element is furnished by the way in which the timber framing is filled in. In place of the primitive wattle and daub, there are inserted, in the grooved framing, sheets of corrugated asbestos. The thickness of the framing is then filled up, on the outside with dense concrete, and on the inside with a porous breeze concrete. Thus is prevented the risk of condensation which follows when a dense concrete is used for the interior face of a wall. There is no reason to fear that this method, which provides a vertical damp-course, will not give a sound and durable wall, but there seems to be a doubtful feature, in the possibility that, with any considerable warping or twisting of the oak frame, a through-joint might develop at some spot. The central asbestos sheet is designed to prevent this, while helping to make the temperature of the rooms independent of the outside temperature, but it is necessary to bear in mind the great twisting tendency of an oak frame, which moreover may continue active for several years. The upkeep should be low, and the work involves the employment of neither bricklayer nor plasterer.

The floor area of this pair of cottages at Wembley (Fig. 81), which had parlours, was about 770 sq. ft. per cottage, and the cost would be, on a normal site, approximately £610 per cottage for one or two pairs. This works out at 15s. 10d. per foot super. But for a group of a hundred or more, built on a normal site, the cost would be only about £480, i.e. 12s. 6d. per foot super of effective floor space. The same cottages, but with one room less (either omitting parlour or one of the three bedrooms), would mean a saving of £35 per cottage.

For the purpose of comparison, I have taken the effective superficial floor area of the two floors of all the Exhibition cottages described in this chapter, but to simplify the calculation the space occupied by internal partitions is taken as floor area.

Another traditional method, which is to be studied in North Wales, Somerset, and Cornwall, is that of the slate-hung wall. It is true that in bygone days slate-hanging was frequently adopted long after the house was built, in order to provide, for a wall which had proved porous, an impervious weatherproof outer skin. There are, however, some old examples of slate-hanging used on a timber-framed house, just as tile-hanging was similarly used during many centuries in Kent and elsewhere.

The all-slate cottage at Wembley was of the five-roomed type, with living-room and scullery and a third room which would be either parlour or third bedroom downstairs, and the two main bedrooms upstairs. It was designed by Mr. Clough Williams-Ellis. The contractors who built the Wembley cottage, Messrs. Humphries of Knightsbridge, estimated that groups of twenty-five detached cottages exactly as this model could be erected on a normal site at any place within fifty miles of London for £405 each.

The all-slate cottage yielded 722 sq. ft., which works out, on the £405 basis, at 11s. 2½d. per foot super. Groups of fifty cottages might mean a deduction of £20 per cottage ; a difficult site, or building in a place not readily accessible, might easily mean 5 per cent. or 10 per cent. increase on the above figures. An all-slate cottage is a little dour in colour, with the walls as well as the roof of grey. As, however, slates take whitewash admirably, there is no difficulty about having the vertical slate-hanging white.

I come now to two sorts of timber houses built by Messrs.

84.—THE " CENTURY " HOUSE (PLANS OPPOSITE).

Henry Boot & Sons at Wembley, both called " The Century House," but distinguished as " shingle type " and " gunite type." In both cases the bones of the house consisted of a stout timber framing. In the " shingle type " this is covered externally on the lower storey with weather-boarding laid over felt, and above with Canadian cedar shingles. Internally, panelling or a pulp board is used as an alternative to plaster. The external boarding was impregnated with Oxylene, a fireproofing solution.

This seems to be a thoroughly sound house and should effectually resist the weather for a century. I am personally doubtful about the use of Canadian cedar shingles ; they give a charming surface, and, of course, are in very common use throughout America and Canada, with, so far as I know, satisfaction. It is, however, possible in our climate of alternating wet and sunshine that some splitting a n d twisting might take place. This, however, is a simple criticism, because the cedar shingles could be replaced by ordinary feather-edged weather-boarding, costing approximately the same and giving an equally attractive appearance.

The alternative method of giving a weatherproof skin to " The Century House " is indicated by the n a m e " gunite." The main timber structure of the cottages is first covered with felt, and a cement and sand sheath is then applied under powerful pressure with a cement gun, and the

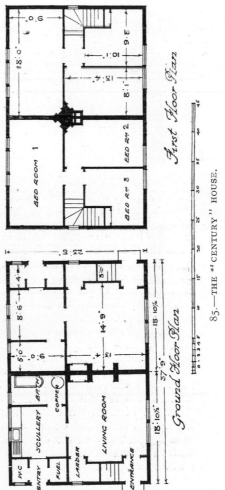

85.—THE " CENTURY " HOUSE.

*First Floor Plan*

*Ground Floor Plan*

plaster skin so formed has a strong steel reinforcement of expanded metal. The speed of constructing either type of house depends, of course, on numbers and on skill in organizing the task, but six months should normally be enough to complete a scheme of 100 houses, and the rate of building ought to increase materially for larger schemes. With regard to price, £450 per house may be regarded as a fair average for not less than 100 at a time, built on normal sites, and excluding foundations, fencing, and drains. Taking the effective superficial floor area of each cottage as 816 sq. ft., the cost per foot super works out at a little over 11s.

The main claim for the Dennis-Wild house is that the method of using a skeleton steel framing with patent cradle roof trusses, clothed with normal materials, makes for such improved speed in building that, although the materials themselves are no cheaper, the saving in time and labour results in a very inexpensive house. In the building of an ordinary brick cottage a considerable amount of time is normally wasted, because men cannot work in the rain. The Dennis-Wild system provides that first of all the steel skeleton is built and the roof forthwith put on. This skeleton is encased as to the lower half of the house with a cavity wall of brickwork and breeze blocks, and as to the upper part with a cavity wall of tile hanging and breeze blocks. The bricklayer is not eliminated, but the amount of brickwork needed is only one-quarter of that required for an all-brick house.

The cost of these cottages built in pairs in groups of about 200 at a time, and assuming a normal site, is £870 per pair, i.e. £435 per single cottage, inclusive of fences, drains, and decorations. The effective floor area of the Wembley house as shown by the accompanying plans was 800 super feet, and at a cost of £435 per cottage this represents 10s. 10½d. per superficial foot of floor. This system is not suitable for single houses, or even a few pairs. Mass production is necessary to secure the economies offered. It is much to the credit of the Dennis-Wild house that it presents a pleasant and traditional appearance.

Perhaps the most novel method of wall-building shown at Wembley was the Billner method of " aërocrete " or aërated concrete. The novelty here consists in the fabric of the wall itself. Instead of using an ordinary aggregate for the concrete, whether gravel and sand or some form of crushed clinker or breeze, a special aggregate is supplied ready mixed with cement and with other materials which profoundly affect its behaviour when water is added.

It can best be described in a popular way by saying that the concrete is made with " baking powder." When water

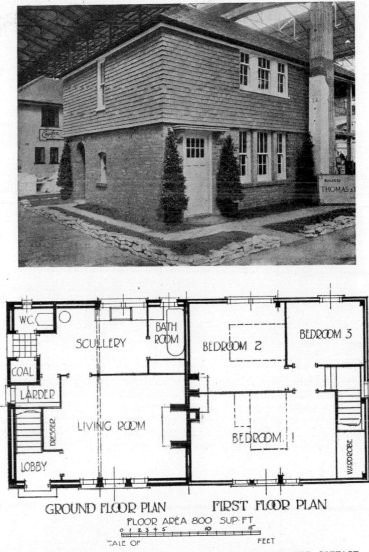

86 AND 87.—PHOTOGRAPH AND PLAN OF THE DENNIS-WILD COTTAGE.

has been added to the special mixture it expands, so that the finished block or slab increases in bulk to double its initial volume. The resulting concrete is something like pumice stone, *i.e.* it is permeated by air cavities, which have the effect of making it impermeable to damp, and of giving it a very high insulating value. Professor A. H. Barker has reported that a solid wall

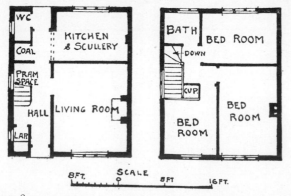

88 AND 89.—COTTAGE OF " AËROCRETE " OR AËRATED CONCRETE.

of " aërated " concrete 8 in. thick has the same insulating value as a $15\frac{1}{2}$-inch wall made up of $9\frac{1}{2}$ in. of dense concrete and 4 in. of coke-breeze concrete, with an air cavity of 2 in., and, alternatively, as solid brickwork of a thickness of $20\frac{1}{2}$ in. The method of building a wall with this novel material is left to the taste of the builder. At Wembley each of the four walls of the cottage was cast flat on the floor, openings being left for doors and windows. When the expansion was complete and the walls thoroughly set in one piece, each in turn was hauled up by very simple tackle to the vertical position, and the necessary jointing done at the four corners. This method of handling pre-cast walls in one piece was, I believe, originally adopted in America, but with the " aërated " concrete the task is as easy as it is difficult with ordinary concrete. Aërated concrete weighs approximately only 42 lb. per cubic foot. It is also claimed that it does not sweat ; that its strength increases with age ; and that it is fireproof. It is just as valuable for casting in moulds for blocks to be built like ordinary masonry as for casting in shuttering for monolithic building.

From lack of experience in this country, it is difficult to say exactly what saving of cost can be secured by this method, but it is claimed that the cost of building a wall 8 in. thick, including labour, the use of shuttering, and external and internal finish, is 11s. per superficial yard, which may be compared with 16s. for a 9-inch brick wall. The material is supplied in bags ready mixed, with all instructions for use. Any kind of shuttering can be used according to the judgment of the builder. So far as foundations are concerned, these can be of ordinary concrete or of the aërated concrete.

The fundamental claim for aërated concrete is that it contains about 70 per cent. of air cavity in very small and finely distributed cells, each cell being a closed compartment.

There were two cottages at Wembley the main claims for which were based on the method of shuttering to take the concrete rather than on the material of the concrete wall so built—namely, those of the Universal Housing Company and the " Easiform " system of Messrs. Laing. There is no doubt that the shuttering difficulty is the main obstacle to a much greater use of concrete for cottage walls than has so far been seen. It really comes to this. The building of a concrete cottage with ordinary timber shuttering means the erection of a hollow wooden skeleton. The filling of the skeleton with concrete almost constitutes the building of a second house, and then the skeleton timber framing is pulled down. That is a rather exaggerated way of putting it, but it is substantially true, and explains why concrete cottages built with ordinary wooden shuttering cost at least as much as

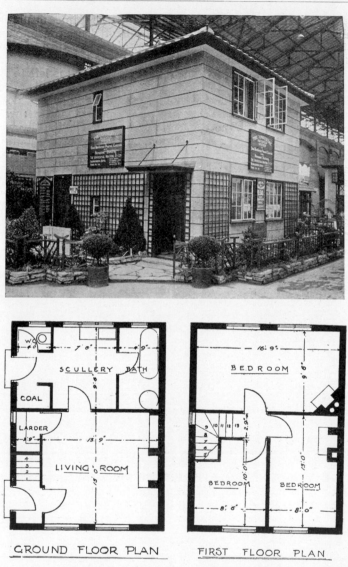

GROUND FLOOR PLAN    FIRST FLOOR PLAN

90 AND 91.—" UNIVERSAL HOUSING " TYPE.

brick, and generally more. Another factor of expense is due to
the necessity of providing, in the thickness of the concrete wall,
either a cavity to stop the passage of damp, or some impervious

vertical damp-course embedded in the concrete that will answer the same purpose. The Universal Housing Company's solution of the problem is to do away altogether with temporary shuttering, and to use instead a permanent shuttering which becomes the finished internal and external faces of the wall. The photograph of their Wembley cottage shows a structure which looks rather as though it were built in masonry ; the horizontal lines mark the joints in the external permanent pieces of shuttering, which are made of a composition consisting of asbestos and cement. Light steel stanchions are fixed after the concrete foundation and plinth have been laid by unskilled labour ; the roof plate is fixed to them, and the roof framed and covered in. Here, as in the Dennis-Wild house, the rest of the work can be carried on regardless of rain. Concrete is filled in between the permanent external shuttering already described and an inner lining of asbestos cement sheeting, and this can be carried up rapidly to the roof plate, which has already been fixed.

It is claimed that the wall so produced is thoroughly permanent, weather-proof and vermin-proof, and that the minimum amount of skilled labour is required. The builders state that the cottage as shown at Wembley, with an effective floor area of about 760 sq. ft., would cost about £40 less than a brick-built house of the same size. The cost of single cottages of the Wembley type should be £500 (14s. a foot super), for a single pair £900 the pair (13s. 2d. a foot super), and for pairs or groups of four in a scheme of 200 houses £400 each (10s. 6d. a foot super).

The points about Messrs. Laing's " Easiform " shuttering are that it is permanent and in large sizes made to fit the design of the cottage to be built. The Wembley exhibition house was a single cottage, but it is more usual to build them in pairs or threes, and certainly less expensive. " Easiform " is mainly applicable to schemes of a certain size : it would not be economic to prepare special shuttering for small quantities. A few, however, can be built if a plan is adopted for which shuttering already exists. The superficial floor area of the Wembley cottage was 729 sq. ft., and the cost of building cottages of this size on a normal site, inclusive of drains, paths, and fences, would be about £430, which gives a price of 10s. 10d. per superficial foot.

As the Exhibition cottage here illustrated is of a somewhat uncompromising appearance, I add a photograph of a pair of cottages built on the " Easiform " system which shows that it is flexible enough (Fig. 94).

In the same category as the aërated concrete cottage is the system known as " Corolite," a concrete made of Portland cement and crushed clinker of such a size that it will pass through

92.—" EASIFORM " CONCRETE COTTAGE BUILT WITH STEEL
SHUTTERING.

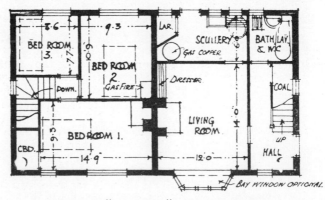

93.—PLANS OF " EASIFORM " COTTAGES IN PAIRS.

94.—" EASIFORM " COTTAGES FOR CUMBERLAND AND WESTMORLAND
MENTAL HOSPITAL.

a $\frac{3}{4}$-inch mesh, with the fine material and dust eliminated by passing this through a $\frac{3}{8}$-inch screen. By this means a wall is formed similar to the " aërated " concrete wall (but for a different reason, namely, the lack of fine material), in so far as it contains an infinite number of small air cavities. The result is that water is not drawn through the concrete, either horizontally or, as happens with ordinary mass concrete, vertically upwards by capillary attraction. The system was first employed in Holland, where it was found to be so effective that builders were able to dispense with a damp-course, since the lack of rising damp made it superfluous.

The " Corolite " wall is poured in a special shuttering, which can be used repeatedly. It is the usual practice for the external walls to be 8 in. in thickness and internal walls 4 in.

It is claimed that the saving on a " Corolite " house, as compared with a similar house built with an 11-inch cavity wall in brick, is from 10 to 30 per cent. on the cost of the carcase. The actual amount saved depends on how much " Corolite " takes the place of other materials than brick, e.g. wooden floors and roof. If the flues, staircase, floors, and flat roof were of " Corolite," the saving on the complete cottage might be as much as 20 per cent. The walls only of a cottage represent about one-seventh of the total cost, so where a material such as " Corolite " is used in place of brick, the saving can only be some part of one-seventh. Taking a cottage as costing £490, there is only £70 on which the saving can be made, if all is normal save the walls.   I am not

95.—HOUSES IN HOLLAND BUILT OF COROLITE.

able to illustrate an English Corolite house at the date I write this, but Fig. 95 shows a pleasant group of flat-roofed houses in Holland in which the design is happily adapted to the material.

An important point to remember in the case of all the costs

given in this chapter is that they are the prices payable to the
builder, from which it is fair to deduct the £75 Government
subsidy before arriving at the net cost to the cottage owner.
All the prices, needless to say, assume a normal site, a reasonable
distance from a railway station, and the absence of special local
difficulties.

This is a convenient place to describe a system which had not
" come out " even as recently as those described above.

It must be confessed that the early essays in what are called
" steel houses " have not brought any great deliverance in the
housing problem. The Dorman Long Housing Company's
latest type is virtually an example of modern steel framed con
struction, familiar to all those who live in cities, reduced to

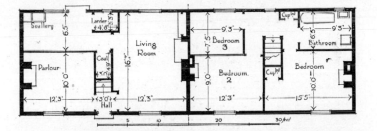

96 AND 97.—DORMAN LONG " CORK HOUSE." PLANS AND
PHOTOGRAPH SHOWING TYPE OF CONSTRUCTION.

cottage proportions, and as such it is claimed to be a concrete house.

References are made elsewhere to the first type of steel-framed house used in part by Messrs. Dorman Long when building Dormanstown. The architectural treatment of the cottages by Professor Adshead and Mr. Patrick Abercrombie prevented that reproach which has not unjustly attached to certain types of steel houses. The constructional system then used has been carefully developed since and the illustrations of the latest type shown in Figs. 96 to 98 mark a great advance. These cottages are constructed with an insulating wall on a steel frame, and the insulating material that is used in the wall is somewhat startlingly novel in its application to housing, namely, cork.

The steel framework of a parlour cottage weighs about two tons, and the members, none of which weigh more than 2 cwt., are fully made up at the factory and marked to facilitate erection at the site.

Erection of the framework of a pair of parlour houses can be done by four men in one day. As the bedroom floor is carried on the transverse members of the steel framework, the partition walls on the ground floor are relieved of any share of its weight. This means that the architect in planning the cottage is left with perfect freedom as to the position of the partition walls on both floors and indeed as to the design generally ; this is a particular feature of the system and should go a long way towards preventing monotony in large housing schemes.

The insulating core consists of cork-board $1\frac{1}{2}$ in. thick, of the same kind that has been used for twenty years in insulating cold storage buildings ; it is, therefore, a proven material ideal for maintaining warmth within the house in winter and keeping it cool in summer, and it is sound-proof.

It is composed of granulated cork that has been highly compressed and baked whilst under pressure, and in this form it is claimed that it resists fire, is damp-proof, does not disintegrate or settle in course of time, and that, enclosed as it is in concrete on both sides, it is vermin-proof.

The way of building is to fill the spaces between the vertical steel stanchions with pre-cast slabs of cork board and clinker-breeze or coke-breeze concrete $3\frac{1}{4}$ in. in thickness, bedded in cement, cork-board $1\frac{1}{2}$ in. thick facing outwards and breeze concrete 2 in. thick facing inwards.

Wire mesh reinforcement is attached to the steel frame on the outer side and kept at its right distance from the insulating slabs by " distance pieces." A concrete skin 2 in. thick is applied on the outer side under pressure by a cement gun, and the steel members are protected from corrosion by a covering of cement

*J. W. Green.*

98.—DORMAN LONG SYSTEM OF INSULATING CORK WALLS.

H

on all sides. The interior face of the slabs is finished with cement or lime plaster applied either by the gun or by hand to a thickness of half an inch, and this in conjunction with the insulating effect of the cork should effectively prevent condensation. The chimney stacks are in brickwork, and the roof is of the usual timber construction, tiled or slated. The bricklayer and plasterer are therefore not entirely eliminated, but if this should be essential, the chimneys can be formed of concrete, and one or other of the numerous plaster boards can be used for wall lining and ceilings.

After much experiment with alternative forms of flooring, Messrs. Dorman Long have returned to wood throughout the house except for the scullery and offices. For the ground floor, the boards are laid in tar directly on the concrete raft which consists of 2 in. of breeze concrete laid over 4 in. of ordinary concrete. For the bedroom floor the boards are attached to light wooden joists supported on the transverse steel members, and all ceilings are covered with lath and plaster or panelled in plaster board.

Although the principle of construction is novel except in so far as the concrete is applied by the cement gun, there is nothing unusual in the actual work of erection, and no operation other than the " gunning," which cannot be performed by the average building trade craftsmen and labourers.

One of the first contracts secured by the Company was with the Air Ministry for forty houses to their own plans for the occupation of married airmen. The Ministry of Health after exhaustive tests by their Research Department recommended the system for adoption by Local Authorities and others, which qualifies it for the Government subsidy.

As with other types of construction, the cost is difficult to estimate on account of the wide variation of conditions, but a parlour type of house of standard type and of maximum subsidy size, i.e. 950 ft. super, should be possible on all except abnormal sites, for £525 or under. In fairly large numbers, say 200, and on average sites, this figure should be reducible to £495. Taking an average of £510, this works out at 10s. 9d. per foot super, and in large numbers, and on a really favourable site, this figure should be still further reduced.

Reviewing the ten methods described above, it is seen that the lowest cost per superficial foot of effective floor space is about 10s. 6d., assuming a scheme of 200 houses, and the most expensive something under 16s. in a single pair. I do no discourtesy to the firms, who gave me the prices set out above, in pointing out that they applied to building on normal sites, i.e. with optimum conditions. In practice, sites have an unpleasant habit of developing abnormal conditions and causing extras which easily increase a rate of 10s. 6d. per foot super to 12s. 6d. or more.

By way of comparing the figures given above with normal pairs of subsidy cottages with 11-inch brick walls, I can quote a group of ten pairs just built at Ashtead, Surrey, the architects being Messrs. Hendry and Schooling. They are good cottages of

*Hendry & Schooling.*

99 AND 100.—BRICK COTTAGES AT ASHTEAD, SURREY.

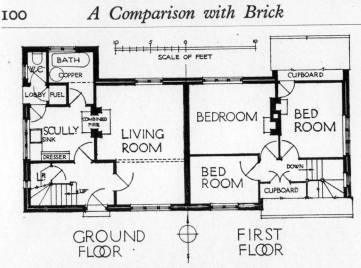

SCALE OF FEET

BATH
COPPER
W.C
LOBBY FUEL
SCULLY
SINK
DRESSER
COMBINED FIRE
LIVING ROOM
CUPBOARD
BEDROOM
BED ROOM
BED ROOM
DOWN
CUPBOARD

GROUND FLOOR ·        FIRST FLOOR

101.—PLAN OF ASHTEAD COTTAGES.

excellent brick with good tile roofs (Figs. 99 to 101). The cost was £525 per cottage, inclusive of drainage, but exclusive of making road, paths, and fences. The effective floor area of each cottage is 776 sq. ft., which gives a price of 13s. 6d. per foot super. Local conditions elsewhere might be more favourable and bring down the cost to £500 a cottage, but I doubt if it could be done for much less anywhere. It, therefore, appears that there is no great monetary advantage in adopting a novel method as compared with ordinary brick, *provided always that bricks and bricklayers are available.* But that proviso rules out many areas, and may be said to operate for the present against brick cottages everywhere in the case of large housing schemes. It follows that, if novel but sound methods are not adopted widely, the housing shortage will not be caught up and we shall have to face, for an indefinite time, the grave social and political evils which are the result of that shortage.

# CHAPTER VI

## FIVE-ROOMED COTTAGES

BY a five-roomed cottage is meant one with kitchen-living-room, scullery, and three bedrooms.

The possible variation in good planning—and freak plans need not be explored—is not great, and the possible types divide themselves roughly into compact plans, two-rooms deep, and extended plans, one-room deep. The former are more suitable for a south aspect, with the living-room looking that way and the scullery facing north. If the main aspect is to the north it is possible to put the scullery facing the front and the living-room facing the garden, but the occupants do not like it, and the one-room deep plan is perhaps the more desirable, especially in

*Carby Hall and Dawson.*

102.—AT BARDSEY : 11-INCH BRICK WALLS.

101

the country, where the longer frontage required by this type
does not affect the cost of the site.   It is, however, more costly
to build and not so warm.   I deal first with the compact type of
plan seen well in the *Country Life* 1914 Competition first prize
designs.   It will be noted how, with almost identical plans, a
totally different character is given to the varying country types
by traditional treatment of
the elevations, modelling of
the roofs, and the use of
local materials.

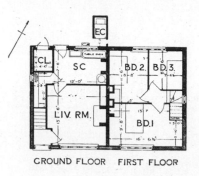

GROUND FLOOR    FIRST FLOOR

103.—WEST RIDING COTTAGES.

The Yorkshire West Rid-
ing cottages were built by
Major G. R. Lane-Fox, M.P.,
one pair at Bardsey, with
11-inch brick walls (Fig. 102),
one pair at Bramham Park
with 9-inch walls rough-cast
(Fig. 104), and another pair
like them at Walton. The
plans of both are given in
Fig. 103.

Built early in the war these cottages cost under £400 per pair.
The sizes of rooms in these cottages follow Schedule I (given

*Carby Hall and Dawson.*

104.—AT BRAMHAM PARK: 9-INCH BRICK ROUGH-CAST.
(*The Walton pair is similar.*)

on page 17) very closely, except that the scullery is 90 ft. super instead of 80 ft.

The plan of the Essex type of cottages built for Mr. Foot Mitchell at Newport, Essex, is very similar (Figs. 105 and 106), but the elevation is more distinctive.

Essex boasts a very definite tradition of cottage-building, the most marked feature of which is pargeting. The exterior plastered walls are decorated with a simple panel treatment which is often diversified by rough patterning of zigzags, basket work, or other simple forms. The first prize design by Mr. Holland W. Hobbiss, with its surface panelling of irregular shapes dictated by the shape of the windows and other features, shows a clear grasp of this tradition, and the panel containing initials and date is an inexpensive bit of decoration, which adds a personal touch to the front.

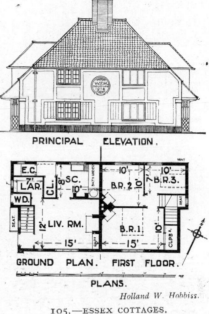

PRINCIPAL ELEVATION.

GROUND PLAN. FIRST FLOOR.

PLANS.

*Holland W. Hobbiss.*

105.—ESSEX COTTAGES.

The photograph reproduced in Fig. 106 does not do justice to a very effective design, and the elevation shown with the plan in Fig. 105 gives a fairer idea of it.

These cottages cost less than £350 the pair early in the war, which was very creditable.

The task of maintaining to-day anything like the traditional character in cottage-building in the face of the over-mastering claims of economy is made all the greater by the shortage of traditional materials. It is therefore the more pleasant to note how successful Messrs. Kieffer and Fleming have been in maintaining the Essex vernacular in the cottages at Debden and Elmdon, designed by them for the Saffron Walden Rural District Council. That part of the uplands of Essex, near such notable places as Thaxted and Newport, has largely retained its old character. Pargeted and thatched cottages still abound, but in view of devastating thatch fires in the neighbourhood during recent years, it was wise no doubt to use tiled roofs in these two schemes. There can just be traced in the picture of the Elmdon cottages the simple panels of pargeting, which was developed so richly in some of the old examples. The elm boarding on the gabled projection, and the interest given by

*Holland W. Hobbiss.*

106.—PARGETED COTTAGES AT NEWPORT, ESSEX.

the diapering of the bricks on the end chimney-stack are also little touches which can have cost practically nothing extra, but show the architects' desire to preserve local traditions. They were obviously fortunate in being able to get tiles of

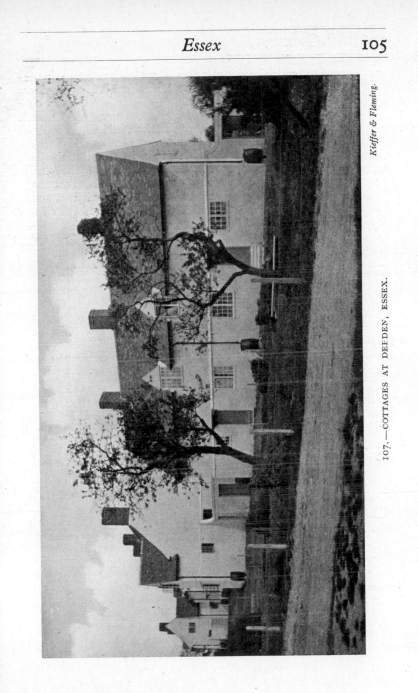

Kieffer & Fleming.

107.—COTTAGES AT DEEDEN, ESSEX.

varying colour, which have given the attractive speckled appearance to the roofs. The Debden cottages make a particularly
attractive group on the roadside.

The "two-room deep" type of five-roomed cottage is well
exemplified by a pair built by Major Charles Mitchell, at Pallins-
burn, Cornhill-on-Tweed, to the designs of Mr. Wilfrid Lawson
(Figs. 111 and 112), which won first prize in the Northumberland
section of the *Country Life* 1914 Competition. As the site is
very exposed this type of plan was well chosen, because a
" through " living-room with windows on the north and south
sides would have been a cold room. The walls are of the hard

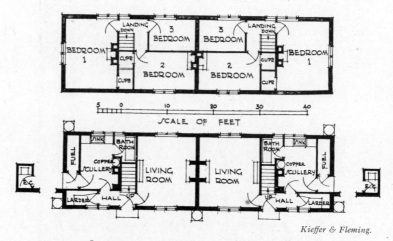

Kieffer & Fleming.

108.—PLAN OF COTTAGES AT DEBDEN, ESSEX.

local freestone, and the roofs were specified to be either of slates,
which were, however, costly, or of pantiles which are strictly in
the Northern tradition. The dormers are rather larger than is
ideal on the grounds of appearance, but they give very well-
lighted bedrooms, and one chimney-stack, common to the pair,
is an economical advantage in stone-built cottages.

The cottages are very comfortable and much liked by their
tenants. In the Competition particulars Mr. Lawson estimated
that the pair would cost £440, but to meet the North Country
desire for a large kitchen-living-room each cottage was extended
2 ft. in frontage length, and when it came to building in 1916,
the pair cost about £700.

Among North Country houses built under the Addison scheme,
those at Newburn-on-Tyne, designed by Messrs. Harvey and Wicks

*Kieffer & Fleming.*

109.—THE ESSEX MANNER AT ELMDON.

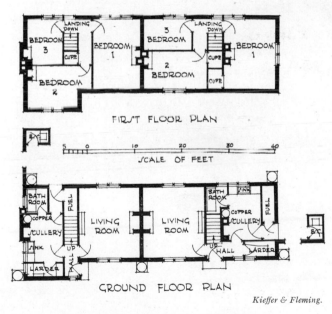

FIRST FLOOR PLAN

SCALE OF FEET

GROUND FLOOR PLAN

*Kieffer & Fleming.*

110.—PLAN OF COTTAGES AT ELMDON.

in association with Messrs. Adshead and Ramsey, are good and simple (Figs. 113 and 114). The bathrooms are on the ground floor and away from the scullery, and the big living-rooms are through-lighted.

*Wilfrid Lawson.*

111.—NORTHUMBERLAND TYPE.

No record of the two-room deep plan would be complete without reference to its use, many years ago, in a scheme which will take an honourable place in the history of English housing.

We are entitled to expect of the cottages at Bournville, one of the earliest places to be laid out on a generous scheme of village-planning, that they shall be attractive, and no less can

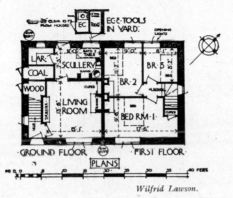

*Wilfrid Lawson.*

112.—NORTHUMBERLAND TYPE: ORIGINAL PLAN.

be said of the two pairs designed by Mr. Alexander Harvey, illustrated (Figs. 115 and 116) with the plan common to both. These contain 22,000 cubic feet, and at 5*d*. a cubic foot cost £230 per cottage many years before the war. Great stress is laid, and wisely, on the needlessness of ornament on such cottages. The Bournville cottages are free from it, but in the nearer pair the sweep of the tiling over the upper windows and the stepping of the chimney give, practically without extra expense, just that touch of character which marks them as architecture when compared with sheer utilitarianism. In the further pair variety has been achieved by carrying the dormers higher and gabling them, and by putting bays to the front windows.

Turning now to the extended cottage plan, one-room deep, a very good example is provided by the Suffolk type (Figs. 117 and 118) for which a first prize in the *Country Life* 1914 Competition was awarded to Mr. C. J. Kay, the cottages being built at Campsea Ashe by Lord Ullswater.

The pair cost in 1916 about £470.

The plan is rather unusual, in that the staircase rises in the middle of the cottage from a little lobby which connects the living-room, scullery and larder. This arrangement has the objection that there are two doors between the living-room and scullery, but there is the corresponding advantage that the living-room has only two doors (one from the outer lobby and one from this internal lobby), and its allowance of 194 square

*Harvey & Wicks and Adshead & Ramsey.*

113.—HOUSES AT NEWBURN-ON-TYNE.

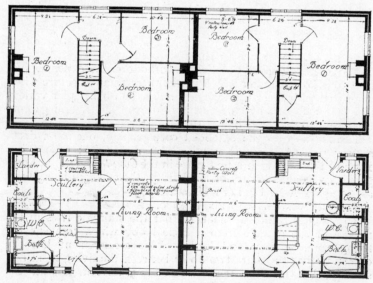

*Harvey & Wicks and Adshead & Ramsey.*

114.—PLAN OF HOUSES AT NEWBURN-ON-TYNE.

feet is all unimpeded space in consequence.  It is, perhaps, the
most comfortable living-room in any of the cottages illustrated

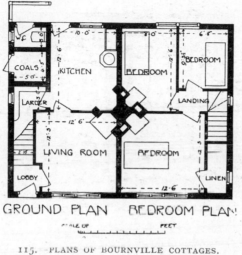

GROUND PLAN    BEDROOM PLAN

SCALE OF        FEET

115.—PLANS OF BOURNVILLE COTTAGES.

in this chapter, and is lighted both from the north and the south.
The scullery is, in part, a passage-room.   This is a good point,

*Alexander Harvey.*

116.—PAIRS OF BOURNVILLE COTTAGES.

in so far as it prevents its being used as a room for meals, but, it is fair to add that where a scullery has a bath in it, the fact that it is a passage-room is an inconvenience.   The bedrooms

C. J. Kay.

117.—LORD ULLSWATER'S SUFFOLK COTTAGES.

upstairs are comfortable and well provided with cupboards.   The simple roof treatment without dormers is thoroughly typical of Suffolk, and looks very well with the plain whitewashed walls. The cottages are very warm because each has only two windows

to the north, all the rest of them facing south, east and west.
For all its simplicity, this design shows considerable skill, and
the break-back of the middle part of the south front not only
much simplifies fenestration by doing away with dormers, but
gives a touch of interest to the modelling of the cottage.

Somewhat similar is the pair built for the Earl of Lytton at
Knebworth, as the first prize design for Hertfordshire, to the
plans of Messrs. A. and J. Soutar (Figs. 119 and 120). Their
conception of a Hertfordshire type was thoroughly simple and

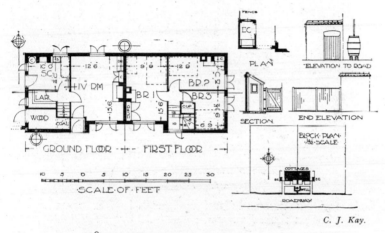

C. J. Kay.

118.—PLANS OF THE SUFFOLK COTTAGES.

effective. There are simple sloping dormers on both fronts,
and ample window space in the tile-hung gable ends. Many
architects waste money by providing dormer windows in the
roofs when they have designed blank gable ends which it would
be much cheaper to pierce with plain windows, as in this case.
Messrs. Soutar adopted what may be called the " through "
principle for their living-room plan, lighting it both from the
east and the west, and put the scullery at the end. The position
of the scullery sink is not ideal with respect to the living-room,
and the scullery itself has a floor of rather larger area than
necessary. Schedule I provides for 80 square feet, whereas
Messrs. Soutar gave 105 square feet. The total area of the ground-
floor rooms could not have been less to allow the three bedrooms
upstairs, but it would have been better if more space had been
given to the living-room and less to the scullery. The bedroom
plan is particularly admirable by reason of the provision of a
large cupboard in each bedroom. There are three chimney

I

stacks to the pair of cottages, so placed as to allow the provision of a fireplace in the third bedroom, if it were desired.   Particular attention may be drawn to the convenient placing of the cot in the largest bedroom.

The pair cost less than £400 in 1916.

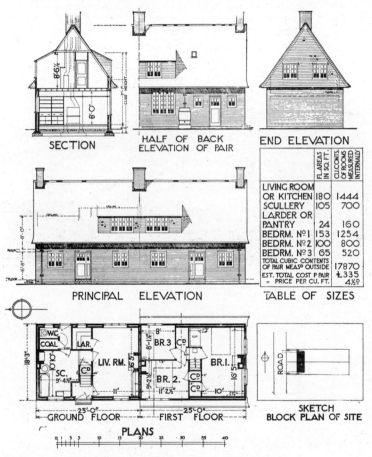

SECTION        HALF OF BACK        END ELEVATION
               ELEVATION OF PAIR

PRINCIPAL   ELEVATION        TABLE OF SIZES

| | FL. AREAS IN SQ. FT. | CU. CONTS. OF ROOMS MEASURED INTERNALLY |
|---|---|---|
| LIVING ROOM OR KITCHEN | 180 | 1444 |
| SCULLERY | 105 | 700 |
| LARDER OR PANTRY | 24 | 160 |
| BEDRM. Nº 1 | 153 | 1254 |
| BEDRM. Nº 2 | 100 | 800 |
| BEDRM. Nº 3 | 65 | 520 |
| TOTAL CUBIC CONTENTS OF PAIR MEASᴰ OUTSIDE | | 17870 |
| EST. TOTAL COST P PAIR | | £335 |
| „ PRICE PER CU. FT. | | 4½ᴰ |

GROUND FLOOR        FIRST FLOOR

PLANS        SKETCH BLOCK PLAN OF SITE

119.—PLANS AND ELEVATIONS OF THE HERTS PAIR.

A pleasant variation in the planning of five-roomed cottages, albeit it involves more cost, is shown in Figs. 121 and 122, which illustrate a pair of Cotswold cottages for the Gyde Charity at Painswick.  The two are of the extended type, but are built to form a right angle on plan.

*A. and J. Soutar.*

120.—THE EARL OF LYTTON'S "COUNTRY LIFE" COTTAGES.

Mr. Sydney H. Barnsley is a master of the building traditions of the district (pictures of other cottages in the group are given

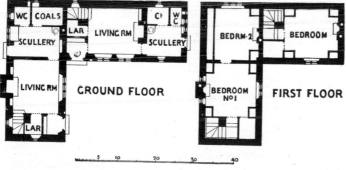

*Sydney Barnsley.*

121.—PLANS OF PAIR OF PAINSWICK COTTAGES.

in Chapter IV) and knows perfectly how to handle the local cream-white colite freestone for the walls and the stone tiles

*Sydney Barnsley.*

122.—AT PAINSWICK : A PAIR RIGHT-ANGLED ON PLAN.

from Stow-on-the-Wold for the roof. I quote Mr. St. Clair Baddeley, who says of these delightful little almshouses :

"It may be averred with some certainty that had the Trustees for this Gyde Charity agreed to expend its moneys in this manner but twenty years ago (as they well might have done) we should have seen arise a red and yellow brick, blue-slated, vermilion-ridged horror perched upon some other beautiful site, to be resembled to nothing so appropriately as to the animal of which at the Zoological Gardens Jerrold said to Lamb : ' That gentleman looks to me as if he had been sitting on a rainbow.' In fact, the latest specimen in this insulting style has been stuck down only seven years ago beside the high road between Painswick and Stroud, face to face with a picturesque old inn, happily to the great distaste of the entire neighbourhood.

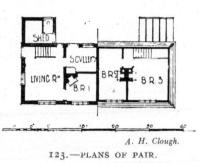

*A. H. Clough.*

123.—PLANS OF PAIR.

"The fundamental advantages of these new Cotswold houses are that in addition to a traditional beauty of line, colour and mouldings, and to the views commanded, all their windows *do* open, and they are supplied with excellent water and a first-rate modern drainage ; while on their north and east sides the windows have been economized as much as reasonably might be done. The delicate curve in the stone door-heads and dripstones sufficiently recalls their Tudor derivation.

"These cottages cost, before the war, £500 the pair, exclusive of laying out the garden, boundary wall, drainage, etc."

I do not like a staircase to rise from the living-room except as a measure of severe economy, which did not rule here, but should have preferred the open porch fitted with an outer door, and the plan re-arranged so that the stair could have risen from the lobby so formed. It is, however, a matter of taste, and

*A. H. Clough.*

124.—PAIR OF FIVE-ROOMED COTTAGES.

followers of tradition can claim much support for the plan
Mr. Barnsley has adopted.

Mr. A. H. Clough has rung another change on this general
type by putting the living-rooms, instead of the sculleries, of
the pair to the outside, in the Hampshire example shown in
Figs. 123 and 124.

He has provided the third bedroom on the ground floor, a
doubtful feature, but almost inevitable where, as in this case,
the mansard roof reduces the floor area upstairs in a pair already
cut down to the minimum. But the least satisfactory point in
the plan is that the living-room fireplace comes between the
doors to the downstairs bedroom and scullery. The external

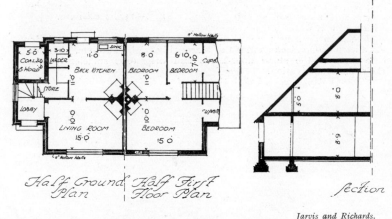

*Jarvis and Richards.*

125.—PLANS OF SUSSEX COTTAGES.

appearance of the pair is very good. Their cost before the war
was £300.

The pair of five-room cottages in Sussex (Figs. 125 to 127)
are interesting for two reasons. They were built, before the war, of
old bricks and tiles from a pair so dilapidated that they had to
come down, and this prevented their ever having the look of
rawness inevitable for a time with new materials.

Secondly, their plan provides for a different way of living than
is generally now liked by the cottager.

Instead of having a working scullery of, say, 80 feet super and
a kitchen living-room of 180 feet, they provide a back kitchen,
which would probably be used as the ordinary living-room, of
121 feet super, and a parlour living-room of 150 feet super. It
would be foolish to dogmatize on this question, but I believe the

*Jarvis and Richards.*

126.—PAIR OF SUSSEX COTTAGES.

weight of evidence is against this method of apportioning the available space.

Among the early groups of subsidy cottages built in a rural

127.—NEWLY BUILT OF OLD MATERIALS.

district under the Addison Act were two blocks each of four cottages at Chobham, Surrey. Their planning as the homes of agricultural folk was based on what was found popular in the neighbourhood prior to 1914. Instead of kitchen and parlour,

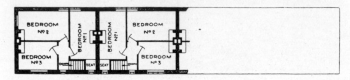

FIRST FLOOR PLAN

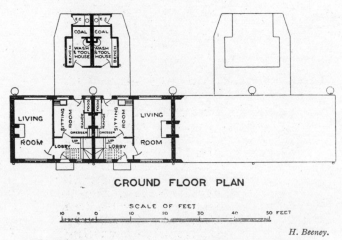

GROUND FLOOR PLAN

SCALE OF FEET

*H. Beeney.*

128 AND 129.—BLOCK OF FOUR COTTAGES AT CHOBHAM.

H. Beeney.

130.—AT CHOBHAM, SURREY: ONE OF THE ADDISON RURAL SCHEMES.

sitting-room and living-room were provided. The cooking-range with dresser were put in the sitting-room, where meals are taken, leaving the living-room free from culinary operations and very agreeable. I feel that the nomenclature of the rooms is a little misleading. The so-called " sitting-room " (*see* plan, Fig. 129) is really a kitchen-dining-room, and the so-called " living-room " is the true sitting-room of the family. Fig. 130 shows what a pleasant elevation these two groups present to the street, and Fig. 128 marks a no less important seemliness in the back elevations with their outbuildings.

*Lawrence Dale.*

131.—RURAL COTTAGES AT ADDERBURY.

I must draw particular attention to Mr. Lawrence Dale's cottages at Adderbury, Oxfordshire, because they represent what is regarded by him, and doubtless also by his clients in typical rural areas, as the final type appropriate to the rural labourer, after his experience gained in erecting about two hundred. The view adopted was that a parlour was a *sine qua non*, because in non-parlour cottages there was too great a tendency for the comfortless little scullery to become the kitchen and living-room. On the other hand, the cottage with kitchen, scullery and parlour was too large and costly, and in that locality at all events the parlour was found superfluous. Mr. Dale has,

*Lawrence Dale.*

132.—"BUTT-AND-BEN" COTTAGES AT ADDERBURY, OXON.

in fact, gone back to the old " butt-and-ben," which may seem
to some people retrograde. The real question is, how do people
live in cottages so planned ? (Fig. 131). They cook in the " ben "
and have their meals very cosily by the kitchen fire. The
" butt " is used for courting and entertaining polite visitors,
but does not tend to become a museum, the danger which
besets the parlour of a real parlour house, because it is a passage-
way. In practice the "butt" is kept as a tidy room, which is
not always the case with the living-room of the typical non-
parlour cottage. I personally regret that there is no bath : a
copper is provided in the scullery (it is not shown on the plan),
but according to Mr. Dale there is no demand for baths in the
neighbourhood, and they were found, when provided, to be used
for storing potatoes. The plan of the larder is a little deceptive,
as it looks as though it had no window, but actually it runs to
the outside window. The upper part has a table top, and the
fuel store runs under this table top, thus utilizing what is not so
valuable as larder space. All the flues are gathered together
in one stack for the pair of cottages. This gives a fireplace in
every room except the third bedroom, and there is an iron chimney for the scullery copper rising just above the low side eaves.
    The claim for this type of cottage is that it combines the merits
of the non-parlour and the parlour cottage in an economical
way. Certainly the amount of brickwork is very small considering the floor area, and there is a valuable bit of accommodation in the large apple-loft over the three bedrooms, a feature
of great value to the rural tenant. The sink in the " ben " is
combined with the dresser to make a presentable piece of furniture. The exterior character of the cottages is very attractive.
Fig. 132, showing a long line of them, marks the fact that there
is nothing wrong with the idea of the standardized pattern,
provided that the standard is a good one.

# CHAPTER VII

## PAIRS OF SIX-ROOMED COTTAGES

A Yorkshire Type—Thatched Pairs in Dorset—Examples by Mr. Clough—Broad and Narrow Frontages—Good Herts and Bucks Types—Lord Riddell's Scheme at Mitcham

THE addition of a parlour to the kitchen, scullery, and three bedrooms of an ordinary five-roomed cottage gives a far larger choice in the possible disposition of the rooms and enables the three bedrooms to be placed on the upper floor without difficulty.

Figs. 133 and 134 show a type for the North Riding of Yorkshire, built by Sir Hugh Bell, Bart., at Ingleby Arncliffe, to the design of Mr. E. Poley. Following Yorkshire custom the scullery is in a back addition. The plan is of the extended type, but with the stairs separating the parlour from the kitchen, and the parlour is entered through the front lobby, a good and practical arrangement. The kitchen is a thoroughly livable room, and the larder and scullery open from it. The

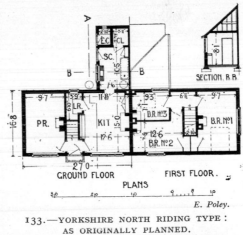

SECTION. B.B.

GROUND FLOOR      FIRST FLOOR.

PLANS

E. Poley.

133.—YORKSHIRE NORTH RIDING TYPE :
AS ORIGINALLY PLANNED.

E.C. is well placed at the far end of the back addition, with the coal cellar adjoining. The bedroom plan is simple and convenient. The external treatment, with the ends half hipped and thus allowing the bedroom window to be in the wall instead of

125

being in a dormer, is well conceived, and the proportions of the front with its two hipped dormers are satisfactory.

134.—SIR HUGH BELL'S COTTAGES : NORTH RIDING TYPE.

*E. Poley.*

The owner of cottages has a good right to be heard on their merits, so I quote Sir Hugh as follows :

" I am sure it will be agreed that the cottages are charming in appearance, and realize the North Country tradition of building. They are certainly all that can be desired in comfort of planning. Their cost has not been as satisfactory, but for that I am mainly to blame. The competition conditions provided that the size of the rooms should be in accordance with Schedule I, with the addition of a parlour 144 ft. (square). To these Mr. Poley strictly adhered, with the result that his design showed a total content, for the two cottages, of 20,901 cubic feet. For the tenants whom I had in mind, however, I thought it better to enlarge the rooms and to add various amenities of equipment, etc., not ordinarily found in labourers' cottages and not essential to decent living. The cottages, therefore, as re-designed and built, have a cubic content of 27,082, a considerable advance on the original scheme.

It is not always that a client admits that increase in cost is the result of his own changes of plan, as Sir Hugh does with characteristic frankness.

In a new hamlet on a Dorset estate there are several pairs of six-roomed cottages built of concrete blocks and thatched (others at the same place are illustrated on pages 127 to 130).

*MacD. Gill.*

135.—DORSET PLAN WITH DORMERS.

In Figs. 135 to 137 are shown back and front and plan of a pair in which the roof starts from the first floor level and the upper windows are dormers. Figs. 138 to 140 similarly show a pair in which the first-floor windows are in the main wall, and there is thus provided a long attic store on the second floor, lighted

*MacDonald Gill.*

136.—CONCRETE AND THATCH : BACK OF DORMERED PAIR.

by a window in the gable. It is interesting to note that the cost of the second pair was only £19 more than the first, so that the two cottages in the second pair got their attic store,

137.—DORMERED CONCRETE COTTAGES IN DORSET: FRONT VIEW.

*MacDonald Gill.*

and more comfortable first-floor bedrooms, at the extra of £9 10s. per cottage, a figure that should be doubled at least to match current costs.

Another pair of cottages on a more modest scale is shown in Figs. 141 and 142, from Mr. Clough's design.   It does not seem

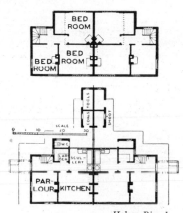

*Halsey Ricardo.*

138.—PLAN OF PAIR WITHOUT DORMERS.

*Halsey Ricardo.*

139.—DORSET CONCRETE COTTAGES, WITH SIDE ENTRANCES :
FRONT VIEW.

good to have the chimneys on the end walls when they could have been placed on the opposite inner walls of the parlours, as in Fig. 133.

K

*Halsey Ricardo.*

140.—DORSET COTTAGES, WITH BACK ADDITION : BACK VIEW.

Of a different sort, and more appropriate for the "week-ender" than the rural worker, is the pair of cottages (Figs. 143

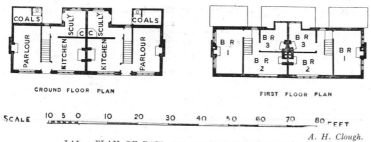

GROUND FLOOR PLAN        FIRST FLOOR PLAN

SCALE

*A. H. Clough.*

141.—PLAN OF PAIR OF SIX-ROOMED COTTAGES.

and 144) at Letchworth, which are characteristic of their designer, Mr. Baillie Scott.

*A. H. Clough.*

142.—PAIR, EACH WITH SIX ROOMS.

They are made picturesque by the wide sweep of roof, and the interiors are markedly pleasant (Fig. 145). The pre-war cost at a time of low building prices was £500 the pair, which removes them from the category of labourers' cottages.

As the cost of land for rural cottages is not usually a serious item in the total cost, the width of frontage taken up is a factor ordinarily determined by other considerations, i.e. as to whether a two-room deep plan or an extended plan best suits the aspect

*Baillie Scott.*

143.—A LONG-FRONTED PAIR.

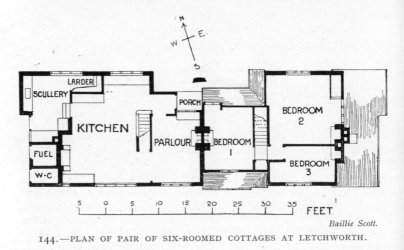

*Baillie Scott.*

144.—PLAN OF PAIR OF SIX-ROOMED COTTAGES AT LETCHWORTH.

or the builder's fancy. Sometimes, however, it is important to save frontage and then the plan needs to be contracted so that the cottage is deeper than its frontage, e.g. a pair of brick cottages at Walton-on-the-Hill designed by Mr. P. Morley

*Baillie Scott.*

145.—INTERIOR OF COTTAGE AT LETCHWORTH.

*P. Morley Horder.*

146.—PAIRS OF COTTAGES AT WALTON HEATH.

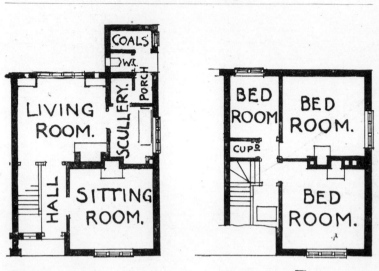

GROUND FLOOR    FIRST FLOOR

*P. Morley Horder.*

147.—PLAN OF NARROW-FRONTED PAIR.

Horder (Figs. 146 and 147). Each cottage has six rooms, including the scullery.

Although the chapter is devoted to six-roomed cottages and a warning has been given that there are already so many four-roomed that more are not needed, it will often happen in new districts that some must be built. They are such small units that it is better to group them with five-roomed or six-roomed. Mr. A. H. Clough has followed the latter course in the block illustrated in Figs. 148 and 149. It will be noticed that in the left-hand six-roomed cottage the space ordinarily given to the parlour is devoted to the purposes of a shop.

Figs. 150 and 151 show a group of three cottages built in York-shire by Major Lane-Fox, M.P., to the designs by Mr. W. T. Lipscomb.

The design is admirable in its simplicity and the walls are of brick rough-cast.

The pair of subsidy cottages built at Town End, Radnage, Bucks, to the design of Mr. Frederick Etchells for Miss Rachel Alexander are below the maximum areas for subsidy cottages, yet give very fair accommodation. The living-rooms are 14 ft. by 11 ft. 6 in., and the parlours smaller but adequate (Figs. 152-3).

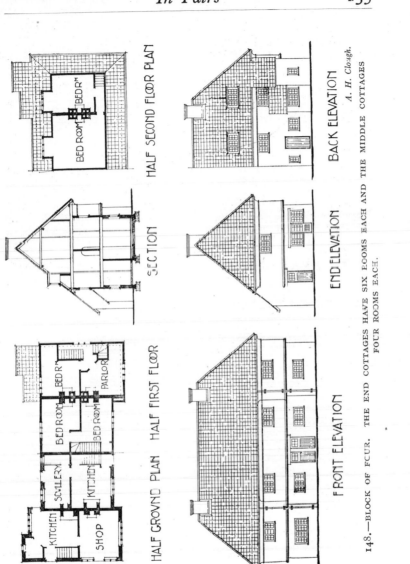

HALF SECOND FLOOR PLAN

BED ROOM | BED R<sup>M</sup>

BACK ELEVATION

*A. H. Clough.*

SECTION

END ELEVATION

HALF GROUND PLAN   HALF FIRST FLOOR

KITCHEN | SCULLERY | BEDROOM | BED R<sup>M</sup>

SHOP | KITCHEN | BEDROOM | PARLOR

FRONT ELEVATION

148.—BLOCK OF FOUR.   THE END COTTAGES HAVE SIX ROOMS EACH AND THE MIDDLE COTTAGES FOUR ROOMS EACH.

*A. H. Clough.*

149.—BLOCK OF FOUR AT BURLEY. TWO WITH SIX ROOMS, TWO WITH
FOUR ROOMS.

*W. T. Lipscomb.*

150.—GROUP OF THREE COTTAGES BUILT IN 1912.

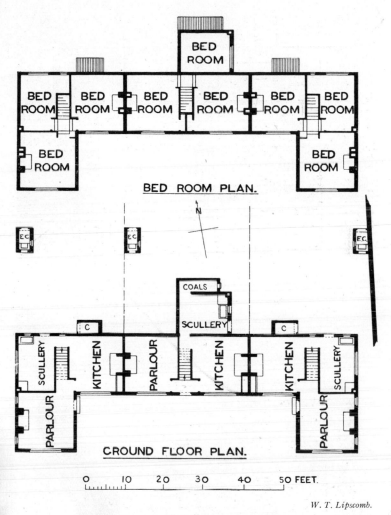

BED ROOM PLAN.

GROUND FLOOR PLAN.

0   10   20   30   40   50 FEET.

*W. T. Lipscomb.*

151.—GROUP OF THREE COTTAGES.

The walls are 11 in. hollow, in stock bricks twice distempered, and the roof of grey-blue Bangor slates. The windows are metal casements set directly into the brickwork. There are no special features otherwise, except perhaps the arrangement of the side and back entrance doors.

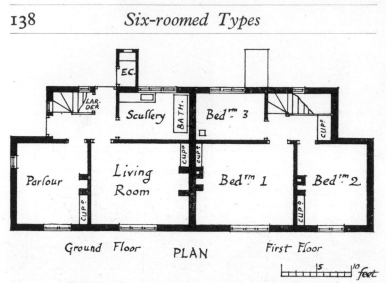

E.C.

LAR-
DER

Scullery

BATH.

Bed^rm 3

CUPD.

Parlour

CUPD

CUP.

Living
Room

CUPD

Bed^rm 1

CUPD.

Bed^rm 2

Ground Floor

PLAN

First Floor

5    10 feet

152.—PLAN OF PAIR AT TOWN END, RADNAGE.

The cost of £1,200 the pair was exceptional, owing to site. Access was by steep and narrow lanes, and the work was about 5 miles from the railway.

*Frederick Etchells.*

153.—PAIR AT TOWN END, RADNAGE, BUCKS.

The parlour houses at Newburn-on-Tyne (Figs. 154 and 155) make a dignified pair with upstairs bathrooms.

The pair of parlour cottages at Hook Norton, designed by

Mr. Lawrence Dale, show a successful use of the mansard roof,
in which a good " boxes " space has been provided. The fuel

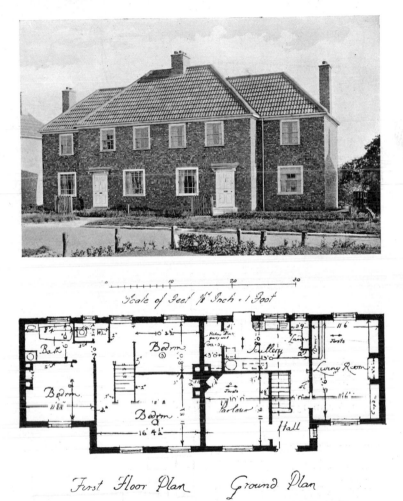

*First Floor Plan*   *Ground Plan*

*Harvey & Wicks and Adshead & Ramsey.*

154 AND 155.—NEWBURN HOUSING SCHEME.

shed is a good size, an important point in the country, where
so much wood is used for firing, and the living-room is " through-
lighted " (Figs. 156–7).

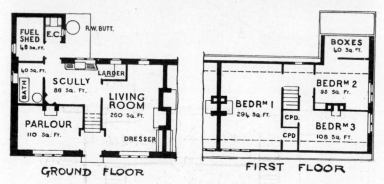

GROUND FLOOR                        FIRST FLOOR

*Lawrence Dale.*

156 AND 157.—PAIR OF PARLOUR COTTAGES, HOOK NORTON.

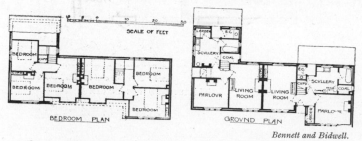

*Bennett and Bidwell.*

158.—PLAN OF COTTAGES FOR HITCHIN RURAL DISTRICT COUNCIL.

159.—COTTAGES AT TEA GREEN FOR HITCHIN RURAL DISTRICT COUNCIL.

The six-roomed cottages at Tea Green, Herts, built to the designs of Messrs. Bennett and Bidwell, are part of the Hitchin Rural District Council's scheme for providing 400 homes in

160.—PAIR OF COTTAGES AT OARE, WILTS.

*C. Williams-Ellis.*

thirty villages. Built at the peak of costliness in 1920, they are of brick rough-cast and colour-washed. In order to meet the custom of the district, each cottage has a small barn behind.

The plans show (Fig. 158) the liberal accommodation that is characteristic of the Addison period, and Fig. 159 reveals the charming architectural character which the same regime made possible.

The successful pair of cottages designed by Mr. Clough Williams-Ellis (Figs. 160 and 161) were built for Mr. Geoffry Fry,

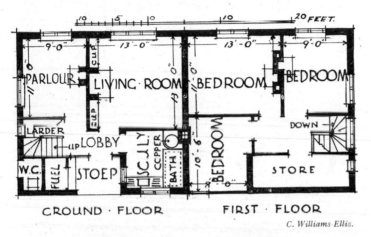

CROUND · FLOOR          FIRST · FLOOR

C. *Williams Ellis.*

161.—PLAN OF PAIR OF COTTAGES AT OARE, WILTS.

C.B., at Oare, near Marlborough. The contract price was £1,187 a pair, a reasonable post-war price for a normal structure of brick cavity wall and tiled roof. Mr. Williams-Ellis has adopted a somewhat unusual way of hanging the windows, namely hopper-fashion, hinged at the bottom and falling inwards, in the belief that in small and often crowded bedrooms the cottager needs to be encouraged in using windows for ventilation. The hopper window gives fresh air without draughts, and has therefore a better chance of being left open. It has the further advantage that there are no complicated fittings to get out of order, an inexpensive catch and a pair of quadrants at the sides being all the equipment necessary. For cleaning, the quadrants can be moved aside and the window brought over into the room.

The two pairs of cottages at Mitcham designed by Messrs. Ewart Culpin and R. S. Bowers were built as part of a housing scheme by *The News of the World,* and mark the practical interest taken by Lord Riddell in all efforts to solve our housing difficulties. The price tendered for them in September, 1922, averaged £662 each, but this was somewhat reduced in execution.

*Ewart Culpin and R. S. Bowers.*

162 AND 163.—TWO PAIRS OF COTTAGES AT MITCHAM FOR
" THE NEWS OF THE WORLD."

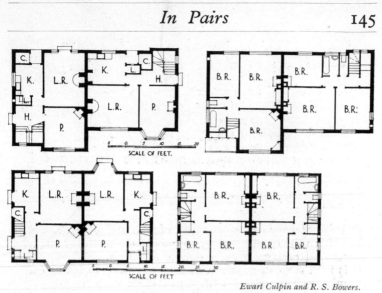

SCALE OF FEET.

SCALE OF FEET

*Ewart Culpin and R. S. Bowers.*

164.—PLANS OF " THE NEWS OF THE WORLD " COTTAGES.

A good feature of their design is the variation not only between
the pairs, but in the two cottages forming a pair. In one pair
both entrance doors are at the side : in the other, one at the
side and one in front. There is a real and reasonable desire
in the minds of would-be house owners to have a home which
is not merely one of a hundred of one type, and these are
very good and economically planned examples of the small six-
roomed house (Figs. 162-4).

L

# CHAPTER VIII

## THE SIX-ROOMED SINGLE COTTAGE

INEXPENSIVE TYPES BY MR. CLOUGH—PRE-WAR SMALL-HOLDINGS BUILD-
INGS—SUBURBAN TYPES AT GIDEA PARK—LIMESTONE COTTAGE AT
CHEPSTOW

THIS category embraces types of widely different character,
from the rural labourer's parlour cottage to the suburban
or week-end cottage costing double as much.

It is for the small-holder who does not want to be, or cannot
conveniently be, grouped with a next-door neighbour, that this
type is mainly needed, and for the small house in garden suburbs.
Wherever building in pairs is practicable there is a marked saving
in cost which puts the single cottage out of court.

Mr. A. H. Clough built many small-holders' single cottages

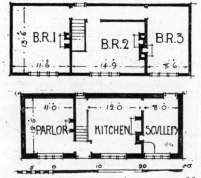

165.—PLANS OF SINGLE COTTAGES (SEE FIGS. 166 AND 167).

before the war, and was a pioneer in their economical contrivance.
Two types are now shown, one with a Mansard roof and the other
with walls carried up higher and with an ordinary roof (Figs. 165
to 167). In both, a central kitchen is provided on the ground
floor, with parlour and scullery on either side. The front door
opens on to a small lobby, with doors to kitchen and parlour,
and there is an outer door to the scullery. Upstairs there are

146

three rooms, all with fireplaces, and all opening from a passage.
The chalk cottage illustrated in Figs. 168 and 169 contains six

*A. H. Clough.*

166.—SIX-ROOMED SINGLE COTTAGE WITH PLAIN HIPPED ROOF.

rooms and has a shed behind. There were provided in connection with it a barn, cowhouse, stable and cart-shed, also shown

*A. H. Clough.*

167.—SIX-ROOMED SINGLE COTTAGE, WITH MANSARD ROOF.

on the plan. The other and similar cottage shown in Fig. 170
was built in timber, steel-lathing, and plaster. It is built on a
similar plan, but is rather larger.

The cottage with roof of Mansard type designed by Mr. Clough Williams-Ellis at Foxcombe Hill, near Oxford (Figs. 117 to 173), was planned to fit a triangular site near the entrance gates. It was so disposed that the main house and its garden to the north-west should be overlooked as little as might be from the frequented windows of the cottage. This involved an irregularity of plan, which usually makes for additional cost, but in this case economy was made possible by putting the bedrooms wholly in the roof, and the joists of the upper floor project under the eaves to form a dentil course to the gutter which does duty as an embryo cornice. With roof-rooms of this sort it is necessary to guard against extremes of temperature ; but as the tiles were laid on felted boarding and an insulating air-gap is provided, they are comfortable in summer and winter.

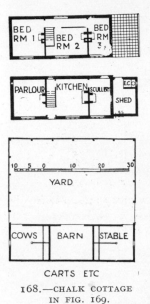

168.—CHALK COTTAGE
IN FIG. 169.

In Figs. 174 and 175 is shown a cottage at Burton Court, Herefordshire, built in 1908, of which Mr. Clough Williams-Ellis was also the architect. The walls are 11 in. thick, and hollow, rendered with cement.

A. H. Clough.

169.—SMALL-HOLDER'S COTTAGE, BUILT OF CHALK.

*A. H. Clough.*

170.—BUILT OF TIMBER AND STEEL-LATHING: PLAN SAME AS FIG. 168, BUT A LITTLE LARGER.

*C. Williams-Ellis.*

171.—COTTAGE WITH MANSARD ROOF.

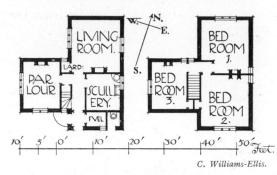

*C. Williams-Ellis.*

172.—AT FOXCOMBE HILL.

*C. Williams-Ellis.*

173.—AT FOXCOMBE HILL.

The tiles are hand-made, and altogether the cottage is of satisfactory appearance. It should be noticed that passages have been eliminated. On the ground floor the parlour can be approached only through the kitchen living-room, and on the first floor the south-east bedroom can be reached only through the principal bedroom. Although this arrangement looks retrograde, there is something to be said for it, as many cottagers think it enables them to keep a sharp eye on the youngsters.

I now pass to a number of single cottages

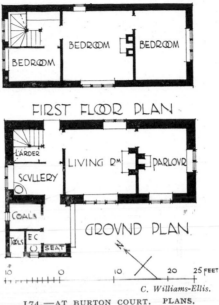

FIRST FLOOR PLAN

GROUND PLAN

*C. Williams-Ellis.*

174.—AT BURTON COURT. PLANS.

*Clough Williams-Ellis.*

175.—AT BURTON COURT.

rather superior in accommodation and design to the six-roomed workman's cottage. They are of a type which before the war cost from £400 to £500. I will deal first with a group built two or three years before the war at Gidea Park, a garden suburb near Romford.

Some of them show the attempt to squeeze in two sitting-rooms in addition to the kitchen, while others show the designer frankly

*C. M. Crickmer.*

176.—AT GIDEA PARK.

accepting the kitchen as one living-room, with the provision, in addition, of a scullery, and another sitting-room pure and simple. Mr. Crickmer's cottage (Figs. 176 and 177) is not only reasonable in plan, but distinctive in elevation. The living-room is large, covering about the same space as the kitchen and scullery together. There is a covered space by the side door which serves to hide the untidinesses which are more or less inevitable near the scullery and coal-house, and this is a distinctly good feature. A door leads from the living-room to the garden front, and the garden itself is made the more private by reason of the trades entrance being at the side. Upstairs there are three good bedrooms, a bathroom, box-room, and linen-room. With regard to the exterior, considerable character is given by a tall gabled projection which lights the stairs. Whereas cooking is done in the kitchen of this cottage, and the living-room is the largest in the house, Mr. Welch contemplated in his cottage (Figs. 178 and 179) that the family would prefer the greatest space being devoted to what he calls on the plan the "living-kitchen," next which is an excellent scullery. Opening from the latter and set under the stairs is a very useful feature—a store for bicycles; while the sitting-room has windows on two sides and a glazed door to the garden. Upstairs there are three bedrooms. In connection with this it may be noted that in practically every cottage built at Gidea Park there was provided in the bathroom a wash-basin with hot and cold tap. This is a very important thing in a cottage, because there is no reason why part at least of the

177.—PLAN.

C. M. Crichmar.

family should not use the bathroom as a dressing-room, and so save the labour of filling separate jugs in the bedrooms. The outside of this cottage is simple and satisfactory, the brick walls having been lime-whited, without first receiving any coat of rough-cast.

Mr. Percy Houfton designed for Gidea Park a very simple and reasonable cottage of red brick banded with grey bricks and covered with dark hand-made tiles. The kitchen is used as a living-room, and there is a good working scullery. A feature has been made of cross lighting and ventilation in the parlour and two chief bedrooms. (Figs. 180 and 181.)

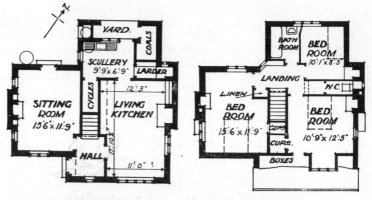

· GROUND FLOOR ·     · FIRST FLOOR ·

178.—MR. H. A. WELCH'S COTTAGE.

H. A. Welch.

179.—ENTRANCE FRONT.

In Mr. Lionel Crane's cottage the planning is very practical, and the range is in the living-room instead of in the scullery.

180.—ENTRANCE FRONT OF MR. HOUFTON'S COTTAGE.

The outside is treated quite simply in plain red brick and red tile. It is doubtful, however, whether it is wise, where only

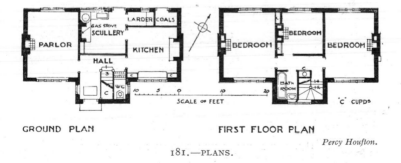

GROUND PLAN      FIRST FLOOR PLAN

*Percy Houfton.*

181.—PLANS.

one W.C. is provided, to have it with a door to the outside air. This arrangement is well enough when there is also an upstairs

W.C., but without one, unsatisfactory, especially for an invalid (Figs. 182-3).

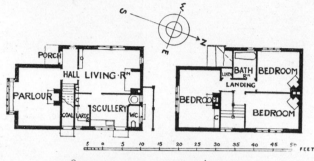

182.—PLANS OF MR. CRANE'S COTTAGE.

Mr. A. P. Starkey's cottage (Figs. 184 to 186) is devised to give the maximum amount of living space on the ground floor.    In

*Lionel Crane.*

183.—AT GIDEA PARK : ENTRANCE CORNER.

some of the other cottages of this type the kitchen range has been put in one of the living-rooms, but in this case it is fixed in the scullery, which thus becomes in practice a working kitchen.

A pleasant little verandah on the south side is reached from the parlour, and has a tool-shed opening from it. The doors between the living-room and parlour fold back, and thus enable

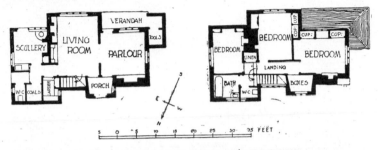

184.—PLANS OF MR. STARKEY'S COTTAGE.

the two to be thrown into one room on occasion. The general treatment of the ground floor is distinctly attractive. Perhaps, however, it is the exterior which is most unusual in its character.

A. P. Starkey.

185.—AT GIDEA PARK: GARDEN SIDE.

On the road front, which faces a little north of east (Fig. 186), there are no windows on the ground-floor level, a feature which adds considerably to the privacy of the house. This is an idea

*A. P. Starkey.*

186.—FRONT TO THE ROAD.

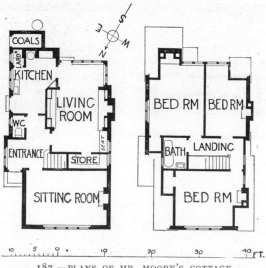

187.—PLANS OF MR. MOORE'S COTTAGE.

very commonly employed in Mahomedan countries ; but there is no reason why it should not have its application on an English roadside, where it is equally desirable that the passer-by should not pry into the occupations of the family. The building, when new, had a ripe air by reason of the employment of old tiles, while the stout proportions of the chimneys and the general simplicity of the grouping make it a very satisfactory little place.

Mr. Arthur H. Moore proceeded on more ordinary lines in the design of his cottage, which has many good points. The

*A. H. Moore*

188.—THE ENTRANCE CORNER.

staircase and the store at one end of the living-room cut the latter off from the sitting-room ; and here again cooking has been banished to a small kitchen, which also serves the purposes of scullery. The three bedrooms upstairs are well planned. (Figs. 187 and 188.)

Practically in the same category as these Gidea Park cottages, but on more economical lines, is one designed by Mr. Harold Falkner, and built in Hampshire. It shows a good type of plan suitable for an average married couple of very limited means who keep a servant.  It is worthy of attention as illustrating an ingenious and economical arrangement of rooms, especially on the bedroom floor.  For people who pride themselves on the simple life, the plan could be further simplified by throwing the ground-floor passage into the living-room ; but this would be at the cost of privacy.  (Figs. 189 and 190.)

*Harold Falkner.*

189.—A COTTAGE IN HAMPSHIRE.

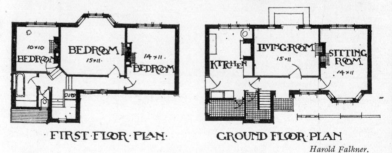

FIRST·FLOOR·PLAN·          GROUND FLOOR PLAN

*Harold Falkner.*

190.—PLANS.

A steep, unbroken descent of old pantiles gives character to the cottage of local limestone near Chepstow (Fig. 191), designed by Mr. Norman Evill.  The object here was, while not producing a habitation beyond the needs of a gardener, if it was required as such, to make it seductive as a sort of week-end cottage for

*Norman Evill.*

191.—LIMESTONE COTTAGE NEAR CHEPSTOW.

one or two people, or a " holiday house " for children. The number of the rooms, therefore, is the same as in a workman's cottage, but the area is larger. It stands on a rocky bank sheltered from the north, but open to the sun and enjoying fine views. It is carefully adapted to its particular purpose and special environment. It therefore gives a sense of belonging to its site, which should always be a fundamental aim in all rural planning. Simplicity and reticence are present, but the design is thought out, and just because the few details have been treated rightly and yet inconspicuously there is that restful completeness which to the man in the street seems so easy of attainment, but to the man at the drawing board so often a cause of struggle and not rarely unachieved.

M

# CHAPTER IX

## THE MINISTRY OF AGRICULTURE'S SMALL-HOLDING COTTAGES

At the Sutton Bridge Settlement—Brick and Concrete—An effi-
cient Shuttering—Omission of Plastered Ceilings—Stoneware
Baths—Doing without a Front Door—H.M. Office of Works
Cottages—A Hampshire Comparison—Other County Types

IN an earlier chapter I have dealt with the experimental
cottages built at the Amesbury Farm Settlement by the
Ministry of Agriculture at the outset of the work carried out

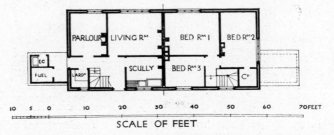

SCALE OF FEET

192.—PLANS OF BRICK COTTAGES SHOWN IN FIG. 193.

by the County Councils and directly by the Ministry under
the Land Settlement (Facilities) Act of 1919. I shall say nothing
here of the administrative task involved in providing about
17,500 small-holdings at a cost of about 15 millions, nor attempt
to review the large schemes of building which were carried out
under the auspices of the Ministry. The curious may find some
account of the latter in a paper by the Director-General of the
Land Department,[1] and of the former in various reports of the
Ministry, notably the Report on Land Settlement in England
and Wales, issued by the Ministry in November, 1925. I
am concerned here only to illustrate some of the more interesting examples of both the Ministry's and the County Councils' cottages as good and typical of what a rural cottage

[1] Printed in the *Journal of the Royal Institute of British Architects*,
Vol. XXVIII, Second Series, April 9, 1921.

should be. They were at least the outcome of the skill and energy of many architects working in close and friendly association and pooling their ideas and experience. I believe I am

193.—THATCH AND BRICK AT SUTTON BRIDGE.

just in saying that none were better than those built at the Ministry's Sutton Bridge Settlement, in Lincolnshire, and I can say it without egotism, for the chief credit was due to Major

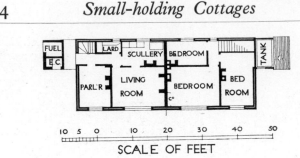

194.—PLANS OF BRICK COTTAGES SHOWN IN FIGS. 195 AND 196.

Maule, D.S.O., M.C., then the Ministry's chief architect, and his devoted staff. Bricks and bricklayers, tiles and tilers were scarce, and the number of cottages so built was limited to the available strength: resort was made to concrete and thatch and to a less extent to elm weather-boarding for the rest. The concrete cottages were built with a continuous cavity for which the Ministry's architects devised an ingenious wooden shuttering. The problem of "cavity" shuttering is how to withdraw the core which makes the cavity. This was overcome by the provision of an oval bar which, by the turn of a spanner, kept the inner face of the shuttering tightly in its place while the concrete was being filled in, but released it immediately with another turn when the concrete had set. Every device of economy was employed, because costs were outrageously high at the time these cottages were built. Moreover, plasterers were very hard to get. Plastered ceilings were therefore omitted, and their omission made up ingeniously. The bedroom floors were laid with the thicknesses of $\frac{5}{8}$-inch boarding with sarking felt between, the boards being laid with broken joints, and both nailed through in one operation to the upper side of the joists. This gave effective headroom up to the upper side instead of to the underside of the joists, and appreciably increased the cubic-air space of the ground-floor rooms. The amount of noise occasioned below by people walking on the first floor is admittedly more than where plaster ceilings are provided, but not enough to matter. The sarking felt prevents water spilt upstairs from coming through. That the internal effect was pleasing is shown by Fig. 201. Internal plastering of the brick cottages was limited to two-coat work in rooms and one coat in passages, instead of the three-coat work of long tradition, and no one was a whit the worse. The bedrooms were fitted with the simplest brick fireplaces with plain brick bottoms, which worked perfectly (Fig. 202). Attention may be directed to the bath arrangements. One of the problems of the rural cottager is to provide enough water

195.—PAIR OF BRICK COTTAGES: NORTH SIDE.

196.—SOUTH SIDE OF COTTAGES SHOWN ABOVE.

197.—SINGLE BRICK COTTAGE AT SUTTON BRIDGE.

or an ordinary-sized bath. Here 4-foot baths of stoneware
were used. It is true one cannot lie full length in such a bath,
but that is a small disadvantage compared with the saved labour
of pumping and heating enough water
for a full-sized bath. The bath and a
copper were disposed, not in the scullery
itself, but in a separate compartment
opening from it and modestly described
on the plans as W.H. (washhouse). The
baths have wooden covers, which are
useful as ironing-boards. They have a
further practical advantage, which would
hardly be guessed. A stoneware bath
has the great merit that it has no enamel
to chip off and expose iron which rusts
in unlovely patches, but it is cold to the
body, and that is as true of the
sumptuous porcelain bath in
the rich man's house as of these
small-holders' baths. A simple
expedient overcomes the difficulty. If one kettleful of

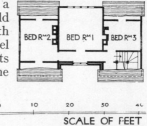

SCALE OF FEET

198.—PLANS OF SIX-ROOMED SINGLE
COTTAGE SHOWN IN FIG. 197.

199.—SINGLE COTTAGE : CAVITY CONCRETE TO EAVES LEVEL,
WEATHER-BOARDING ABOVE.

boiling water is poured into the bath and the wooden cover shut down and left for five minutes the whole bath is ideally warmed, and it can then be seriously filled from the copper, for the family bath. Other practical advantages of a 4-foot stoneware bath are that it is a far better washing tub than an ordinary enamelled iron bath, it is indestructible, and it takes less room. Altogether the Sutton Bridge cottages seem to me to have solved the bath question, and the arrangements are popular with the tenants. A point of planning is worthy of note. It will be seen that the plans of the pair of cottages shown in Fig. 192

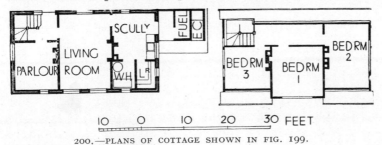

200.—PLANS OF COTTAGE SHOWN IN FIG. 199.

201.—LIVING-ROOM SHOWING JOISTS AND UNDERSIDE OF FIRST
FLOOR.

202.—A SIMPLE AND EFFICIENT BRICK FIREPLACE.

reveal two external doors, a front and a back door, while those
of Fig. 194 show a single door only. The latter arrangement
economizes space, but that was not the reason for it. Sutton

Bridge is in a flat and open country across which the wind blows shrewdly. It was found that the provision of a single door only, especially when it was masked by the side addition containing larder and E.C., baulked the searching wind and obviated the draughts which were too frequent in the cottages with front door and back. When all is said a front door is a rather ceremonial appanage. The small-holder and his family rarely use it save on state occasions, for they do not enter with muddy boots save at the back door, and when are boots not muddy near a farm-yard? The particular merit of the single cottages (Figs. 197 and 199) is that their living-rooms are "through" rooms, lighted from two sides. I think it may be claimed that all these cottages, whether of brick or concrete, and whether tiled or thatched, are of seemly aspect and worthy to house the new class of post-war English yeomen.

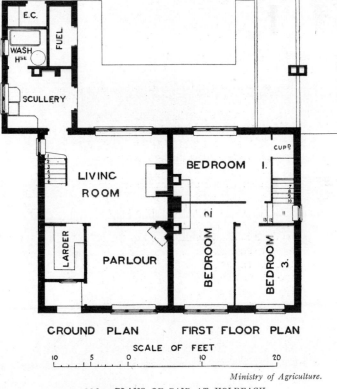

GROUND PLAN       FIRST FLOOR PLAN

SCALE OF FEET

*Ministry of Agriculture.*

203.—PLANS OF PAIR AT HOLBEACH.

The pair of parlour cottages at the Holbeach Settlement of the
Ministry of Agriculture have a special interest (Figs. 203 and 204).
They owe their sound, but by no means ideal, form to the fact
that previous cottages on the estate had been built of this back-
addition type, and it was thought unwise to break away from
it in new adjoining cottages.    The older ones had no bath, but
in the new cottages this is seen to be well provided as an annexe
to the scullery, with the copper handily placed behind the
scullery range.   It is not good planning in a cottage of this
size to have the staircase rising from the living-room, but here

*Ministry of Agriculture.*

204.—A PAIR AT HOLBEACH, LINCS.

again it was inadvisable to make too marked a change.   The
internal front porch with the parlour door at right angles to
the main opening is a desirable arrangement in so windswept a
district (for plan see Fig. 203).

Each of the examples, designed by H.M. Office of Works for
the Ministry of Agriculture (Figs. 205 to 208), is a pair of cottages
at the Rolleston Settlement.

The 1925 Report of the Parliamentary Agricultural Committee on cottage holdings seems to contemplate that villagers,
such as smiths and carriers, as well as agricultural labourers,
shall have the benefit of a cottage and a piece of land.    If this
could be carried into effect, it would mean a wide amelioration
of village life.   When the equipment of the Rolleston Estate
was under consideration there was a need for a village shop, and

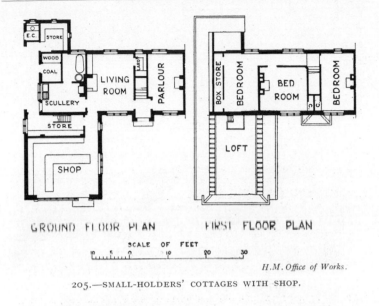

GROUND FLOOR PLAN     FIRST FLOOR PLAN

SCALE OF FEET

*H.M. Office of Works.*

205.—SMALL-HOLDERS' COTTAGES WITH SHOP.

*H.M. Office of Works.*

206.—PAIR OF SMALL-HOLDERS' COTTAGES WITH SHOP AT ROLLESTON
FOR MINISTRY OF AGRICULTURE.

*H.M. Office of Works.*
207.—PAIR OF SMALL-HOLDERS' COTTAGES AT ROLLESTON, NOTTS.

a suitable ex-Service man willing to run it, in conjunction with
a small holding. The accompanying plan (Fig. 205) shows how the
left-hand cottage of the pair was arranged with the shop projecting towards the road as a single-storey addition to a normal
cottage plan. The interest of the other Rolleston pair (without
a shop) is in the planning. Broadly speaking, all simple cottage
plans fall into one of two categories, one-room deep and two-
rooms deep. The Rolleston cottages belong to the former.
The advantages are obvious ; the parlour, the living-room and
two of the three bedrooms are windowed on two sides, and thus
catch what sun there is and are readily ventilated. Such rooms,
however, are apt to be cold, and there is the overwhelming
objection that an attenuated plan of this type means a greater

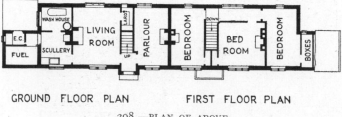

GROUND FLOOR PLAN          FIRST FLOOR PLAN

208.—PLAN OF ABOVE.

209.—AN INSTRUCTIVE COMPARISON.

On the left, a pair of Hampshire County Council cottages for small-holders (designed by Major Roberts). On the right, a pair built by the local District Council.

proportion of external wall, and, therefore, higher cost for every foot of effective floor area in the cottage.  But, on the grounds of appearance, there is everything to be said for this type, the long roof line being very attractive.

During the equipment of the County Councils' small-holdings for ex-Service men, under the Land Settlement (Facilities) Act, the Ministry of Agriculture laid no less stress on seemliness than on economy.  The Councils rose well to the occasion, and their cottages up and down the country are, with few exceptions,

FRONT VIEW OF COTTAGES

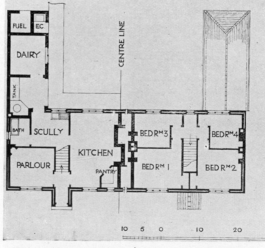

210.—BRETTON ESTATE (FLINT COUNTY COUNCIL).

a credit to their architects. It seems useful, therefore, to record some of the results of a real effort to maintain the amenities of the country-side, especially as the efforts of individual builders of bungalows have, during the last two or three years, produced an outrageous rash of shacks of mean

*J. M. Hotchkiss.*

211.—BUNGALOW IN BRICK ROUGH-CAST.

materials and worse design. Any policy of rural housing must be based on rigid economy, but a war must steadily be waged against the idea that economy inevitably means ugliness and meanness. Economy and seemliness are inseparable if they are cemented by brains. I have chosen examples of unusual as well as normal character in order to mark the fact that the essence of good architecture is fitness for purpose, and that standardization will not meet rural needs, however feasible it may be in a mining village.

Fig. 209 points the moral. Here are shown on the left of the picture a pair of cottages built by the Hampshire County Council, to the design of their architect, Major Roberts, for small-holders. There is nothing striking about them, but they fit modestly and reasonably into the landscape, which is all that need be asked. On the right of the illustration is seen a pair of cottages built under the auspices of the

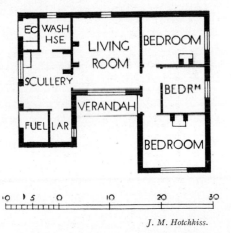

*J. M. Hotchkiss.*

212.—PLAN OF BUNGALOW FOR DISABLED EX-SERVICE SMALL-HOLDER, SHROPSHIRE COUNTY COUNCIL.

*A. L. Roberts.*

213.—MATTINGLEY, HANTS: COTTAGE WITH SLEEPING BALCONY
FOR DISABLED MAN.

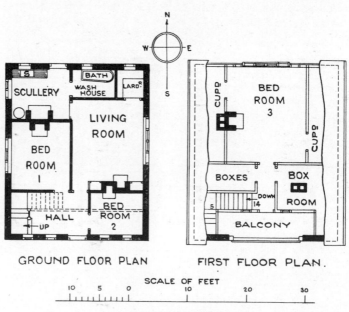

GROUND FLOOR PLAN          FIRST FLOOR PLAN.

SCALE OF FEET

214.—MATTINGLEY, HANTS.

*Mathews, Ridley & Pearce.*

215.—RINGMER, EAST SUSSEX; SINGLE COTTAGE FOR SMALL-HOLDER.

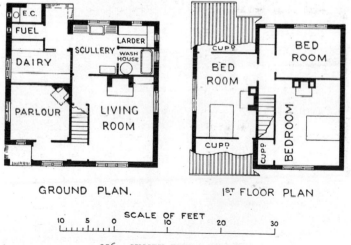

GROUND PLAN.     1ST FLOOR PLAN

SCALE OF FEET

216.—SUSSEX TYPE: SINGLE.

N

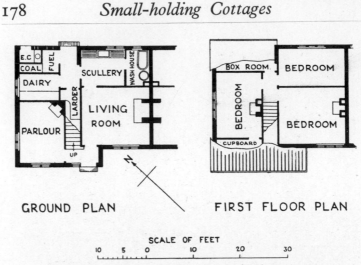

GROUND PLAN        FIRST FLOOR PLAN

SCALE OF FEET

217.—SUSSEX TYPE : ONE OF A PAIR.

*Mathews, Ridley & Pearce.*

218.—RINGMER, EAST SUSSEX : PAIR OF SMALL-HOLDERS' COTTAGES.

local Rural District Council as part of a housing scheme. It may well be that the accommodation is as good as in the County Council's cottages, but what is to be said of the design? The proportion of the front is destroyed by meaningless horizontal

*A. Barker, County Land Agent.*

219.—KENT COUNTY COUNCIL SMALL-HOLDER'S COTTAGE AT CHALKSOLE, ALKHAM.

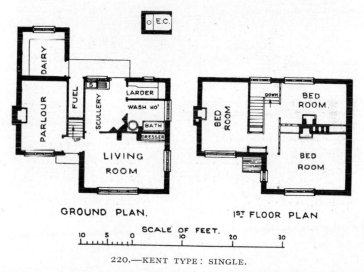

GROUND PLAN.      1ST FLOOR PLAN

SCALE OF FEET.

220.—KENT TYPE: SINGLE.

stripes, the windows are needlessly ugly, and the roof planning is neither seemly nor economical. There could scarcely be a better picture of how and how not to build a pair of cottages.

*John Stuart.*

221.—GREAT BENTLEY, ESSEX: A PAIR IN TIMBER AND PANTILES.

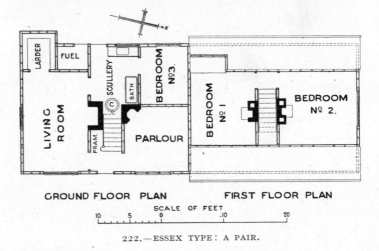

GROUND FLOOR PLAN          FIRST FLOOR PLAN

SCALE OF FEET

222.—ESSEX TYPE: A PAIR.

The small-holders' cottages on the Bretton Estate of the Flint County Council are notable for the rather lavish provision of four bedrooms as well as a parlour (Fig. 210). The grouping of the dairy and washing space in a long back addition enables the housewife easily to take her share in the dairy work.

Among the special problems which arose in the settlement of ex-service men on the land was the provision for the disabled man. Some County Councils took this duty very seriously and provided a number of small cottage holdings for poultry. Among them was Staffordshire, which considered the case of the many men whose disablement made stairs a difficulty. For them they built five-room bungalows, one of which is illustrated in Figs. 211 and 212.

The cottage at Mattingley, Hants, is also of a special plan well worth recording. The Hampshire County Council had to consider the case of ex-Service men, partly disabled by tuberculosis, to whom sleeping in the open air was a necessity. That explains the sleeping balcony, which, with the chief bedroom and a box-room, occupies the whole of the small first floor, the other two bedrooms being downstairs. The cottage is in effect a bungalow with the space in the high-pitched roof utilized to meet a special need (Figs. 213 and 214).

The Sussex cottages illustrated in Figs. 215 to 218, both a single and a pair, are of interest as marking a detail of planning to be considered in dairy holdings. Assuming that a dairy is properly to be placed under the main roof, it is here planned suitably in relation to the scullery and well away from the living-rooms of the cottage. Its door opens on to an external porch, and not an internal passage. The plain white walls and the tiled roof give a pleasant effect.

The small-holder's cottage at Chalksole, Alkham (Figs. 219 and 220), provided by the Kent County Council, has the dairy in a single-storey back addition, entered from outside. The parlour, 9 ft. by 14 ft., is rather liberal. Cottages of L-shape plan as this are not an economical type. Very different are the weather-boarded timber cottages at Great Bentley, provided by the Essex County Council. There is a parlour (see plan, Fig. 222) and the third bedroom is downstairs. Each cottage manages with one chimney stack to get a fireplace in every room but the third bedroom, but the bath is in the scullery—not the best arrangement. However, the cottages have a seemly look, and the same design is seen as a single cottage in Chapter IV.

# CHAPTER X

## THE EIGHT-ROOMED COTTAGE

EXAMPLES FROM GIDEA PARK—VARIOUS TYPES OF PLAN—NOTES ON
SLATING—SOME WELSH EXAMPLES—USE OF OLD MATERIALS—
ROCKYFIELD—HEIGHTS OF WINDOW-SILLS—A SEMI-BUNGALOW

THERE is a wide circle of readers interested in the cottage which used to cost about £500 and now costs rather more than double, because it includes people of small means who want an inexpensive permanent home, and also those town-dwellers of larger income who dream of a week-end cottage in the country or by the sea. For £500 it used to be just possible, before the war, given reasonably cheap building materials, to provide two small sitting-rooms, four bedrooms, kitchen, scullery, and offices—the eight-roomed cottage. A study of some of the more successful eight-roomed cottages at Gidea Park should be helpful in establishing valid comparisons between varying types, because the group now illustrated all cost the same within a few pounds.

*Geoffry Lucas.*

223.—GARDEN FRONT.

182

Mr. Geoffry Lucas, of Messrs. Lanchester Lucas and Lodge, has been a particularly successful designer of cottages and small

*Geoffry Lucas.*

224.—ENTRANCE FRONT.

houses at the Letchworth Garden City, at the Hampstead Garden Suburb, and elsewhere, so the planning of the cottage shown

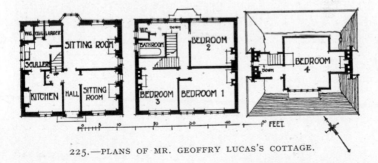

225.—PLANS OF MR. GEOFFRY LUCAS'S COTTAGE.

in Figs. 223 to 225 may be taken as the result of accumulated experience. The walls are of simple whitewashed brick, and the roof of red tiles. The arrangement of the rooms is admirable in its simplicity, for the whole house is contained within four square walls without any attached outbuildings ; the little pavilions at the back are tool-shed and summer-house, which

R. T. Longden.

226.—AT GIDEA PARK.

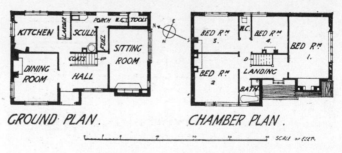

227.—MR. R. T. LONGDEN'S PLANS.

add much to the privacy of the garden by screening it from adjoining houses. We enter a small hall, from which there open the two sitting-rooms. The staircase is not only wide and easy-going, but screened from view of the front door, which is all to the good. The kitchen and scullery are spacious for the size of the house, and compactly arranged. On the first floor are three good bedrooms, all big enough to take double beds, a

*Curtis Green, A.R.A.*

228.—SOUTH-WEST SIDE.

bathroom with lavatory basin, and a large warmed linen cupboard. On the attic floor is a large bedroom with a fireplace and a roomy store for boxes.

The house designed by Mr. R. T. Longden (Figs. 226 and 227) showed his desire to give to the elevation those bold and simple characteristics which we associate with the cottages of the seventeenth century. This has been successfully done without importing into the plan any of those haphazard quaintnesses which designers sometimes think are essential to this type of house. Through the porch we enter a hall, distinctly spacious for the size of the house ; indeed, a captious critic

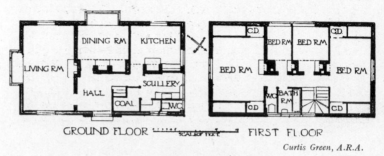

GROUND FLOOR      scale of feet      FIRST FLOOR

*Curtis Green, A.R.A.*

229.—MR. CURTIS GREEN'S PLANS.

might complain that a smaller hall would be as useful and allow more space in the sitting-rooms. The staircase is shielded from the door. The sitting-room is to the right of the hall, the dining-room and kitchen to the left. All four bedrooms are on the first floor, grouped round the central landing, and there is also adequate box storage. The general treatment

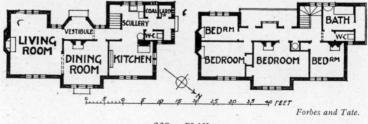

*Forbes and Tate.*

230.—PLAN.

of the rooms is made to accord with the external architecture by the use of open beams and rafters, and by the rather rough finish to the plastering of the walls, while all the woodwork is stained and wax-polished. The bricks and tiles used for walls and roof are of mingled colours, happily chosen and casually mixed.

The house designed by Mr. Curtis Green, A.R.A. (Figs. 228 and 229) stands on a corner site, and exhibits rather more variety

*Forbes and Tate.*

231. EXTERIOR OF COTTAGE AT GIDEA PARK.

of treatment than the last two described, in that it is partly
of red brick and partly rough-cast; but the latter has been

*Forbes and Tate.*

232.—FROM DINING-ROOM TO LIVING-ROOM.

well managed, and an added touch of interest is given by a
moderate use of a wavy outline tooled on the plaster. The
projecting bay window, bracketed out on corbels, built of tiles,

is a good feature from the point of view of accommodation. Here again may be noted the commendable arrangement of keeping the whole accommodation within four walls without outbuildings. The kitchen and scullery are very practically arranged with reference to the dining-room.

The house designed by Messrs. Forbes and Tate (Figs. 230 to 232) is distinctly good, and has a quite impressive appearance when its cost is considered. The dining-room and living-room are in effect one apartment, as there are no doors between. This arrangement makes possible the pretty vista which appears in Fig. 232 ; but it is doubtful whether it is a very practical arrangement or generally popular.

A word must be said as to the clever treatment of the walls internally. Instead of being plastered, they have been covered with a rough paperhanger's canvas, which is stuck firmly to the wall and shows the outlines of the brick joints. The finish

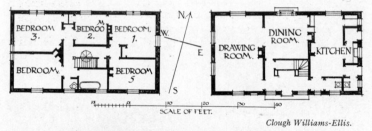

*Clough Williams-Ellis.*

233.—PLAN OF A COTTAGE AT GIDEA PARK.

is a coat of distemper. This was practical before the war, but infinitely more so now with plasterers so scarce. All the wood-work has been stained a very pleasant grey. Interesting features of the exterior are the porch, which is covered by the main roof, the shape of the chimneys and the brick mullions of the windows. There has been an evident desire to reduce the cost of upkeep. The casements are of steel, the front door is of oak, and, indeed, the only part of the outside that needs painting is the back door.

Into the house illustrated in Figs. 233 to 235, Mr. Clough Williams-Ellis has imported a flavour of design which more usually belongs to buildings larger in scale. The plan is a plain rectangle, and the front elevation is strictly symmetrical. A good feature is that one of the four bedrooms has an adjoining dressing-room, which can be used as a fifth bedroom. The ground-floor plan is satisfactory. The dining-room has a bay opening out at one corner, and on the other side of it are folding doors to the drawing-room. The service hatch to the kitchen

*Clough Williams-Ellis*

234.—AN INTERIOR.

235.—MR. CLOUGH WILLIAMS-ELLIS'S COTTAGE.

is ordinarily a doubtful feature, because it means that practically
everything said at the dinner-table can be heard in the kitchen ;

236.—MR. QUAIFE MAY'S COTTAGE.

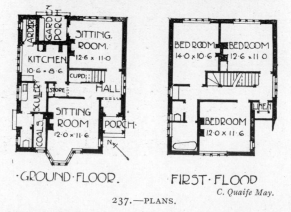

·GROUND·FLOOR.        FIRST·FLOOR

C. Quaife May.

237.—PLANS.

but in this case there is a special air-lock arrangement devised
by the architect, which should overcome the usual objections

to the transit of cooking smells. It is a good point that all the
plumbing should be concentrated in one corner of the house,
which makes for cheapness in first cost and maintenance. Ex-

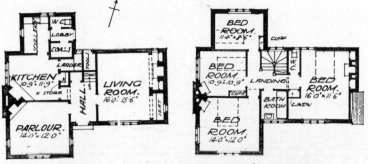

238.—PLANS OF MR. HERBERT WELCH'S COTTAGE.

Herbert A. Welch.

239.—COTTAGE AT GIDEA PARK.

ternally, the slopes of the roof are covered with pantiles, and
there is a flat deck in the middle. The design would be more
successful in a house of about twice the cubic capacity, but it

shows thought and a fresh outlook on the problems involved.
There is an air of individuality about the house built to the
designs of Mr. C. Quaife May (Figs. 236 and 237), and its plan

H. L. North.

240.—WHYLOME, LLANFAIRFECHAN.

is the more interesting because there has been a successful
attempt to provide a garden porch, which is in effect a tiny
loggia opening out of the sitting-room. Though the plan is a
little broken up and is rather lacking in simplicity, it has distinct

merits. The windows are ample in size and well proportioned, but would have been better if the sills had been rather nearer the floors.

In the house designed by Mr. Herbert A. Welch (Figs. 238 and 239) no attempt has been made to reproduce what may be called the " cottage feeling." It is well planned, but if, as seems likely, it was proposed to have meals in the living-room rather than in the parlour, it is, perhaps, not altogether convenient to have it separated from the kitchen by the hall. The exterior is well treated, and a pleasant feature is made of the big chimney.

I have elsewhere in this book referred to Mr. H. L. North's faithful use of Welsh materials, and now illustrate others of his little houses. Whylome (Figs. 240 to 242) is a cottage of

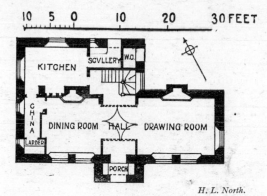

H. L. North.

241.—PLAN OF WHYLOME.

admirably simple plan. The doors from hall to dining- and drawing-rooms are both in double leaves, and throw almost the whole ground floor into a single room. As will be seen in the picture of the hall (Fig. 242), Mr. North clings closely to Gothic traditions.

The pair of cottages on the shore at Llanfairfechan, Talfer and Gorsfield (Figs. 243 to 245) are like Whylome in having their chief sitting-rooms treated as a single suite with folding doors, but they are a little larger, with nine rooms each, a study being provided at the back. The view of the interior at Gorsefield (Fig. 244) shows not only the spaciousness secured by the big folding doors, which yield at will a room 30 feet in length, but the charming effect of simple stencilling on the ceiling beams. In the distance we notice on a table the ever-welcome little bronze Narcissus. Externally the cottages are simply designed, with long roofs which serve their practical purpose in throwing off

O

the blustering sea breezes.  Despite the character which marks
these cottages and separates them from the usual buildings of

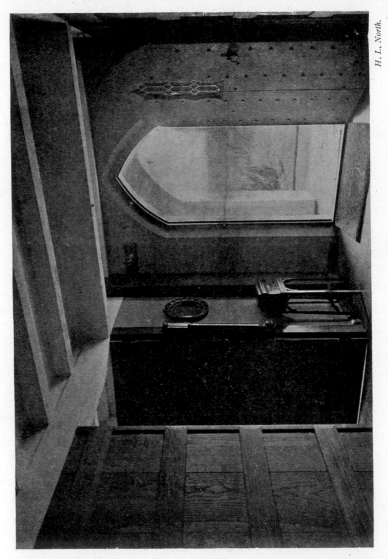

*H. L. North.*

242.—WHYLOME, LLANFAIRFECHAN: INTERIOR OF HALL.

North Wales, the virtue of economy has not been neglected.
They serve, in fact, to show that it costs no more to impart

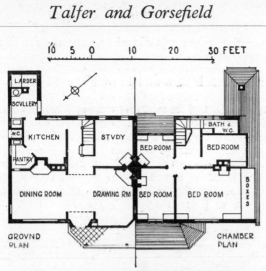

10 5 0 10 20 30 FEET

LARDER

SCVLLERY

W.C. KITCHEN STVDY

BATH & W.C.

BED ROOM

BED ROOM

PANTRY

BED ROOM

BED ROOM

BOXES

DINING ROOM DRAWING RM

GROVND PLAN

CHAMBER PLAN

243.—PLANS OF TALFER AND GORSEFIELD.

H. L. North.

244.—INTERIOR AT GORSEFIELD.

the right feeling to domestic architecture than to leave it in the old slough of ugliness and pretence.

They had an unsatisfactory subsoil of nothing more than mud, and a concrete raft had to be laid over the whole site to ensure

H. L. North.

245.—TALFER AND GORSEFIELD: A PAIR OF COTTAGES ON THE SHORE AT LLANFAIRFECHAN.

structural safety and freedom from damp. In order to reduce the weight, brick was employed for the walls instead of the local stone.

The cottage shown in Figs. 246 and 247 can hardly be regarded as a normal type. It was built almost wholly from the very admirable materials, including the oak for the half-timber work, which already existed on the site in the form of the wreckage

Unsworth and Triggs.

246.—A COTTAGE AT PETERSFIELD BUILT OF OLD MATERIALS.

of an older house. It was designed by Messrs. Unsworth and Triggs.

Among the cottage designers who clung tenaciously to the

old traditions of building, and have indeed done much to give them a new life, none showed a more convincing art than the late Ernest Gimson. Rockyfield (Figs. 248 to 251) is in Charn-

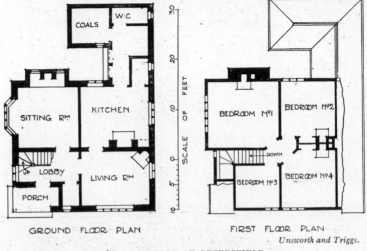

GROUND FLOOR PLAN      FIRST FLOOR PLAN

*Unsworth and Triggs.*

247.—COTTAGE AT PETERSFIELD.

wood Forest, Leicestershire. The roof is covered with Swithland slate saved from demolished buildings. Indeed, had none been available from such a source, some slate foreign to the district

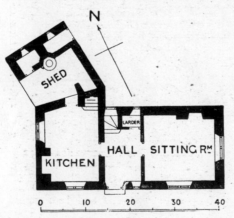

248.—ROCKYFIELD : GROUND-FLOOR PLAN.

must have been used, for the old local quarries are no longer worked, more the pity. Rough in texture and rich in colour, their many tones of purple, green and blue have already become flushed with gold on the shaded side of the cottage where lichens grow. Old Leicester was wholly roofed with these Swithland slates, and it is very unfortunate that they are no longer to be had. The disused quarries are, however, still stores of wealth

to those who, like Ernest Gimson, can rightly use what they offer.
Great flakes of slate, discarded years ago, because of some flaw,

The late Ernest Gimson.

249.—ROCKYFIELD FROM THE WEST.

have been used in the walls, as lintels, hearthstones, and the
like. The mass of the building is of granitic stones mostly

gathered up from neighbouring fields. Rockyfield does not bear its name without good reason. It sits bravely on a great rock between a spinney and a greenish black, lichen-covered outcrop.

The cottage was built simply for week-ends and summer holidays, and its plan is admirably adapted for the purpose.

250.—ROCKYFIELD : FROM KITCHEN TO SITTING-ROOM.

When the owner is away a caretaker lives there, and the kitchen is her living-room. From it a short stair leads to her bedroom above, which is thus cut off altogether from the rest of the cottage. From the hall another staircase leads to the remaining three bedrooms. There remain only the useful shed (where a copper is fixed) and the sitting-room. The latter, in common with the whole of the ground floor, is paved with red tiles, and upstairs the floors are of hard white plaster, clean and warm to the feet. The woodwork throughout is of oak, and the walls are all white-washed. The furniture accords with the atmosphere of the cottage, and has that gracious quality which Ernest Gimson knew so well how to give to the simplest things, a quality visible also in the internal fixtures. Goldsmith makes one of his characters say that a marble chimney-piece will "inflame the bill confoundedly," and any sort of luxurious equipment is fatal to the attempt to get a reasonable amount of accommodation for a small sum. Not that the red-tile flooring on the ground floor was adopted for motives of cheapness, but rather because

*The late Ernest Gimson.*

251.—ROCKYFIELD : FROM THE ROAD.

it is a pleasant colour and dries promptly after being washed. Deal wood-block flooring costs about the same.

Oak flooring is markedly more expensive and, whether in

*Clough Williams-Ellis.*

252.—MARBURY COTTAGE.

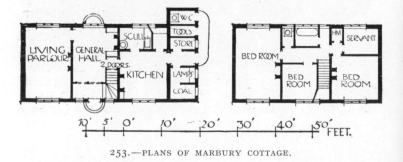

253.—PLANS OF MARBURY COTTAGE.

tongued and grooved planks or in blocks laid as parquet, cannot be laid complete even in foreign oak for less than two and a half times the cost of deal-block floors. In the use of parquet, moreover, it is usual to lay it, in the case of ground floors, on a layer of fine cement concrete, which is itself laid on the rough concrete bed covering the ground area of houses. Departure from simple flooring materials, therefore, means considerable

*E. Turner Powell.*

254.—A COTTAGE IN ESSEX.

additional expense. The use of oak blocks on the ground floor at Rockyfield would have involved an extra of 7 per cent. on the total cost of the building. When people are building a little cottage and decide to have little extras like oak floors, they are apt to forget how " confoundedly they inflame the bill "

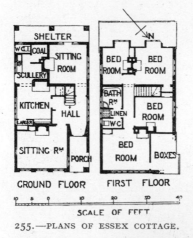

GROUND FLOOR FIRST FLOOR

SCALE OF FFFT

255.—PLANS OF ESSEX COTTAGE.

until the day of reckoning comes at the finish of the contract, when the schedule of " extras " is sometimes known to cause astonishment and pain. In the case of week-end cottages such added luxuries are altogether superfluous.

Marbury Cottage, designed by Mr. Clough Williams-Ellis, is a successful eight-roomed cottage. There is a little sitting hall and a parlour in addition to the kitchen and its offices, which are provided on an ample scale for the size of the place. The bedrooms are small, but there are four of them. The treatment is simple and pleasant, and as an open outlook was permanently assured only to the back and front, no windows were provided in the end gables. (Figs. 252 and 253.)

Figs. 254 to 257 show a cottage by Mr. Turner Powell, in which variety is given to the ordinary whitewashed wall by having the plaster tooled in the manner which is indigenous to Essex, and the rich surface of the pantiles adds a touch of interest.

*E. T. Powell.*

256.—BRICK FIREPLACE.

*E. Turner Powell.*

257.—AN ESSEX COTTAGE : GARDEN FRONT.

The plan of the house is good. The picture of the sitting-room next the porch shows a cupboard and book-recess next to the fireplace (Fig. 256). Upstairs there are four good bedrooms and a box-room. Criticism is often directed against the practice of placing the window-sills rather too high above the floor-level. It is claimed that if a man goes to live in the country or a village suburb he does so because he wants the benefits of the country. While his wife is working her needle, she should be able to look out of the window and see green things growing. If there is an invalid in the family, he or she equally needs an outdoor view when lying in bed. These demands are hopelessly defeated if the level of the window-sill is unduly raised above the floor-level. All this sounds very reasonable, but it need not be assumed that architects are ignorant of people's wishes. Houses on a small scale, especially if they are of gabled type, seem to demand casement windows rather than sliding sashes. Casements rarely look well if more than 4 ft. high, and are better proportioned if shorter. Building by-laws almost universally demand a minimum height of 8 ft. for bedrooms, and it is not an unreasonable provision, though some latitude should be given where floor space

R. Longden.

258.—COTTAGE AT NEWCASTLE-UNDER-LYME.

and window openings are ample. It is not good for the head
of the window to be more than a foot below the ceiling-level,
as otherwise the air in the room tends to stagnate, and a good
many people like the windows carried up to the ceiling. Unless,
then, the casements are to be unduly elongated, or fitted with
a transom, which looks ill in cottage architecture, the sill must
be 3 ft. or more above the floor. The difficulty can, of course,
be avoided by using sliding sash windows, which look the better

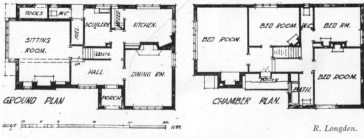

R. Longden.

259.—AT NEWCASTLE-UNDER-LYME.

*P. Morley Horder.*

260.—AT BROMBOROUGH, CHESHIRE.

the taller they are, but they do not fit in with the gabled type of cottage, and it is not possible always to get the best of both worlds. In the cottage now illustrated, Mr. Turner Powell fixed the glass-line about 3 ft. 6 in. above the floor-line, a compromise which is satisfactory and ensures good proportions for the elevations of the cottage. People who want to sit in low chairs and still to be able to see out of the window must realize that their wish may involve either an imperfectly ventilated room or an ill-proportioned front.

In Figs. 258 and 259 is illustrated an attractive cottage at Brampton Farm, Newcastle-under-Lyme. Mr. Reginald Long-

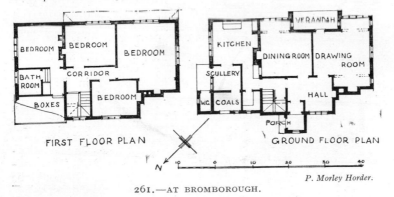

FIRST FLOOR PLAN

GROUND FLOOR PLAN

*P. Morley Horder.*

261.—AT BROMBOROUGH.

P. Morley Horder.

262.—AT STROUD, GLOUCESTERSHIRE.

P. Morley Horder.

263.—AT STROUD.

den made an interesting feature of the sitting-room chimney, and the half-timber work is well and reasonably designed.

Figs. 260 and 261 show an interesting cottage at Bromborough, Cheshire, designed by Mr. P. Morley Horder. The arrangement of the verandah is distinctly good.

Another little place, designed by the same architect, at Stroud, Gloucestershire, is illustrated in Figs. 262 and 263. Within a narrow limit of expenditure Mr. Morley Horder contrived to provide three sitting-rooms and four bed-rooms. It should be

noted that very little space is occupied by the staircase, an
economic point in planning which is of importance in all cottage-
building. The low cost of the building is the more notable
seeing that it is of rubble masonry with ashlar quoins, and there
are iron casements. The Cotswold traditions of building have,
indeed, been faithfully observed.

*Halsey Ricardo.*

264.—DORSET COTTAGE IN CONCRETE AND THATCH.

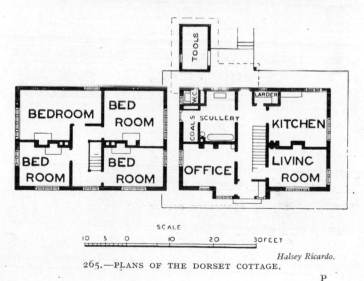

SCALE

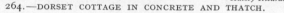

10  5  0      10      20      30 FEET

*Halsey Ricardo.*

265.—PLANS OF THE DORSET COTTAGE.

P

Very inexpensive, for it was built early in the war for the now incredible figure of £147, is the admirable eight-roomed cottage

*Halsey Ricardo.*

266.—BACK OF THE DORSET COTTAGE.

*Leonard Martin.*

267.—A BERKSHIRE COTTAGE: BACK VIEW.

in Dorset, seen in Figs. 264 to 266. The walls are of concrete blocks and the roof of thatch. It serves to house one of the people on the estate, who needs an office as well as a parlour.

268.—A BERKSEIRE COTTAGE.

Leonard Martin.

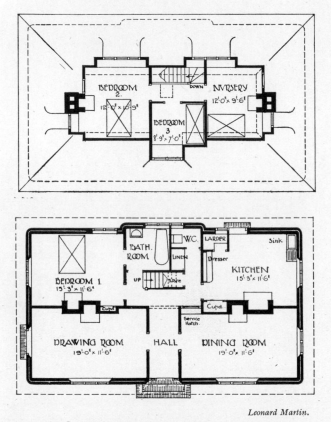

*Leonard Martin.*

269.—PLANS OF SEMI-BUNGALOW IN BERKSHIRE.

Figs. 267 to 269 show a type of cottage which has a delightfully modest appearance and is very suitable where the bedroom space required is rather small in proportion to sitting-rooms. It is half-way between a bungalow and a two-storey cottage. Mr. Leonard Martin has managed with a minimum of passage-way, which ordinarily eats up a lot of floor space in bungalows. Built with an 11-inch cavity wall of brick, rendered in cement and finished with a " float " to give a pleasant texture, it represents a more economical type than the pure-blooded bungalow with no accommodation above the ground floor.

# CHAPTER XI

## DESIGNS FOR AN EIGHT-ROOMED HOLIDAY COTTAGE WITH GARAGE AND LARGE GARDEN

THE "COUNTRY LIFE" 1912 COMPETITION—THE CONDITIONS—THREE
SOLUTIONS OF A TYPICAL PROBLEM—PLANNING OF THE GARDEN

THE preceding chapters have been devoted in the main to cottages which were designed to be the sole home of their occupants, who, whatever their avocations, may be assumed to be people of small means. The war, however, has not destroyed, but rather increased, interest in the cottage which, while small and comparatively inexpensive, is built in a holiday atmosphere, provided with a garage and set in the midst of a comparatively large garden for people who want a country retreat, although the high cost of building may well postpone or modify many such projects. This chapter is given mainly, therefore, to a consideration of the special problems which it raises. Such a cottage throws open a field of design so large, and offers matter for illustration so overwhelming in amount and diversity, that some limitation is needed. It seems well, therefore, to give chief place to the consideration of the various ways in which a single problem may be solved. This can be done conveniently by discussing some of the designs submitted in a *Country Life* Competition for Designs of a Holiday Cottage and Garden. The conditions laid down that the cottage should cost £550, a motor-house £100, and the work in forming the garden £150. The cost limit for the cottage itself determined its accommodation, i.e. two sitting-rooms, four bedrooms, kitchen and scullery, which gave an eight-

*→ FIRST FLOOR PLAN ←*

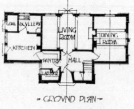

*→ GROUND PLAN ←*

*C. F. W. Dening.*

270.—FIRST PRIZE COTTAGE.

213

271.—THE FIRST PRIZE DESIGN, BY C. F. W. DENING.
*(Perspective drawn by the late Charles Gascoyne.)*

roomed cottage. Needless to say, the pre-war prices should be multiplied by from 2 to 2¼. As two of the three judges who awarded the prizes were Sir Edwin Lutyens, R.A., and Mr. Arthur Bolton, the decisions are worthy of respect. The third judge was the present writer.

In view of the somewhat liberal provision of accommodation by some of the competitors, the average pre-war cost of the cottages illustrated would no doubt have been £600 rather than £550, and I again remind readers of the heavy addition that must now be made. The plans are also valuable because of the light thrown on the possibilities of design for a garden on an acre plot.

The long axis of the site (*see* Fig. 272) selected for the competition ran due north and south. Its north end was protected from east and west winds by trees. The ground was practically level

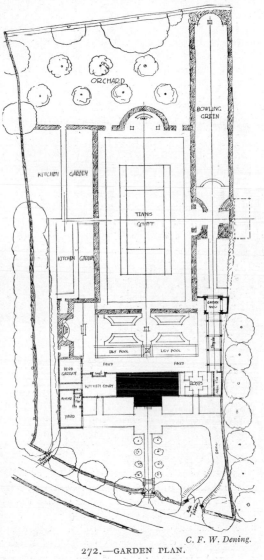

C. F. W. Dening.

272.—GARDEN PLAN.

except for a rise of a few feet from the road at the north end, and a feature was to be made of the garden design. It seemed obviously desirable that the cottage should be placed as near to the road as conveniently possible, having regard to proper access for vehicles and a due distance from the few trees on the north or road boundary. By this disposition undue expense in carriage-ways is avoided, and the cottage and its outbuildings serve to screen the garden from the road. The latter purpose is best served by a long, low, oblong type of house which has the further advantage of providing a sunny south aspect for the maximum number of rooms.

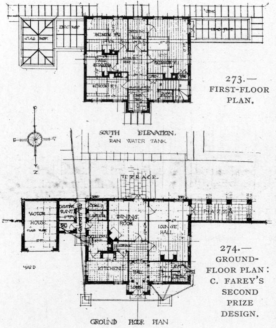

273.— FIRST-FLOOR PLAN.

274.— GROUND-FLOOR PLAN: C. FAREY'S SECOND PRIZE DESIGN.

The winning designs, now illustrated, show a clear grasp of the problems. If they are criticized, it is only with a view to showing how difficult was the problem set, viz. of devising a convenient and artistic cottage within severe limits of cost.

Mr. Dening's design, placed first, was marked by a practical solution of the problems (Figs. 270 to 272). He provided four bedrooms on the first floor, all facing south and looking down the garden, and the staircase and bathroom are adequate. Downstairs there are two useful sitting-rooms. It might be better to transpose the names of living-room and dining-room, so that meals would be served in that which is nearer the kitchen, but the hall is so small that the point is negligible. The kitchen is a sensible size, but the range is not well placed for light. The larder also has an east light, but doubtless Mr. Dening took into account that the trees serve as a screen against the sun. He has obviously been pleased with the idea of a blank north elevation, and he has contrived to obtain it without any violent departure from general convenience. Such a treatment has the

advantage of help-
ing towards a
warm cottage.
The side elevations
are ingeniously
contrived within
his scheme of
design.

The south eleva-
tion is particularly
satisfactory. It
is composed of
simple elements,
and very broad in
effect. There re-
mains an attic
space from which
an extra bedroom
could be contrived,
by the provision
of two dormer
windows on the
south front, which
would, if anything,
add to the value
of the design and
entail a compara-
tively small extra
expenditure. The
choice of materials
and the working
out of the details
of the cottage
would need to be
thoughtfully man-
aged to bring out
the effect of the
design. The
garden scheme is
very simple (Fig.
272). The ten-
nis court runs
north and south,
the correct dispo-
sition. The bowl-
ing green on the

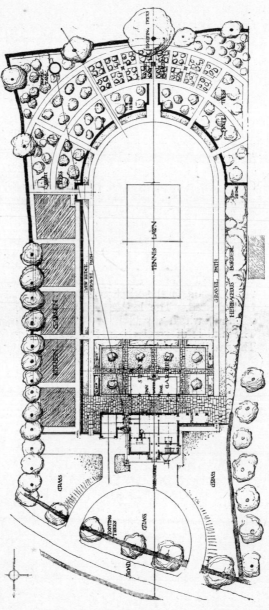

275.—GARDEN DESIGN BY C. FAREY.

west side is a pleasant idea, and there would be an element of surprise in reaching it through the green parlour. It is a good point that the kitchen courtyard and motor-yard are all grouped together, and that the other end of the house is left free for a rose garden. The kitchen garden is a little bit on the small side. It is doubtful whether Mr. Dening quite fully considered the point of getting the motor into its house and back again, but he is entitled to assume that the car used at such a little cottage would be a runabout which can turn in a small space. A slight modification of the plan, by which the motor could go out where the tradesmen's entrance is shown, would be an improvement.

The design to which the second prize was awarded is by Mr. Cyril A. Farey. It represents a different idea (Figs. 273–276), and is a version of the rural Italian manner, reminiscent of a present phase in American domestic architecture. This cottage is more ambitious than the last, and the hall and staircase are somewhat beyond the needs of the case. It would be unwise to put pillars into a hall measuring only six feet in width, in the attempt to suggest a minute Italian *cortile*. The kitchen is not as practical as could be desired. The projection of the range would make the position of the kitchen table a difficult problem ; but it is well lighted. The larder and coals have monopolized a south window, which would have better been given to the scullery. The hall is of good size ; but the dining-room is rather small. The small service space off the hall would not be of much practical value. A ground-floor W.C. has been provided—a good point in cottages of this type. There is one very good bedroom, but it is doubtful if it was wise to provide a dressing-room in addition to the four bedrooms, as it uses valuable space. The exterior of the cottage has a frankly cement treatment. Turning to the garden adjuncts, the piazza opening from the lounge hall is well placed, and an attractive feature. Undue space seems to have been given to the tennis lawn, and the radiation of the kitchen garden (Fig. 275) is rather ambitious for the surroundings of a small house. Mr. Farey seems to have attempted rather too much, and the double approach drive is a little suburban. The pool and paved paths are more satisfactory features.

The scheme to which the third prize was given is by Mr. Geoffry Lucas and Mr. Lodge (Figs. 277 to 279). It shows a very good plan, but in order that it should balance, the lighting plant has been divorced from the motor-house and included in the east pavilion with the coal space and W.C. On the other hand, the hall is attractively arranged with the staircase, and is very well lit by a window on the upper landing. The middle bedroom is satisfactory in size, and there are two good bedrooms on either

276.—PERSPECTIVE OF SECOND PRIZE DESIGN BY CYRIL FAREY.

277.—GARDEN SCHEME.  THIRD PRIZE DESIGN BY GEOFFRY
LUCAS AND ARTHUR LODGE.

side of it, and one small one behind. The design is of a typically
English character, and is most successful on the entrance front,
where there is a quietly treated doorway and hood. The chimneys
are well placed. The designers gave a detail of the interior of
the hall and staircase which would have been pleasing. The
garden, like Mr. Farey's, has too large a games lawn. The
water ponds placed on the south side are well contrived. An
alcove masks the motor-house on the adjoining site, and a small
rose garden is arranged opposite. The fruit trees are well dis-

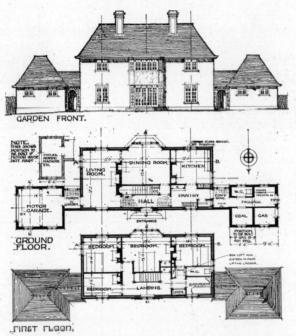

GARDEN FRONT.

GROUND FLOOR.

FIRST FLOOR.

*G. Lucas and A. Lodge.*

278 AND 279.—PLANS AND ELEVATIONS.

posed at the ends of the subsidiary paths. The bird's-eye perspective so admirably illustrates the scheme that it is reproduced
instead of the plan. It makes it plain, however, that the
great size of the lawn is out of scale with the cottage (fig. 277).

By way of summing up, the least that can be said is that
the designs proved the existence of abundant ingenuity and
considerable versatility in the treatment of an eight-roomed
holiday cottage. It is a mark of the present tendency of
design that the successful competitors decided to rely on

regularity of plan, austerity of elevation and a conscious balance of features, coupled with a classical note in the treatment of detail.   It might be suggested that the cottage tradition calls for something less conscious, but that is to beg the question. There is a note of insincerity in the attempt to reproduce the haphazard planning and quaintly projecting features which give us so much satisfaction when we see them in old cottages. They are generally the result of casual accretions, of a room or a shed added here, and an extra window opened out there. There exist, indeed, an ample number of examples of small eighteenth-century cottages, both in red brick and covered with a skin of plaster.   It is just as reasonable to adopt them as models for a modern cottage as it is to revert to earlier types and traditions.   The fact remains that a holiday cottage of to-day—for which are demanded such modern and artificial adjuncts as a motor-house, a place for a lighting plant, and a room for outdoor meals, like a loggia—offers a problem altogether as much detached from the conditions which created the little cottage of bygone days built for those who worked on the soil, as from the needs of the labourer's cottage of to-day.   This difference in the people who occupy such a holiday cottage, and the uses to which they put it, amply justify a more sophisticated character in its treatment.   We do not play at the simple life with so strenuous an attention to the rules as did Prince Florizel in " The Winter's Tale," and we may therefore be excused if we give to the scene of our pleasures a setting less rigidly rustic.

# CHAPTER XII

## COTTAGES FOR ESTATE SERVANTS AND GATE LODGES

For Gardeners and Chauffeurs—Cottage combined with Garden-
House—Planning and Treatment of Gate Lodges influenced
by design of Main House—Double Cottages with Archway—
A Group of Three

I T seems desirable to devote a few pages to considering cottages
intended for the accommodation of estate servants, in cases
where such use affects their planning or treatment. This is
specially seen in gate lodges, which involve in their design
questions of axial planning, etc., in their setting with reference

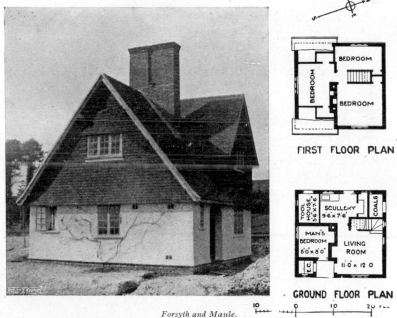

FIRST FLOOR PLAN

GROUND FLOOR PLAN

*Forsyth and Maule.*

280 AND 281.—AT BOURNE END.

223

to the larger houses which they serve. Considered by themselves they are generally no more than cottages built by the side of

*Sir Robert Lorimer.*

282.—A SINGLE-STOREY CHAUFFEUR'S COTTAGE AT HILL OF TARVIT.

entrance gates, and as such they may properly take their place in this survey of the cottage problem.

The cottage at Bourne End, designed by Messrs. Forsyth and Maule, was built for the gardener, in connection with a week-end home, and an extra bedroom is provided on the ground floor for a chauffeur. The arrangement of the first-floor rooms, with its ingenious avoidance of waste space in landing or passage, determined the plan downstairs, which is convenient, except that the placing of the E.C. facing the entrance to the living-room is hardly fortunate. A good point is the inclusion of a tool-house within the main walls. It is a thoroughly

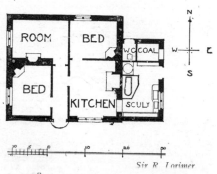

*Sir R. Lorimer*

283.—SINGLE-STOREY COTTAGE.

*Forsyth and Maule.*

284.—GARDENER'S COTTAGE AND LODGE AT THREE FIELDS, BOXMOOR, HERTS.

*Ascough Chapman.*

285.—FOUR-ROOMED STONE COTTAGE.

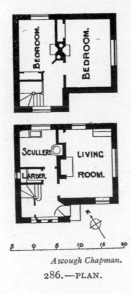

*Ascough Chapman.*

286.—PLAN.

attractive cottage, with a stout chimney, and throughout of brick rough-cast, except at the base, and above the first-floor level tile hung (Figs. 280–1).

The chauffeur's cottage designed by Sir Robert Lorimer (Figs. 282 and 283) is unusual in so far as it is of one storey only. It is a good example of its type, which is practical where two bedrooms only are required. If, as is usually the case, it is desired to provide accommodation for a larger family, it is more economical to provide the extra rooms on an upper floor.

The lodge at Three Fields, Boxmoor, Herts, another by Messrs. Forsyth and Maule (Fig. 284), is a characteristic example of the skill with which Major Maule plays with thatch and weatherboarding and achieves with them an

effect which escapes the reproach of being "quaint" or "old-
world." These words imply too often that the architect has set
himself to construct an "antique," which is unlikely to be
convincing, and if unconvincing is pointless. Late mediæval
architects did not put a gardener's cottage alongside the gate
which opens on to a drive, and it is silly in such a situation
to ape the mediæval. Major Maule has been content to build
this lodge simply and unaffectedly with traditional materials :
it tells its story without affectation and misleads no one.

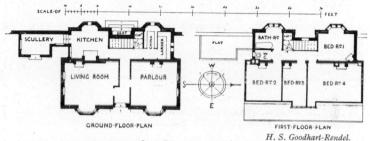

H. S. Goodhart-Rendel.

287.—AT GOLDINGS.

H. S. Goodhart-Rendel.

288.—ENTRANCE FRONT, GARDENER'S COTTAGE.

289.—GARDENER'S COTTAGE AT GOLDINGS, SHOWING TREATMENT OF ELEVATION FACING THE GARDEN.

*H. S. Goodhart-Rendel.*

290.—AT GOLDINGS : RECESS ON GARDEN FRONT.

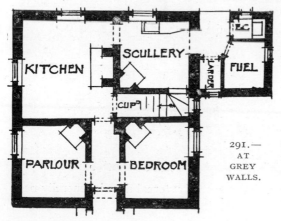

291.—AT GREY WALLS.

The example shown in Figs. 285 and 286 was built for estate servants —a middle-aged couple— and in stone to accord with the main house which it adjoins. It is unusual in having only one external door ; but its architect,

Mr. Ascough Chapman, attached importance to this arrangement because of the freedom from draughts thereby ensured.   It may

*Sir Edwin Lutyens, R.A.*

292.—COTTAGE AT GREY WALLS, GULLANE.

be noted, however, that a second external door is generally necessary to give access to an adjoining E.C. under the same roof. In this case, however, the E.C. is altogether separate, and the provision of one outer door only is thereby made practicable. Not least of the problems which face the designer of cottages for estate servants is the right placing of them with relation to

*Eric Francis.*

293.—COTTAGE FORMING PART OF HUNTING STABLES.

the architectural scheme of the main house and gardens. There is therefore a good deal to be learnt from the cottage which Mr. H. S. Goodhart-Rendel added at Goldings, near the great house designed by the late George Devey. A feature to which attention may be drawn is the skill with which he has made it serve, not only its primary use as a cottage, but also a decorative one as an ornamental feature of the garden. The illustration on page 228 shows that the building has been set on the line of a garden wall, and that to its western front, with its open parapet, has been given a definitely Elizabethan character which recalls the brick garden-houses of the beginning of the seventeenth century. The middle of this elevation has been treated as a large niche with steps leading up to a seat. There are only two very small windows on the ground-level, one for the pantry and the other for the kitchen, the chief lighting of the kitchen being by a window on the south side.

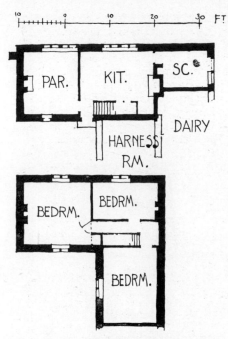

294.—PLAN OF MR. ERIC FRANCIS' COTTAGE.

There is therefore nothing which militates against the use of the recess as a place where one may rest in the course of a walk round the extensive gardens of Goldings. Though this front is conceived on somewhat stately lines to fit it as a decorative adjunct to the garden, the

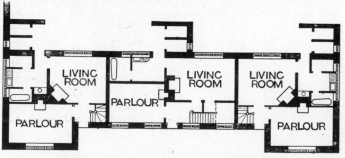

295.—PLAN OF THE MOUNTON COTTAGES.

east side relapses, and very properly, into a more ordinary cottage manner (Fig. 288).

296.—COTTAGES ON THE DRIVE AT MOUNTON HOUSE.

Very delightful in the treatment of its masonry and grey pantiled roof is the cottage at Grey Walls, Gullane, designed by

Sir Edwin Lutyens. In such a building, which has a definite relationship with the main house, and can be seen from it, economic considerations do not press, but it is well to emphasize that building in stone is almost invariably more costly than in brick (Figs. 291 and 292).

The cottage designed by Mr. Eric Francis shown in Figs. 293 and 294 is part of a quadrangle of buildings built for Miss Clay of Piercefield. It was unnecessary to build over the washhouse, as the third bedroom is accommodated over the harness-room. The skyline of the general group is thus improved, and character given at small outlay by putting a little pavilion roof over the outhouse. The cottage was intended for a headman, and is roomy. Limestone, quarried close by, formed the principal

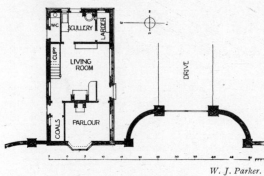

material, and a general appearance of solidity is given by its liberal use in the chimney-stacks. The slates are from Delabole, thick, rough-edged, grey with a russet tinge. They harmonize very well with the stone and melt into the landscape.

*W. J. Parker.*

297.—AT FERNHILL PARK.

The group of three cottages (Figs. 295 and 296) is part of the extensive architectural scheme of Mounton House, near Chepstow. Occupying a bare tableland, all the buildings were necessarily visible, and therefore Mr. Tipping arranged them to form, as it were, a connected and interdependent entity that included house, offices, bothy, garage, workshops, yards, walled gardens and cottages for married employés. Fig. 296 shows the last named in the foreground opening on to the drive, and beyond them the kitchen-garden wall and the garage quadrangle. The treatment of the cottages had to be architectural and in sympathy with, though subsidiary to, the house itself. There are the same massive quoins and thick walls, the same unbroken roof of stone tiles. The windows are leaded iron casements in oak frames, the latter, for these humbler dwellings, being unmoulded. The same quarry which provided thick strata of stones up to 5 ft. long for the quoins, lintels, etc., also gave thin laminated courses that could be effectively used for relieving arches over the windows and other like purposes. But there is no ornamentation or unnecessary detail, and no material beyond limestone, oak, and stone tiles. Tone and texture, form and line are relied

W. J Parker.

298 —FERNHILL PARK, BERKSHIRE.

upon to produce the desired effect. The planning of the end cottages is good and practical, and the exigency of exterior symmetry has not seriously interfered with the convenient disposition of the central dwelling. The living-rooms all look out on to the yards and gardens, get the early morning sun, and are

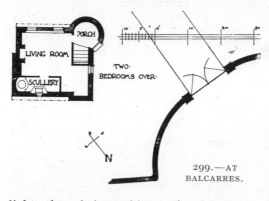

near to wash-house, bathroom, and out-offices. The parlours face the drive and a fine view over the Severn estuary. Each cottage has three roomy bed-rooms upstairs. The low windows to the front main-ly light staircases, and all the bed-rooms have high

299.—AT BALCARRES.

light, there being gables to front and ends and a row of five dormers at the back. The stone is warm and varied in tone.

*Sir Robert Lorimer, A.R.A.*

300.—AT BALCARRES.

The gate lodge at **Fernhill** Park, Berkshire (Figs. 297 and 298), was designed in the same manner as the big house, which is of the period of William and Mary, with bold chimneys and big pedimented dormers that make the three bedrooms upstairs very light and airy. An attractive feature in the wall is the bull's-eye opening, filled with an iron grille, to the left of the small lodge gate. The main gates are all the more impressive for being well set back from the line of the road (*see* Fig. 298).

The two interesting Scottish examples at Balcarres and Pitkerro (Figs. 299 to 302) are both smaller than the Fernhill lodge, having a single living-room with small scullery on the ground floor, and two bedrooms over, ample enough, however, to house a married couple with one or even two children. At Pitkerro the characteristic turret-like projection is used for the staircase, and at

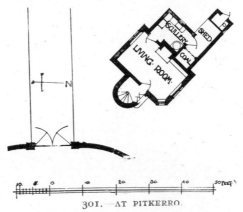

301. — AT PITKERRO.

*Sir Robert Lorimer, A.R.A.*

302. — AT PITKERRO.

Balcarres as a porch.   The design of gates and posts gives infinite room for the translation of heraldic fancies into stone and iron.

303.—AT WITLEY PARK.    *Edward Warren.*

At Pitkerro the over-frame is ornamented with a small shield of arms, and the two gateposts are surmounted by the halves of a broken pediment.   At Balcarres the heraldic idea is more largely developed, for pleasant beasts hold up iron bannerets. In both these lodges the gates are set back so that the curved wing walls form a little segmental entrance court.

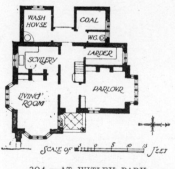

304.—AT WITLEY PARK.

Ormiston Lodge, designed by Mr. Edward Warren, is at one of the gates of Witley Park. It is a more ambitious building, of stone, and with a parlour as well as living-room and scullery on the ground floor, and three bedrooms, bathroom and cupboard upstairs (Figs. 303 and 304).

An altogether different idea, and an excellent one, has been

*Walter Brierley.*

305.—COMBINED LODGE AND STABLES AT BISHOPTHORPE.

adopted by Mr. Brierley for a house at Bishopthorpe, near York, viz. the grouping under one roof of lodge, coach-house and stables. This gives an imposing block of entrance buildings

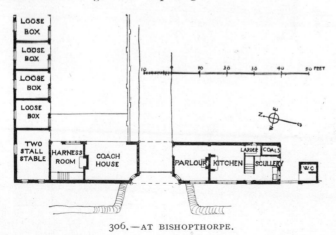

306.—AT BISHOPTHORPE.

*Sir Edwin Lutyens, R.A.*

307.—DOUBLE LODGE AT BARTON ST. MARY, EAST GRINSTEAD, FROM THE ROAD.

and has a practical side, because the coachman is living close to his work. The illustration on page 239 shows well what an attractive vista is seen through the open gateway, while the

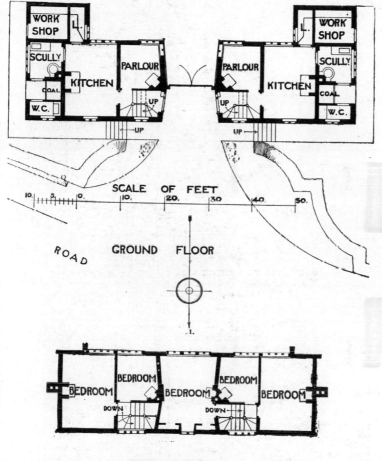

*Sir Edwin Lutyens, R.A.*

308.—PLANS OF DOUBLE LODGE, BARTON ST. MARY, EAST GRIN-STEAD, WITH CARRIAGE-WAY THROUGH.

low-pitched pantiled roof gives a sense of welcoming comfort. The lodge accommodation upstairs amounts to three bedrooms. The Victorian idea was to plan the entrance lodge without

R

309.—THE LODGE ENTRANCE, BARTON ST. MARY, FROM THE ROAD.

reference to the house, which was approached by a wriggling road that in point of design rose no higher than the ideals of a cemetery. By giving regard to planning on axial lines, so that

*Sir Edwin Lutyens.*

310.—DOUBLE LODGE, BARTON ST. MARY, FROM THE SOUTH.

the entrance from the road has a direct relation to the entrance to the house, that air of respectable mystery which was so beloved

*Alan Royds.*

311.—TWIN LODGES AT DORE MOOR HOUSE, DERBYSHIRE.

in the middle of the nineteenth century is sent to the limbo reserved for pretentious futilities.

It may be added that the system of grouping employed at

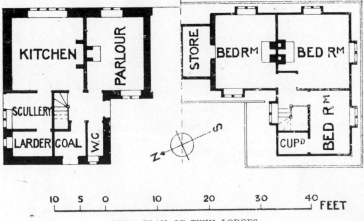

312.—PLAN OF TWIN LODGES.

Bishopthorpe necessarily effects economies as compared with building lodges and stables in separate blocks.

A pair of lodges, one on either side of the entrance gates to an estate, is a usual arrangement, but it would often be better to treat them as one building, a method employed by Sir Edwin Lutyens at Barton St. Mary, East Grinstead (Figs. 307 to 310). A marked aspect of dignity belongs to this pair of cottages with its central opening for the carriage-way to the main house. The treatment of the building follows the vernacular traditions

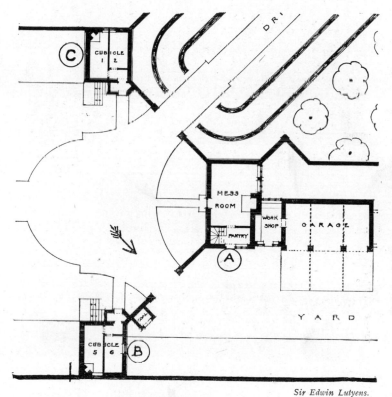

*Sir Edwin Lutyens.*

313.—PLAN OF THREE LODGES AT GREY WALLS, GULLANE.

of the neighbourhood—white rough-cast walls for the ground storey and tile-hanging above. The inner walls of the carriage passage through the building are of half-timber work, but Sir Edwin was very wisely economical of this type of construction, which becomes more and more an anachronism in modern work. The space in both halves of the lodge has been well utilized. The kitchens have windows to north and south and

the parlours to the south only.   A practical provision is a work-
shop for each cottage.   Upstairs there are two bedrooms for
one family and three for the other.

A similar arrangement was devised by Mr. Alan Royds for the
gate lodges at Dore Moor House, Derbyshire (Figs. 311 and 312).

In the case of a large house, the lodges at the entrance may
fulfil a very important function in the general development of

314.—AT GREY WALLS : LODGE A (SEE PLAN, FIG. 313).

the architectural scheme by masking awkward lines of approach.
This is seen very well at Grey Walls, Gullane (Figs. 313 to 315).
The entrance to the grounds from the road bore no sort of reference to any important axial line of the house or of the carriage-
approach.   Sir Edwin Lutyens got over the difficulty, with his
usual ingenuity, by building three lodges, which are perfectly
balanced, as seen from the main entrance (to the left of the plan
shown in Fig. 313) and also from the house.   The way to the
latter is between the lodges marked A and C on the plan, and the

opening between lodges A and B leads to the yard of the garage. The photograph reproduced in two halves in Figs. 314 and 315 was taken from the point of view shown on the plan by an arrow. It shows (in Fig. 314) the lodge A, which consists of a mess-room for the men employed. The garage block is behind it. Fig. 315 (the other half of the photograph) shows lodge B, the accommodation in which is four bedrooms. Lodge C, which is not illus-

*Sir Edwin Lutyens.*

315.—AT GREY WALLS : LODGE B (SEE PLAN, FIG. 313).

trated by photograph, also has cubicles. By distributing the accommodation, which is a perfectly practicable arrangement for outdoor servants who are single men, a difficult architectural problem was solved in an interesting and wholly successful way.

It is one of the good things about a gate lodge that it gives just opportunity to the designer to invest a little building with a marked architectural character which would be inappropriate and, indeed, pretentious in a cottage built for ordinary purposes.

*Frank Verity.*

316.—LODGE AT ELMSTEAD GLADE, CHISLEHURST.

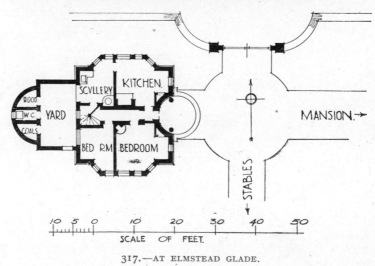

317.—AT ELMSTEAD GLADE.

It is, in effect, an outpost of the mansion, the needs of which
it serves. It may properly strike the same note of design and
prepare the mind of the visitor for the character of the main

*The late Sir Ernest George.*

318.—LODGE AT ESHER.

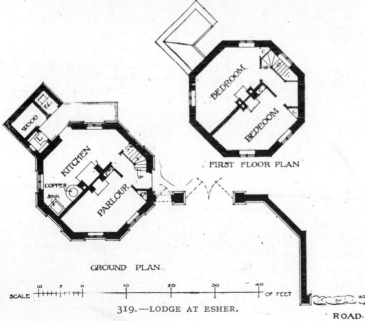

FIRST FLOOR PLAN

GROUND PLAN

SCALE |++++|++++| OF FEET

319.—LODGE AT ESHER.

ROAD.

building. It is permissible, moreover, to indulge, not only in especial richness in the treatment of materials, but also in a

*The late Sir Ernest George.*

320.—OCTAGONAL LODGE AT MOORE PLACE, ESHER.

more conscious variety in planning than is appropriate in simple cottage work. The lodge at Elmstead Glade, Chislehurst (Figs.

316 and 317), designed by Mr. Frank Verity, is a good exercise
in an early eighteenth-century manner. The ground floor is
occupied by kitchen, scullery, and two bedrooms, and there is
a room in the roof. The coal space, etc., are contrived at the
far side of a little yard, and the semi-circular plan of this little
group adds to the interest of the scheme. The bold cornice
and the rusticated brick quoins are noticeable features.

Another very good gate lodge, at Moore Place, Esher, is
shown in Figs. 318 to 320, and was designed by the late Sir Ernest
George. Its octagonal plan makes it an interesting variant
on the more usual types. The rooms are ingeniously contrived.

*The late Dan Gibson.*

321.—LODGE AT HOLE HIRD, WINDERMERE.

A tiny hall at the entrance door gives access to kitchen and
parlour, and there are two bedrooms upstairs.

The last two lodges illustrated show the happy effect of a
markedly architectural treatment, but sometimes the surroundings of an entrance lodge suggest a building of very modest
character. At Hole Hird, Windermere, for example, the late
Dan Gibson designed a low spreading cottage, which is illustrated in Fig. 321. The site is richly wooded, and from the
road wide views are obtained across the lake to the hills beyond.
Doubtless Gibson felt that it would be unwise at such a spot to
put up a building which drew attention to itself and away from
the natural beauties of the scene. Whether that was so or not,
he designed a lodge which is wholly unobtrusive and nestles
quietly in its bower of trees.

# CHAPTER XIII

## REPAIR AND ALTERATION

IT may be admitted that it is often, but not always, as expensive to repair a little old building as to pull it down and build afresh. None the less, every nerve should be strained to save the old work, for it is an expression of craftsmanship that can never be reproduced ; it is, in fact, a piece of history. Words to this effect have so often been written and spoken that there is a risk of their repetition being wearisome. Nevertheless, all who love the English countryside and what it represents, all who see our market towns and villages continually marred by the ignorant builder with his hideous sham villas, purple-slated, will appreciate that the writer on architecture must feel " woe is me if I preach not the gospel." Not only is the neglect of old village buildings bad art and the sign of an inert civic conscience, but it is bad business from the point of view of the landowner and everybody else. Let us take a case in point. There is a Worcestershire village (its name will occur to many) that has escaped the besom of destruction. It was always a beautiful place, and its beauty has been allowed to remain. A century ago, no doubt, there were a score or more villages in the same county quite as beautiful. It is possible to walk their broad streets and forget the hideous blots that now deface them, to imagine them as a whole as they now appear only in the fragments that remain. Who, though, wishes now to live in them, defaced as they are in their old features, and polluted by new vulgarities ? What, on the other hand, of the undefaced village to which reference has been made ? It has become a focus of new life, because its old beauties have remained. Folk are drawn to it, buy land, build new houses—but reverently and in the light of old traditions. It is alive with a new prosperity, and has taken on a new pride. Fortunately the place was obviously picturesque as a whole. It is necessary, however, if villages that have been defaced are to be recreated in a new

252

spirit of beauty, that people should look into their buildings a little closely. In this connection we may listen to Mr. C. R. Ashbee, for his writings on the subject are helpful: " People

322.—AT BROAD CAMPDEN, GLOS.

will appreciate an old building if it be picturesque, or if it be built by somebody whose name they have heard: that is, if it appeal to their pictorial sense or to their literary sense. They

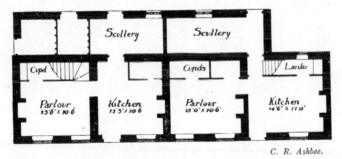

C. R. Ashbee.

323.—FOUR ROADSIDE COTTAGES TURNED INTO TWO AND REPAIRED AT BROAD CAMPDEN.

do not understand it for its construction or beauty. If it happen to be disguised, as old buildings often are, with bad or commonplace additions, they may ignore it altogether. The name of Sir Christopher Wren has saved many a building, and the fact that he could not be proven its author has lost us many more. We are a foolish and half-cultured people ; and the principle of ' beauty in all things,' which we enjoy in the poetry of Keats, we deface, obliterate and forget in the poetry of Thorpe, of John of Padua, of Gibbs, of Pugin, of the hundred and one little lyrics of stone that such as they have inspired by the wayside." All this is exceeding good sense, but it is in no way a plea for the preservation of damp and insanitary cottages *as such.* Damp and bad sanitation must obviously be destroyed, but every effort should be made before the cottages are destroyed with them. If the principles upon which the Society for the Protection of Ancient Buildings works were widely known, many a cottage could be saved and made perfectly habitable for less money than would be spent in building anew. At the same time the village would retain its beauty and interest, which even now have a money value, and will be worth more as education in taste covers a wider field.

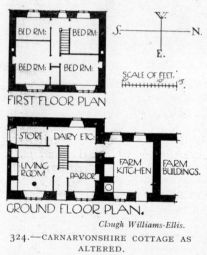

FIRST FLOOR PLAN

GROUND FLOOR PLAN.

*Clough Williams-Ellis.*

324.—CARNARVONSHIRE COTTAGE AS ALTERED.

This point may be illustrated by reference to the accompanying pictures of four roadside cottages at Broad Campden (*see* page 253), repaired by Mr. C. R. Ashbee. They had become unfit for human habitation, and were so small that the four only made two satisfactory homes. The plan shows how well the remodelling has been accomplished. The total cost of reconstruction was no more than £158 (pre-war), so not only were the amenities of the village preserved by rescuing the old work, but less money was spent than on a new building.

An interesting example of the remaking of a small holding is to be seen on the Glasfryn Estate, Carnarvonshire. It indicates what can be done with property which has been rightly condemned. The old cottage was of one storey, and contained practically no more than two rooms. It was hopelessly insanitary, cramped and dilapidated, but, as Fig. 325 shows, quite romantic in appearance. Mr. Clough Williams-Ellis restored and enlarged it (Fig. 326). He used a great deal of the old materials and built as much as possible on the old foundations, only

325.—COTTAGE AT GLASFRYN BEFORE RENEWAL.

*Clough Williams-Ellis.*

326.—SAME COTTAGE AFTER ALTERATION.

increasing the width on one half of the west side.  About six feet in height of the old walling was retained.  The new work continued above all the window openings, the frames in which are new and enlarged. Such of the old slates as were good sufficed to cover about half of the reconstructed roof, but nearly

327.—CONVERTED FROM A RUINED BARN.

all the timber-work had to be new. The interior partitions and ceilings are all of tongued and grooved match-boarding, and the partitions are stiffened by a horizontal rail half-way up their height. The ceilings are clear varnished. Mr. Williams-Ellis claims that this treatment effects a saving in first cost, upkeep and space as compared with studding and plaster. The total cost of rebuilding the cottage was less than eighty pounds, a very small sum even for pre-war days.

Near Chepstow stood a little

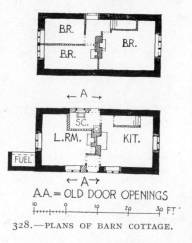

A.A. = OLD DOOR OPENINGS

328.—PLANS OF BARN COTTAGE.

barn, disused and fast falling into ruin, its tiles slipping and rafters rotting. Its walls were retained, but, as it had to be

*G. H. Kitchin.*

329.—YEW TREE COTTAGE AS ALTERED.

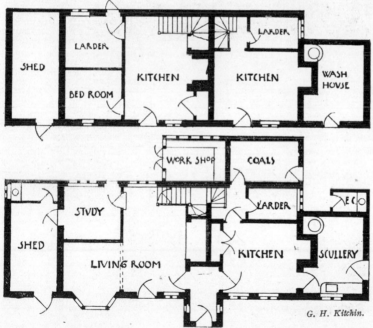

*G. H. Kitchin.*

330.—YEW TREE COTTAGE, COMPTON, WINCHESTER: GROUND-FLOOR
PLAN BEFORE AND AFTER ALTERATION.

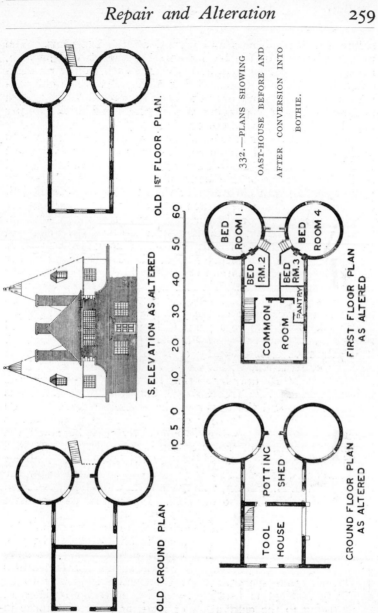

OLD 1ST FLOOR PLAN.

S. ELEVATION AS ALTERED

332.—PLANS SHOWING OAST-HOUSE BEFORE AND AFTER CONVERSION INTO BOTHIE.

BED ROOM 1.

BED RM. 2

BED ROOM 4

BED RM. 3

PANTRY

COMMON ROOM

FIRST FLOOR PLAN AS ALTERED

OLD GROUND PLAN

POTTING SHED

TOOL HOUSE

GROUND FLOOR PLAN AS ALTERED

new roofed, the walls were raised 18 in. and the roof given a steeper pitch ; board and felt, moreover, were introduced to secure weather-tightness and warmth in the bedrooms. The unbroken oblong of the barn dominated the planning, which, nevertheless, gives the required accommodation quite conveniently, the smaller bedrooms being 8 ft. wide. The old pantiles were re-used, and only the little time required for garden making and creeper growing was needed to make the former barn look like an ancient cottage (Fig. 327).

The remodelling of labourers' cottages to bring them up to modern standards of accommodation and sanitary equipment would doubtless be attempted more often if the expense could be kept within reasonable bounds. It is a more satisfactory way of dealing with old property than the frequent method of altering a group of two or three cottages into a little home for people who want to spend their week-ends in " simple " fashion. Sometimes, but rarely, when the character of a district changes, there is justification for this course. Before the war there were cases when old cottages would have become altogether derelict for lack of some one to put them in good repair for their normal occupants, but with a forward agricultural policy and a grave shortage of decent homes for rural labourers, it is to be hoped this diversion of cottages to playtime uses will not be continued. It should be a point of honour that no one should acquire a labourer's cottage for holiday purposes merely because it is attractive architecturally or historically, or by reason of its view or situation, without first building a new and wholly satisfactory cottage near by so that the total of available homes is not reduced. Yew Tree Cottage, Compton, Winchester, was originally two, and the upper of the two plans reproduced on page 257 shows them as they were. The lower plan indicates the additions and alterations. Especially may be noted the ingenious treatment of the two staircases, which were retained and joined at the first landing. The original builder had put his bedroom windows at the floor-level to get them below the eaves. Mr. G. H. Kitchin, who devised the alterations, corrected this by changing them to dormers. Fig. 329 shows the result of his work.

An interesting example of the alteration of a type of building which tends to outlive its usefulness is illustrated in Fig. 331. Oast-houses have the peculiar charm of enshrining the spire form in domestic building, and they make such delightful features in English landscape that their destruction is greatly to be deprecated. Kent is turning from the uncertain business of hop-growing to the cultivation of fruit, and the oast-house in consequence begins to fall into disuse. At Godinton, Sir Reginald Blomfield has added to one and made of it an attractive bothie. Fig. 332 shows the plans of the building before and after the

333.—DRINKSTONE COTTAGES, IN 1921.

334.—AFTER MR. WILLIAM WEIR HAD REPAIRED THEM.

alterations were made. Mr. Clough Williams-Ellis has also
preserved an oast-house in a block of buildings at Hildenborough,
Kent, used for Princess Christian's Farm Colony.

Another admirable work of salvation was carried out in 1921
by Mr. William Weir on behalf of the Society for the Protection
of Ancient Buildings to demonstrate to all and sundry that not
only is such an enterprise worthy as saving the humble heritage

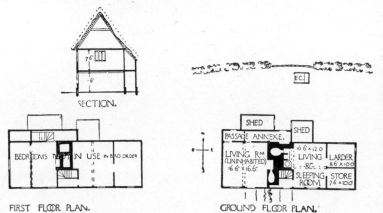

335.—DRINKSTONE : PLANS AND SECTIONS BEFORE ALTERATION.

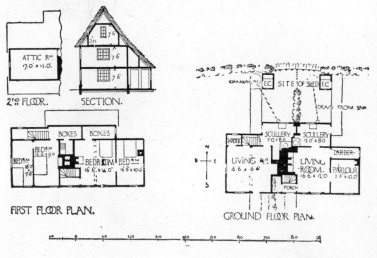

*William Weir.*

336.—DRINKSTONE : PLANS AND SECTIONS AFTER ALTERATION.

337.—DRINKSTONE : THE OLD FOLK IN THEIR REJUVENATED LIVING-ROOM.

of the countryside, but economically sound. The pair of timber-built derelicts at Drinkstone, Suffolk, are shown in Fig. 333 as they were and in Fig. 334 as they are. Their state could hardly have been worse. First of all, the roof was put right. The main timbers were still sound, thanks to the ample margin of safety allowed by the old builders. A new thatch 2 feet thick was put on. The lath and plaster was not wholly stripped, but repaired where needful. The ground-floor rooms had been floored with bricks which were badly worn and cracked, and they were taken up. The ground was excavated

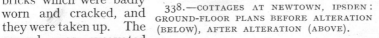

338.—COTTAGES AT NEWTOWN, IPSDEN : GROUND-FLOOR PLANS BEFORE ALTERATION (BELOW), AFTER ALTERATION (ABOVE).

enough to allow for a layer of hard core and then 6 inches of concrete faced with tile paving. New sculleries with sink and copper were added at the back and a modern range put in each cottage. A few windows were renewed, and the total cost worked out at about half the cost of new cottages.

Amongst the virtues incidental to the reparation of old cottages

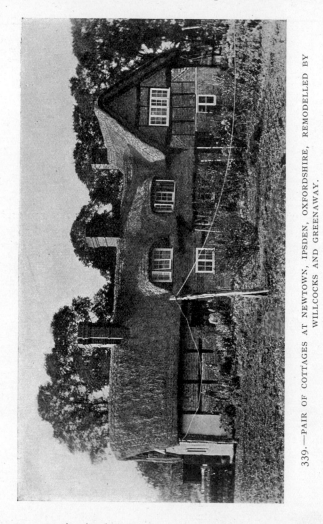

339.—PAIR OF COTTAGES AT NEWTOWN, IPSDEN, OXFORDSHIRE, REMODELLED BY WILLCOCKS AND GREENAWAY.

is the opportunity it gives to amend ancient defects of planning, as is well seen by an examination of the plans of a pair of thatched cottages at Newtown, Ipsden, Oxfordshire, altered by Messrs. Willcocks and Greenaway (Figs. 338 to 340). The arrangement of the

cottages before alter-
ation was not only
awkward but very
wasteful, the pas-
sage in the right-
hand cottage being
almost big enough
for a room, and it
was turned into a
parlour. The left-
hand cottage had at
one time been a pair
of tiny dwellings
which gave it two
staircases, each ris-
ing from a room.
One was removed,
and the unneces-
sarily large larder
turned into a scul-
lery. Upstairs in

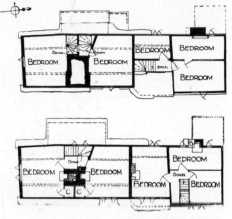

*Willcocks and Greenaway.*

340.—COTTAGES AT NEWTOWN, IPSDEN: FIRST-
FLOOR PLANS BEFORE ALTERATION (ABOVE),
AFTER ALTERATION (BELOW).

a similar way much better use was made of the available
floor area. The oversailing courses on the chimneys show
the immense thickness of the original thatch. This was wholly
removed, and it will take a generation or two before future additional coats so increase the thickness that the oversailing
courses will once again resume their original function. One
practical point does not appear in the illustration, viz. the excavation of a sunk path round the cottages, in order to keep the
bases of the walls dry. In two or three hundred years the level
of a cultivated garden rises considerably, and unless this is
corrected by digging down near the house trouble is bound to
develop from sodden walls.

It is rarely that the opportunity arises to save a house so com-
pletely derelict as was Wangfield Farm (Figs. 341 to 343). It
had, however, a skeleton of distinction, and Major Roberts,
County Architect for Hampshire, was sound in his instinct for
history and economy alike when he proposed to renew the fabric
rather than destroy and build afresh. The result was more than
justified, for the expense of reparation, which incidentally involved
re-planning, was less than the cost of a new building.

The alterations and additions to a pair of cottages at Bledlow
Ridge, Bucks, for Sir William Lister, K.C.M.G., devised by
Mr. Frederick Etchells, are another good example of reparation.

The cottages, probably about 120 years old, were in an
extremely bad condition, and would not have stood much longer.

FIRST FLOOR PLAN

GROUND FLOOR PLAN

*Major Roberts, County Architect.*

341, 342, AND 343.—WANGFIELD FARM,
BOTLEY (HANTS COUNTY COUNCIL.): RE-
CONSTRUCTION OF DERELICT HALF-TIMBER
HOUSE.

As soon as door frames were removed large portions of the walls at once fell down. This necessitated a great deal of expensive shoring, and the ultimate rebuilding of nearly all the walls, with the exception of the gable ends, one of which had to be buttressed in brickwork.

The headroom downstairs was a bare 6 ft. 3 in. This involved excavation to give a final headroom of 7 ft. 6 in. All ground round the cottages was excavated to suitable depth and carefully drained. Floors were laid in mastic on concrete for the ground floor, and new floors provided above. New metal casements were fixed throughout, set into wood frames. New doors and skirtings were needed everywhere, and mostly new plastering.

The new portions were built in 9-inch brickwork, and the whole of the exterior rendered in cement, trowel finish, and distempered two coats. The original roof was left intact,

except for necessary repairs, and for the new portion similar
hand-made tiles were used.

Drainage was a heavy item, owing to the lie of the land. The
cottages are over five miles from a building centre, and access
was by a steep narrow lane, which made transport a heavy item.

The new work cost about £500, and the rebuilding of the old
£626. Drainage, etc., cost £80.

344.—PAIR OF COTTAGES AT BLEDLOW RIDGE, BUCKS.

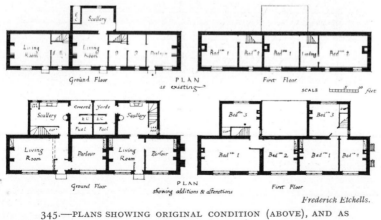

*Frederick Etchells.*

345.—PLANS SHOWING ORIGINAL CONDITION (ABOVE), AND AS
REMODELLED (BELOW).

The total of about £1,200 for the pair of cottages as they stand to-day was heavy, but the conditions were exceptional, and it is at least clear that a pair of wholly new cottages would have cost far more, for they are very roomy.

# CHAPTER XIV

## THE GROUPING OF COTTAGES

THE grouping of cottages in blocks of three or more has advantage in cheapening the cost as compared with single cottages, but it is well to consider it also from the point of view of architectural amenity. It is difficult to make the small single cottage look attractive, because the designer is deprived of the conspicuous advantages obtained from a long roof-line, from the interesting skyline created by several chimney-stacks, and from large breaks in the lines of the plan. All these features can be secured by building several cottages in a block. The illustrations of this chapter are chosen to lay stress on æsthetic possibilities, rather than economic difficulties. The group of three dwellings illustrated in Figs. 346 to 349 cannot pretend to answer any economic problem, but its artistic success is sufficiently demonstrated. We may hope that there may still be some landowners who will be prepared to face loss rather than lose the opportunity of putting a satisfying building on some prominent village site. For setting there must be imagined an ideal Oxfordshire village remote from the railway, and, as yet, undefaced by thoughtless modern buildings. All around are old cottages of flint, brick, and half-timber. The task of the architect, Mr. Maxwell Ayrton, was to provide a building that should be in perfect accord with its surroundings, and his success was complete. He was hampered by no local by-laws, such as often before the war prevented building being carried out in the manner consecrated by centuries of Oxfordshire usage. The cottages are entirely of timber construction, save for the brick base on which they are set. There is no brick-nogging between the oak timbers ; the spaces between them are narrow and filled in with lath and plaster. The oak was all felled on the estate, split and axed in the woods and then carried to the site. This work was done exclusively by the local woodmen, and the home construction of the cottages was further emphasized by the making of the casements and their fittings, the door latches and the

bolts at the blacksmith's forge in the village.   In connection with
the woodwork, it may be of interest to add that in this part of

*Maxwell Ayrton.*

346.—GROUP OF THREE OXFORDSHIRE COTTAGES, SEEN FROM VILLAGE STREET.

Oxfordshire, just south of the Chilterns, the woodmen do not
use the adze, as is common in most parts of the country, but

an axe with a short handle.   Turning now to the cottages themselves, it may be noted how much attractiveness is gained by
the setting forward towards the road of the third cottage, so as
to give an internal angle on the main front.   Reference to the
plans Fig. 349 will show that the design to secure a picturesque

*Maxwell Ayrton.*

347.—GROUP OF OXFORDSHIRE COTTAGES : VIEW FROM SOUTH-EAST.

effect has not impaired in any way the convenient arrangement of the rooms.  By the provision of dormer windows of
adequate size the best use possible has been made of the roof
space.  The interior walls are left untouched to show their
natural construction of oak and plaster, and the usual garish

wall-papers beloved of villagers are taboo. Perhaps no higher compliment can be paid to the skill with which Mr. Ayrton has

*Maxwell Ayrton.*

348.—GROUP OF OXFORDSHIRE COTTAGES : BACK ELEVATION.

caught the spirit of the old work near by than the fact that anyone, when first seeing. the building, would suppose that it was old work carefully restored and underpinned. The cottages were not intended to solve the economic problem of the rural cottage, but their pre-war cost of $7\frac{3}{4}d$. a cubic foot included the value of the timber supplied from the estate, and the cost of its felling and preparation. By so much, therefore, the landlord brought into beneficial use the timber on his own property, employed local labour for its conversion into building material, and saved transport. These are advantages

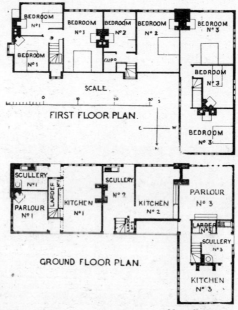

*Maxwell Ayrton.*

349.—PLANS OF GROUP OF THREE COTTAGES IN OXFORDSHIRE.

which now more than ever should be taken into consideration. The greatest merit of Mr. Ayrton's work, however, remains in the fact that the new buildings

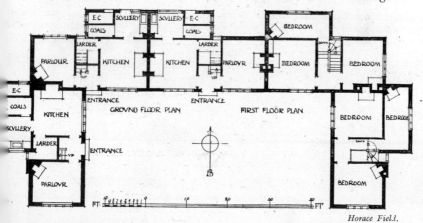

*Horace Field.*

350.—GROUP OF FIVE COTTAGES AT MAYFORD, WOKING : LEFT-HAND HALF SHOWS GROUND FLOOR, AND RIGHT-HAND HALF THE BEDROOM FLOOR.

added to the beauty of the village, instead of introducing, as is too often the case, a note of modernity fatal to the charms of old-world surroundings.

The next example is a group of cottages at Mayford, Woking, designed by Mr. Horace Field (Figs. 350 to 353). It happened

351.—AT MAYFORD : PRINCIPAL FRONT, LEFT-HAND HALF.
*See opposite page.*

often enough that old country cottages became the habitation of people of educated taste after they had been altered and enlarged to suit the views of their new owners. It is less usual, however, to find thus occupied a modern dwelling which was built for

labourers. Croswell Cottages form a group of five which under-
went this change. Two of them had partition walls removed, so
as to make them into one week-end home. The other three stand
as they were built, and very charming they are. The accommo-

*Horace Field.*

352.—AT MAYFORD : PRINCIPAL FRONT, RIGHT-HAND HALF.
*See opposite page.*

dation of all was originally the same, parlour, kitchen, scullery
and offices, and three bedrooms, as will be seen by the plan, which
shows on its left side the disposition of the ground-floor rooms,
and on the right the arrangement above stairs. They are all
under one roof, the cottages at each end making projecting wings,
which form a quadrangle with the south side open. This way
the view is over Smart's Heath, and very delightful it is. The
garden growth was so vigorous as to make it impossible to get
one general view of the principal front ; but the two separate
pictures side by side on these pages (Figs. 351 and 352) answer
the same purpose. The garden was very wisely treated as a whole,
and is common to all. The treatment of the general scheme is

unaffectedly simple—whitewashed walls and red-tiled roofs without, and white paint and whitewash within.   The refinement

353.—FIVE COTTAGES AT MAYFORD :   VIEW FROM SOUTH-EAST.

*Horace Field.*

which Mr. Horace Field brings to his simplest work was enriched
by charming furnishing, when I saw the cottages before the war.

*Baillie Scott.*

354.—TWO COTTAGES AT GIDEA PARK.

Altogether Croswell Cottages provided a happy example of what is possible to a group of friends of sympathetic tastes desiring a little country dwelling and ample garden space at the minimum of yearly cost.

355.—GROUP OF FOUR COTTAGES AT CATBROOK, CAMPDEN.

*C. R. Ashbee.*

Even when only two cottages are to be built together, considerable opportunity is given for attractive grouping, as is shown by Fig. 354. Mr. Baillie Scott has connected these two cottages in a markedly picturesque way, without giving them the banal air of the "semi-detached." Attention is also drawn to

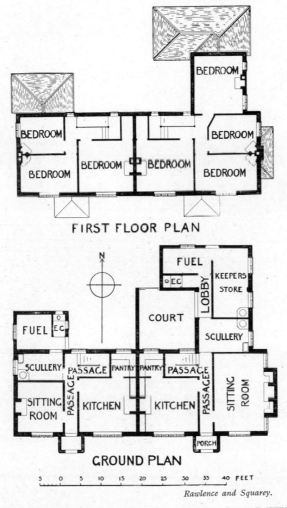

FIRST FLOOR PLAN

GROUND PLAN

*Rawlence and Squarey.*

356.—PLANS OF PAIR OF COTTAGES ON THE HILL AT IWERNE MINSTER.

the very attractive group of four cottages with thatched roof, built from the designs of Mr. C. R. Ashbee, at Catbrook, Campden, Gloucester (Fig. 355). The end cottages are rather larger than the two in the middle, but all have three bedrooms, and there are only two chimney-stacks in all.

*Rawlence and Squarey.*

357.—IN IWERNE MINSTER VILLAGE.

Other delightful examples of the grouping of thatched cottages are to be seen at Iwerne Minster, where Mr. James H. Ismay has done much towards preserving the ancient character of the village. The cottages are built chiefly in pairs (Fig. 357). Two on the hill are occupied by a keeper and a farm labourer, two in the

358.—AT ASHBY ST. LEDGERS: AT THE BACK OF THE COTTAGES.

*Sir Edwin Lutyens, R.A.*

village street by a carrier and the mail-driver. As appears clearly enough from the plans (Fig. 356), these cottages have ample accommodation, and their general treatment is markedly superior to what can be expected from landowners in the ordinary way. Mr. Ismay, however, was not thinking of an economic rent, but of the amenities of the village. It may be hoped that there will still be landowners who can afford to wink at a low

359.—AT ASHBY ST. LEDGERS: PART OF STREET FRONT.

return on capital expenditure and follow such a good example. At Ashby St. Ledgers, Northamptonshire, Sir Edwin Lutyens designed a most attractive group of thatched cottages for Lord Wimborne. One detail of this block is illustrated in the frontispiece, and other views are given in Figs. 358 and 359. The

plan is broken up in the most delightful way, and produces a
street picture of pleasant diversity, but the amount of accommodation is the same in all of the cottages. Each boasts a
kitchen, scullery, parlour, and three bedrooms. There is a porch
at the back which serves as a covered way from the cottage

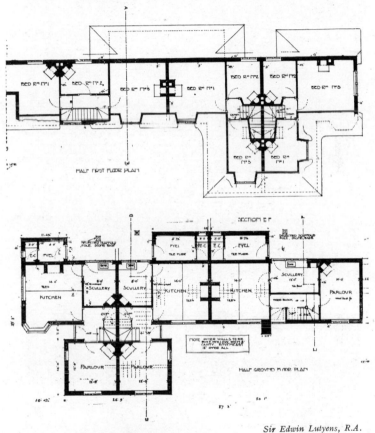

*Sir Edwin Lutyens, R.A.*

360.—AT ASHBY ST. LEDGERS : PLANS OF BOTH FLOORS AND OF
ROOF OF HALF THE BLOCK.

proper to the fuel-house, and the E.C. is approached through
the latter. This arrangement has the advantage of putting the
E.C. at a considerable distance from the living-rooms, while
making it accessible under cover. A feature of the block is
the arched passage-way through the middle of it, which leads

from the village street to the cottage gardens at the back. A certain amount of old masonry was available, and Sir Edwin Lutyens made use of this for the lower parts of the walls, as far

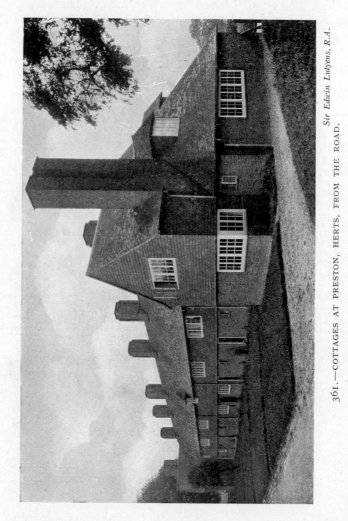

*Sir Edwin Lutyens, R.A.*

361.—COTTAGES AT PRESTON, HERTS, FROM THE ROAD.

as it would go, building the upper parts of the walls with brick rough-cast. The thick thatched roof, with its admirable dormers and ridge, the unbroken roof-line and the stout brick chimneys produce an effect altogether picturesque and satisfactory. The cottages are large, but the planning of the chimneys has been so carefully thought out that only eight stacks were required for the six cottages, which form a very satisfactory example of

362.—AT PRESTON : THE BACK OF THE COTTAGES. *Sir Edwin Lutyens, R.A.*

what can be done by a landowner not only to preserve but to increase the amenities of a typical English village. The work was done in 1906.

Another group by the same designer at Preston, Herts (Figs. 361

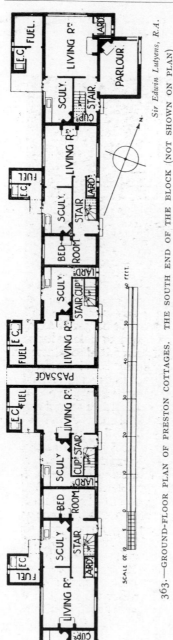

*Sir Edwin Lutyens, R.A.*

363.—GROUND-FLOOR PLAN OF PRESTON COTTAGES. THE SOUTH END OF THE BLOCK (NOT SHOWN ON PLAN) EXACTLY MATCHES THE NORTH END.

to 363), was influenced in its character by the neighbouring house of Temple Dinsley. The six cottages were intended mainly for pensioners and others connected with the estate. The two at the ends of the blocks are rather larger than the rest and include a parlour as well as a living-room and scullery. Two others have a small bedroom on the ground floor, as well as two above stairs, so that ample variety is provided in the accommodation. One difficulty in the design of a long range of cottages is to provide convenient access from front to back of the block; another is to ensure an orderly back elevation. The architect provided an opening in the middle of the block which leads through, and Fig. 362 shows that the back elevation is in no way less dignified than the front to the road.

The secret of success in a long range of this kind is to preserve an unbroken roof line, which is also maintained here in the projecting wings at either end. Nowhere is there a break in any horizontal line, save only in the dormer window at the middle of the road front. This determination to avoid anything in the nature of contrived picturesqueness gives a restful effect altogether satisfactory. The detail of the chimneys rising from the main roof is attractive, and the tall stacks at either end give the effect of buttressing the whole range in a pleasant fashion.

Our last example is a humble group which Mr. A. H. Clough built in a Hampshire village (Figs. 364 and 365).

A. H. Clough.

364.—BLOCK OF SEVEN COTTAGES AT CORNER OF TWO ROADS.

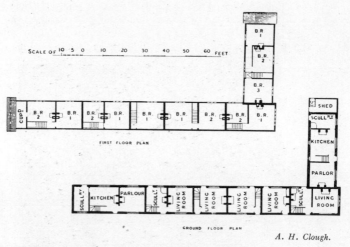

SCALE OF 10 5 0   10   20   30   40   50   60 FEET

FIRST FLOOR PLAN

GROUND FLOOR PLAN

*A. H. Clough.*

365.—BLOCK OF SEVEN COTTAGES.

Among the post-war housing schemes there are many in which great care has been given, not only to the larger considerations of lay-out in regard to roads and open spaces, but to the equally important factor of grouping of houses either in quadrangles or crescents, or in the modelling of a block of four or more. Good examples are to be seen at Swanpool, Lincoln, in a big scheme by Messrs. Hennell and James (Figs. 366 and 367). The big square has the quality of dignity without monotony : the setting of the end houses in the other block off the main axial line gives a note of interest, but it probably gave rise to some rather light-hearted planning of rooms. Any angle but a right-angle is difficult to deal with in a very small house.

Mr. Clough Williams-Ellis is as successful and personal as usual in the grouping of houses in a village street in Antrim (Fig. 368), where he lets go the Gaelic element in his Snowdon blood and forgets the overwhelming virtues of his moments of lanky and altogether amusing Baroque.

This chapter on groups of cottages cannot be closed with anything better than an examination of a large number of groups of four, designed for Lord Riddell by Mr. Paxton Watson, and built very recently at Merstham and Walton Heath. They are not only admirable in appearance and planning, but certainly the best value for money in 1924, of which I know anything. The blocks of four comprise two parlour cottages and two non-parlour. The modelling of the group with the non-parlour cottages

set back a little in the middle and the ends roofed at a rather
lower pitch gives variety with any sense of contrived picturesque-

*Hennell and James.*

366.—AN OPEN QUADRANGLE OF COTTAGES AT SWANPOOL, LINCOLN.

ness, and the total cost including everything but the site worked

out at less than an average of £500 per cottage, which means that
the non-parlour type were nearer £450 than £500. The best

367.—A GROUP OF HOUSES AT SWANPOOL, LINCOLN.

*Hennell and James.*

bricks and tiles were used—no mean substitute materials helped
to bring down the cost—and the accommodation is above the

368.—GROUPING OF COTTAGES AT CUSHENCAN VILLAGE, CO. ANTRIM.

*Clough Williams-Ellis.*

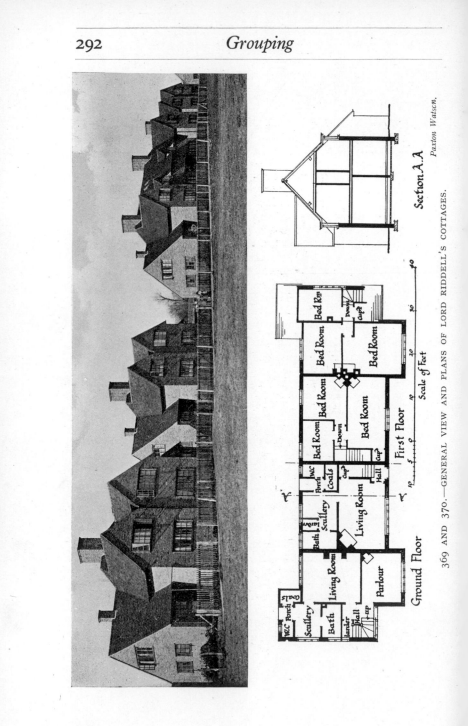

Section. A. A

*Paxton Watson.*

Bed Rm
Bed Room
Bed Room
Bed Room
Bed Room
Bed Room
Bed Room
WC
Porch
Coals
Cup
Down
Hall
Cup
Down
Cup
First Floor

Scale of Feet

Coals
WC
Porch
Scullery
Bath
Bath
Scullery
Larder
Living Room
Living Room
Hall
up
Parlour
Ground Floor

369 AND 370.—GENERAL VIEW AND PLANS OF LORD RIDDELL'S COTTAGES.

average floor area of " subsidy cottages." The interior finish
is plaster and distemper,—again no savings by the use of fancy

*Paxton Watson.*

371.—BLOCK OF FOUR COTTAGES FOR LORD RIDDELL AT MERSTHAM.

The area of the parlour cottages is 806 ft. super, and of the non-parlour cottages 751 ft. super. The former let at 11s. 6d. a week plus rates, which brings them up to about 15s., and the latter let at 9s. 6d. a week.

materials. This result is got in the only way best results in
cottage building are to be got, by employing an architect who

is widely experienced in cottage design. Mr. Paxton Watson
uses his materials with as full a knowledge of what lengths and
scantlings of timber work out cheapest, as the wise speculative
builder, but without the temptation to "scamp" anything.
The planning shows that not an inch is wasted. There are no
passages on either floor, but each cottage has its separate bathroom
(adjoining the scullery), with a copper fixed at the end of the
bath. The back door has a porch to give access to coals and
W.C. under cover. The cooking range is in the living-room, and
the flues are gathered together so that there are only four stacks,
two large and two very small, to each group of four cottages.

It is always tempting to believe that a particularly cheap
pair or group of cottages are a freak, not to be repeated in
ordinary conditions. But as Lord Riddell has built forty or
fifty cottages like those illustrated and in two districts, the
virtues of the design are obviously inherent and not accidental.
Economical cottage building is based on common sense and the
most rigid supervision of every detail, cutting out every feature
that does not directly minister to a reasonable standard of
comfort for the tenant.

# CHAPTER XV

## VILLAGE AND SUBURB PLANNING :
## EXAMPLES BEGUN PRE-WAR

The Lesson of the Hampstead Garden Suburb—Squares and Crescents—Absence of Garden Walls—New Eltham—Ruislip—Earswick—A Co-partnership Scheme at East Grinstead

THUS far we have considered cottages as individual buildings or as groups of two or more ; but it would be unwise, even in so small a book as this, to neglect the larger aspect of the question, viz. their relation to each other by the roadside or as grouped round a village green. It would be easy enough to illustrate scores of English villages where, partly by accident and partly by design, the setting of cottages on their site has fallen so happily that every point of view gives a picture. It will be more helpful, however, to look for illustration to purely modern schemes. Among them I deal first with the Hampstead Garden Suburb, as a pre-war example. Gretna as the most complete of the Munition Villages, but now, unhappily derelict, comes in the next chapter. At Hampstead, though it is frankly a suburb and not a village, the principles on which the earlier sites were planned were derived from the example of old villages. The aim has been to give cohesion and character to what might otherwise have been a mere confusion of streets. This has been secured by wise grouping of the cottages in relation to the ground appropriated to open spaces. There is, for example, Co-partnership Square, with one side open to the adjoining road. It presents something of that pleasant architectural character which we associate with old almshouses and other buildings of collegiate type. This treatment, of course, involves a larger aggregation of houses than is possible or desirable in a small village, but it is one that is very proper to be imitated in the new industrial suburbs which must be widely built if the housing shortage is to be caught up.

Lucas Square is pleasantly named after its designer. Mr. Geoffry Lucas, by building on three sides only and leaving the quadrangle open to the street, has prevented the striking of any false note of community life, which would be inappro-

372.—CO-PARTNERSHIP SQUARE, HAMPSTEAD GARDEN SUBURB.

priate in a scheme where each house is of separate ownership. He was left free, however, to secure a balance of architectural features such as we find, though in less sprightly fashion, in some London terraces of the early nineteenth century.

A simpler arrangement, which can be adopted for a much smaller number of houses, is shown by the picture of Lucas Crescent (Fig. 373), where several pairs of cottages are thrown back from the line of the road in crescent form. Greater cohesion is given to the design by connecting the adjoining pairs by short walls. These have arched openings which give access to the

*Geoffry Lucas.*

373.—LUCAS CRESCENT, WILLIFIELD WAY, HAMPSTEAD.

gardens at the back. The ground slopes away from the road, and two trees have been spared to add beauty to this reminiscence of an old village green. Prominent in the photograph are the posts and chains, and here may be mentioned a most important feature of the Hampstead Garden Suburb, to which, to a large extent, its charm is due. There are no dividing walls or fences to block the view or emphasize divided ownership, save those of a natural sort. Hedges of sweetbrier, yew and holly are growing freely everywhere, and during their early growth an invisible wire fence is enough for the practical needs of separating

374.—BACK OF LUCAS CRESCENT, HAMPSTEAD, SHOWING ABSENCE OF GARDEN WALLS.

plots.   A visit to the suburb gives a good idea of the revolution
in appearance which follows the absence of the dwarf walls and

375.—VIEW DOWN ASMUN'S PLACE, HAMPSTEAD GARDEN SUBURB.

cast-iron railings and gates which have too long been the accepted
symbol of ownership in English suburbs.   It must, though, be

understood that the old-world air of this Lucas Crescent would have been impossible before the war under the usual by-laws which choked the artistry out of suburban site-planning. The Hampstead Garden Suburb Trust Company, which owns the land, obtained from Parliament an Act exempting them from the usual regulations as to widths of metalled roads and flagged paths. In exchange, the company are bound to provide those amenities which it was their purpose to give in any case, which are, in fact, the root principles of a garden suburb. Perhaps the effect of the no-garden-wall method is best illustrated by Fig. 374, which shows the back of Lucas Crescent. The many gardens comprised in the view are quite adequately delimited, but there is as well an air of spaciousness which is altogether to the good.

*The late Basil Stallybrass.*

376.—AT WOLVERHAMPTON.

A picture of Asmun's Place (Fig. 375), designed by Messrs. Raymond Unwin and Barry Parker, indicates how carefully a rural character has been given to the suburb by the retention of old trees, by the planting of new and by the wide grass borders that divide roadway from footpath. Of much the same character is the grouping of some cottages at Wolverhampton (Fig. 376), designed by the late Basil Stallybrass.

The design of Linnell Close at the Hampstead Garden Suburb, by Mr. Michael Bunney, is based on the quiet traditions of the eighteenth century, but this sort of building is apt to work out more expensively than the more definitely cottage type with gabled ends. Still more severe in treatment, and wholly delightful, is the North Square. This square, its immediate surroundings and all its buildings were designed by Sir Edwin Lutyens, and the whole scheme achieves a simple dignity which makes it well worthy of examination. The rest of the suburb suggests an attempt to reproduce the casual irregularities of an English village. While no one can be insensible to the charms of an old village street, winding, perhaps, round the side of a hill to secure the easiest gradient, or to the medley of jutting fronts and broken roofs that enshrine the history of a village community, it is difficult to manufacture these effects anew. A good idea

*Sir Edwin Lutyens, R.A.*

377.—THE NORTH SQUARE FROM ERSKINE HILL.

of Sir Edwin's design for the square can be obtained from the study of the plan (Fig. 378). This shows that the intellectual and religious life of the new suburb is centred in the square. The garden space is bordered on one side by the Institute, on another by St. Jude's Church, and on the third by the Free Church, while the fourth side is left open. Adjoining St. Jude's is the vicarage, and next to the Free Church is the manse for its minister. To the west of the Free Church there is a group of houses, planned as half a square, and a view of this range is

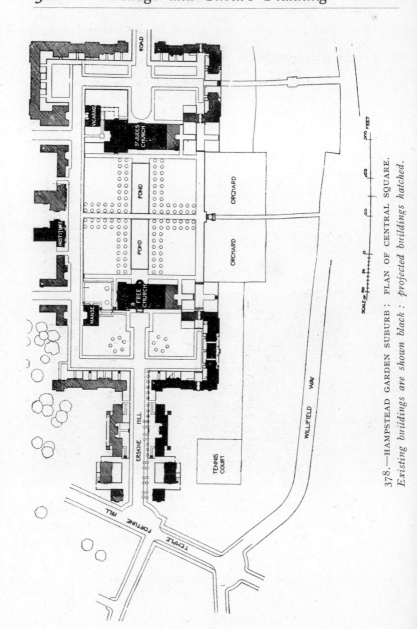

378.—HAMPSTEAD GARDEN SUBURB : PLAN OF CENTRAL SQUARE.
*Existing buildings are shown black : projected buildings hatched.*

now given (Fig. 377). By the side of the road which leads north-west to existing parts of the suburb is a series of detached and grouped houses, which serve as an architectural connection between the central square and the rest of the suburb. The particular points to be noted are that the square and its surroundings are laid out strictly on axial lines, and that the site is a large plateau which commands the whole suburb.

Two housing schemes on land belonging to Cambridge Colleges

*G. L. Pepler.*

379.—GREEN LANE, ELTHAM.

must be described as showing how the great responsibilities resting on large landowners can be met by those who are ready to control the lay-out of their estates in the interests of health and amenity.

The New Eltham Estate of Clare College was a small, and the Ruislip Manor Estate of King's College a large, example of what can be done by landowners of good-will. At New Eltham Clare possessed twenty-seven and a half acres of well-timbered meadow land, admirably adapted for a village community. A

*G. L. Pepler.*

380.—HOUSES OF THE ELTHAM TENANTS' SOCIETY.

Co-partnership Tenants Society was formed, to which the College agreed to sell the estate at a reasonable price and on terms

381.—WINDMILL WAY, RUISLIP.

382.—IN MANOR WAY, RUISLIP.

which enabled the building scheme to be developed in an un-hurried and satisfactory fashion. These terms enabled the

x

383.—A QUADRANGLE AT RUISLIP.

Cecil H. Hignett.

Society to provide an adequate garden for each house, and play-grounds and open spaces for the common use of the tenants, the lay-out of the whole being designed by Mr. G. L. Pepler, F.S.I. (Figs. 379 and 380).

All tenants are shareholders in the Society, and, as all have a stake in the undertaking, the utmost care is taken of the property. All profits over and above the payment of moderate dividends on shares and loan stock go, after the provision of proper reserves, to reduce rents and to provide additional amenities.

The Ruislip Manor enterprise was on more ambitious lines. King's College owned about 1,300 acres at Ruislip and Northwood, which were made the subject of a town-planning competition. Messrs. A. and J. Soutar won the first prize with an admirable scheme (Figs. 381 to 383), which is being carried out by a limited company formed to develop the estate on ideal lines. It has also served as the core of a wider town plan laid down by the district council for the 6,000 acres included in its jurisdiction. The college arranged that the company shall be obliged to take over blocks of land only as they are needed for development, and the enter-prise is not, therefore, burdened with interest payments on capital which for the time being would necessarily be " dead." It is infinitely to the credit both of King's and Clare that they have

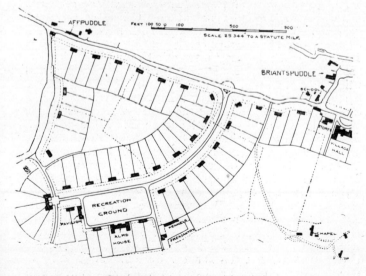

384.—A NEW HAMLET IN DORSET.

given such facilities for the development of their land on proper lines. No doubt it will be found in the end that their foresight has been as profitable to their exchequers as it has been beneficial in the public interest. The private landowner is beginning to see that, in the matter of estate development, his private interest is, in the long run, identical with the public weal. Nothing better could happen than the general adoption of the policy of these two Cambridge colleges, who are at once serving the best interests of those for whom they hold their estates in trust, and for the wider public to whom they also owe some duty of stewardship.

But the principles of town-planning are no less applicable to far smaller schemes, and as thousands of cottages are still being added to our villages, it is a disaster when those principles are not applied by architects of skill and judgment. The scattering of cottages on any road frontage without regard to the village tends rapidly to destroy such amenities as the heavy hand of the nineteenth century contrived to spare.

Fig. 384 shows a hamlet created on a single estate in Dorset. If landowners would follow this example and have a coherent scheme prepared, the haphazard development that is generally seen would be avoided. Such a scheme may take many years to complete, but a coherent plan to start with will prevent much avoidable ugliness.

I add to this chapter two schemes, the village of Earswick, and a co-partnership enterprise at East Grinstead, because both were started before the war, though both have had their most interesting developments since.

Earswick is a peculiarly interesting example of the benefits of sound design, because development has been and will be continuous and steady, and it has been in the same hands from the start. In 1904 the Joseph Rowntree Village Trust was created by Mr. Rowntree, and the capital with which the enterprise has been carried on was his free gift. All income derived from the village must be devoted to its improvement and extension. Each year, therefore, the income increases snowball fashion, and the speed of growth increases. Given a thousand years and Earswick will spread all over Yorkshire. Also, it is not reserved for employés of the Rowntree works, who only represent about half the Earswick population. The trustees' motto is "First come first served." The original lay-out was by Dr. Raymond Unwin and Mr. Barry Parker, and when Dr. Unwin placed his experience at the disposal of the Government, Mr. Parker carried on. So Earswick has been the field of countless experiments and developments in detail.

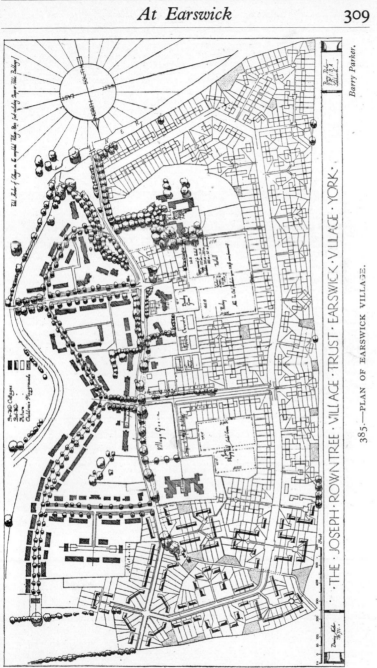

385.—PLAN OF EARSWICK VILLAGE.

*Barry Parker.*

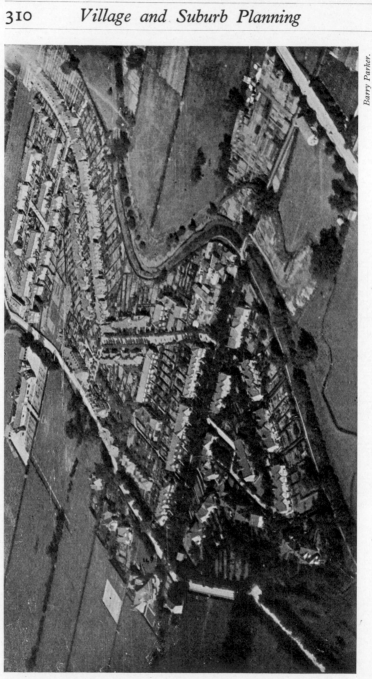

*Barry Parker.*

386.—A BIRD'S-EYE VIEW OF EARSWICK.

The plan of the village is on open lines, but that does not mean extravagant lines. If speculative builders knew their business, Earswick would be a Mecca for the shrewdest of them, because it shows that the old way of laying out houses in dreary terraces in parallel streets is not only ugly and unhygienic, but uneconomical. Mr. Barry Parker claims that the crowding of more houses on an acre than the amenities demand is only an ignorant way of wasting money, and that is true of an ordinary village or suburb where land is a reasonable price. It would obviously not be true of costly land in a city. But in most housing schemes the cost of the land is not the important factor, but the money spent on roads, sewers and other services. The old speculative builder was devoted to "back additions," but they shut out sunlight, whereas a projection of the plan to the front absorbs

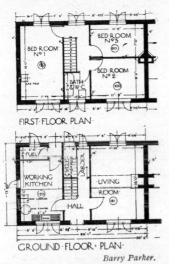

FIRST·FLOOR·PLAN·

GROUND·FLOOR·PLAN·

*Barry Parker.*

387.—PLANS OF NON-PARLOUR COTTAGES, EARSWICK, FOR SOUTH ASPECT.

*Barry Parker.*

388.—NON-PARLOUR COTTAGES: A PAIR.

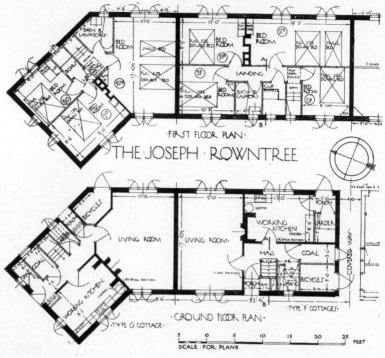

·FIRST FLOOR PLAN·

THE·JOSEPH·ROWNTREE

·GROUND FLOOR PLAN·

SCALE·FOR·PLANS

*Barry Parker.*

389.—PLANS OF TWO COTTAGES OF THE FOUR FORMING ONE FRONT
OF THE OCTAGON, EARSWICK.

*Barry Parker.*

390.—ONE PART OF THE OCTAGON, EARSWICK.

no more frontage and eliminates waste passage-space. Intelligent planning of sites and roads, moreover, actually saves cross-roads without reducing the number of houses per acre, and yields vistas and street pictures instead of a dreary uniformity. The view of Earswick taken from the air shows a lay-out of infinite variety, yet a minute study of economy in road-planning has given the results stated below.

The cost per house of roads, sewers and services, compared on the same basis, has dropped as the village plans have been modified in the light of experience as follows :

In pre-war Earswick    ..    ..    .. £50 13   0
In Mr. Parker's first post-war plan ..   47 13   0
In his second ditto    ..    ..    ..   45 10   0
In his third ditto      ..    ..    ..   43 15 11

and he hopes and believes his next revision will bring the cost down again.

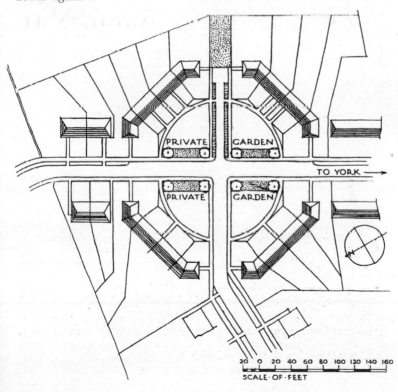

TO YORK →

20 0 20 40 60 80 100 120 140 160
SCALE·OF·FEET

391.—PLAN OF THE OCTAGON, EARSWICK.

392.—PAIR OF COTTAGES FACING SOUTH.

*Barry Parker.*

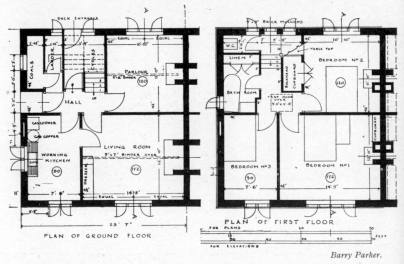

PLAN OF GROUND FLOOR

PLAN OF FIRST FLOOR

*Barry Parker.*

393.—PLANS OF PAIR OF PARLOUR COTTAGES, EARSWICK, FOR SOUTH ASPECT.

An attractive feature of the village plan is the Octagon, with the end houses of each quartette splayed. This gives an odd-shaped, but by no means uncomfortable, living-room (Figs. 389 to 391).

I come now to the planning of the houses. Mr. Parker has always before his mind the following facts: A tuberculosis germ will live for two years out of the direct rays of the sun and not more than ten minutes in the sunlight. A typhoid germ has the same life out of the sun and two minutes in the sun. He regards a "through living-room"—i.e. one with a window at each end—as indispensable in a non-parlour cottage.

Everything is standardized in the Earswick cottages, except the plan, which is varied within very wide limits to suit aspect and prospect in single cottages, pairs and groups of three and four. The plans now reproduced show the main types devised for different aspects. As to general treatment, Mr. Parker works in the main on the basis of the plain oblong, without breaks, and with hipped roofs. All the quaintnesses and prettinesses that used to be beloved in garden suburbs are eschewed, partly because the quaint is of doubtful prettiness, but mainly because it costs money and makes no return in pleasure or profit. On details of arrangement Mr. Parker is urgent that a space be provided under the main roof for cycle or perambulator. That space should be distinct and not a part of the hall, for no housewife can clean a hall into which either machine is wheeled daily. A detached shed to take domestic vehicles is a costly afterthought and an eyesore. Another fundamental point, in Mr. Parker's view, is that no room should be a passage to another.

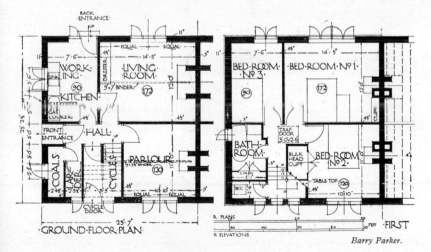

Barry Parker.

394.—PLANS OF PAIR OF PARLOUR COTTAGES, EARSWICK, FOR NORTH ASPECT.

He dislikes extremely the bathroom opening out of the scullery, and in all the plans now shown the bathroom is upstairs. This is well and good in an urban area where there is a public water supply. In rural cottages there are grave objections to the bath being in the scullery, but the bathroom opening out of the scullery seems to me a reasonable, and often an inevitable, arrangement. As to staircases, straight flights cost less than turned stairways, but in cottages " two rooms deep " Mr. Parker claims that straight flights mean a waste of space in passage-way. So he builds them straight in houses one room deep, and turned in houses two rooms deep, but without " winders " at the head of a staircase, where they are especially dangerous, or indeed anywhere.

On the subject of materials, Mr. Parker has the most definite views. The Earswick Trustees wished him to explore most

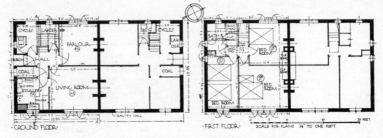

395.—EARSWICK PARLOUR COTTAGES.

carefully all alternatives to brick, and he has done so fully and methodically, but in the end he has kept to brick. With that decision I am in the fullest sympathy, but I do not know what Mr. Barry Parker would do at Earswick if he could get neither bricks nor bricklayers. If he had suddenly to proceed with the prompt building of, say, another two thousand houses, I am persuaded he would need to find some alternative. I am equally sure that many would like to know his choice, for he is one of the Early Fathers in the whole art and mystery of garden city and garden village and cottage plan and building, and it is an art in which an ounce of experience is worth any quantity of brilliant improvisation.

A word about cost, illuminating the nightmare of expense which housing entailed in the first years of peace. In 1920 the parlour cottages cost £1,665 the pair, and in 1921 £1,726 the pair. In 1922 the non-parlour pairs cost £1,254, whereas to-day they have dropped to about £1,000.

The building scheme of the Co-Partnership Society, called East Grinstead Tenants Limited, is typical of various schemes which were set on foot before the war. The Committee of the Society acquired ten acres of land just before the war broke out, but had to stop when nine houses had been built. In 1923 they went forward again, and the general plan (Fig. 396) shows the good lay-out prepared by the architects, Messrs. Crickmer & Foxley. Altogether forty-seven cottages and five bungalows have been or are now being built, and the complete scheme will contain sixty-five cottages, five bungalows, and eight flats. A site was reserved for a small Institute, but it is now probable that it will be occupied by more cottages. The cost is varying from £425 to £480 for cottages with three bedrooms, down to £403 for those with two bedrooms, which must be regarded as low, as they include a hot-water system and paths and fences. The walls are of 11-inch hollow brick. The planning in almost all cases provides for a good living-room with a separate combined

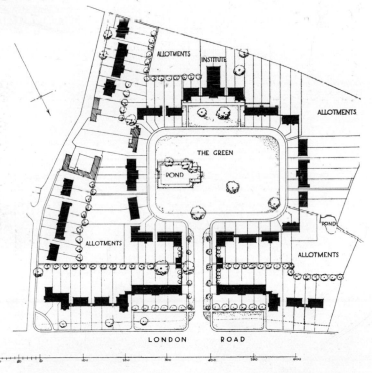

*C. M. Crickmer and Foxley.*

396.—EAST GRINSTEAD : LAY-OUT PLAN OF GROUP OF COTTAGES.

397.—HOUSES FOR A CO-PARTNERSHIP SOCIETY AT EAST GRINSTEAD.

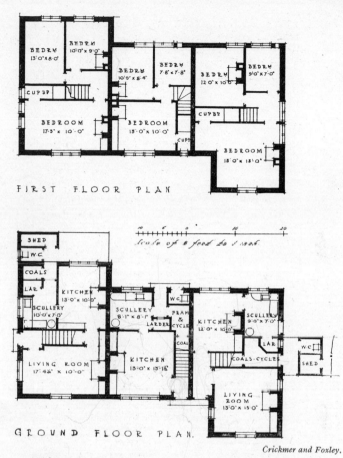

FIRST FLOOR PLAN

GROUND FLOOR PLAN.

*Crickmer and Foxley.*

398.—EAST GRINSTEAD : PLANS OF A BLOCK OF THREE
COTTAGES OF VARYING ACCOMMODATION.

kitchen-scullery and a separate bathroom (Fig. 400). One set of plans reproduced shows a pair of three-bedroom houses costing £631 each in 1924, with living-room accommodation in excess of what is customary or indeed feasible for accommodating a working-class family. There is a combined kitchen-scullery, general living-room and a dining-room (Fig. 401). A good feature of this, as of many Co-Partnership Schemes, is the mingling of houses of varying accommodation and rentals instead of grouping separately all the parlour cottages in one quarter and all the non-parlour elsewhere, an anti-social system to be avoided.

399.—EAST GRINSTEAD : A PLEASANT GROUP OF GABLES.

The most popular plan at East Grinstead is that which provides a good living-room with separate combined kitchen-scullery

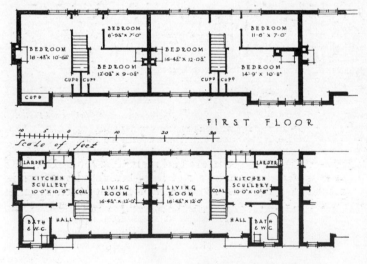

*Crickmer and Foxley.*

400.—EAST GRINSTEAD : PLANS OF HALF OF A BLOCK OF FOUR
COTTAGES WITH CENTRAL THROUGH PASSAGE.

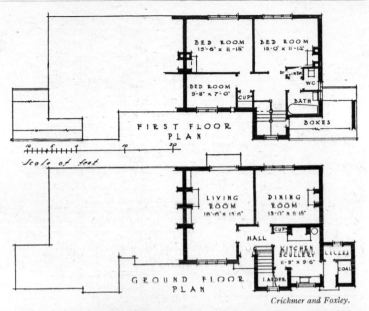

BED ROOM
15'-6" x 11'-18"

BED ROOM
15'-0" x 11'-12"

BED ROOM
9'-8" x 7'-0"

LINEN

W.C

CUP⁰

BATH

FIRST FLOOR
PLAN

BOXES

Scale of feet

LIVING
ROOM
18'-0" x 15'-6"

DINING
ROOM
15'-0" x 11'-15"

HALL

CUP⁰

GROUND FLOOR
PLAN

KITCHEN
SCULLERY
11'-9" x 9'-6"

CYCLES

COAL

LARDER

*Crickmer and Foxley.*

401.—EAST GRINSTEAD : PLANS OF A PAIR OF LARGE COTTAGES.

402.—EAST GRINSTEAD : CO-PARTNERSHIP SCHEME.

and a separate bathroom (Fig. 400). Despite the economical
character of the scheme, the architects have not sacrificed the
amenities of design, and the central ground will always be a
delightful feature.

# CHAPTER XVI

## VARIOUS VILLAGE AND SUBURB SCHEMES:
### WAR AND POST-WAR

GRETNA—DORMANSTOWN—STANMORE ESTATE, WINCHESTER—
DURLOCKS, FOLKESTONE

IT is hard enough to find any good thing which came out of the war, but it is at least true that the need for housing vast munition populations in new areas led in some cases to the planning of towns and suburbs in which the experience laboriously gained at Letchworth, the Hampstead Garden Suburb, Ruislip, and elsewhere, was used with admirable effect.

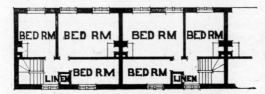

FIRST FLOOR

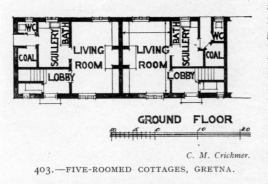

GROUND FLOOR

C. M. *Crickmer.*

403.—FIVE-ROOMED COTTAGES, GRETNA.

The war village at Gretna, the home of a great industrial army engaged in making explosives, gave great opportunity, which was well grasped by Dr. Raymond Unwin and those who worked with him, notably Mr. C. M. Crickmer, who acted as resident architect. Three sets of typical house plans are reproduced without further comment in Figs. 403 to 405, to show the general character of the cottages provided, but detailed comment can be better centred on the scheme as a whole. It involved the solution in an incredibly short time, not only of great housing

322

and engineering problems, but also of perplexing social questions known generally as "welfare." I cannot do better than use the words of a description written during the War by my friend Sir Robert Lorimer, whose own great skill in such matters made his appreciation the more valuable.

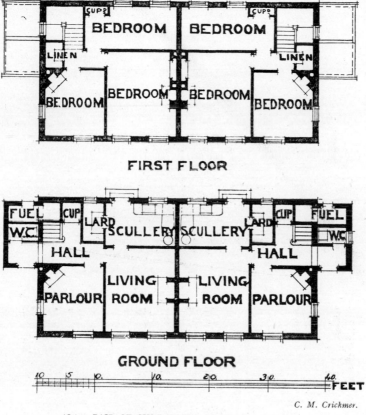

FIRST FLOOR

GROUND FLOOR

*C. M. Crickmer.*

404.—PAIR OF SIX-ROOMED COTTAGES, GRETNA.

"Here was a great tract of country near a considerable town with good railway connections, but with few natural advantages to recommend it. The most that could be said of it was that it had no conditions that made it impossible for the purpose required.

"Roughly speaking, the idea of the lay-out was as follows: More or less in the centre of the area was the old Gretna village;

south of this the principal township of new Gretna was planned with its central avenue, in the neighbourhood of which are the principal buildings, the institutes, halls, cinemas, post office, shopping centre ; at vantage points the churches are placed.

"In touch with the west end of the factory the township of East Riggs was laid out, while to the south, nearer the Solway, and running east and west, the factory spreads itself dog-leg fashion for a distance of about nine miles.

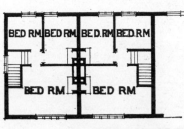

FIRST FLOOR

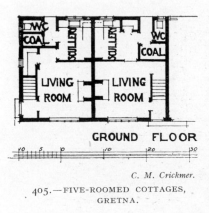

GROUND FLOOR

*C. M. Crickmer.*

405.—FIVE-ROOMED COTTAGES, GRETNA.

"What in the lay-out and management of Gretna are the freshest and most interesting points to note ? In what does it differ from the old type of industrial centre ? In what way does the carrying on of the factory production differ from what would have been found a generation ago ?

"The interesting point is that out of the necessities of the time here was a State-owned town and factory, and here was a population, turning out a deadly explosive, but working under conditions more humane, more enlightened, and also more calculated to result in productive efficiency than in pre-war days was ever thought possible. How was this result arrived at ? By squarely facing the fact that if you are to get the maximum of efficient work out of people you must see to it that they live in healthy, cheerful conditions, that they are well fed, that they breathe pure air and drink pure water, and that they are provided with the possibility of mental and physical refreshment.

"There are five permanent churches, and two schools of most excellent design. There are hospitals, fire stations, a club, the inevitable cinema, three recreation halls, institutes and club-rooms for men and women workers, and in all these buildings, simple and straightforward in design, the social life of the place was carried on.

" The sane and extremely simple type of permanent house that was erected shows what a far road has been travelled since

406.—EAST RIGGS : HOUSES ROUND A COURT.

the days of the first cheap cottage exhibition at Letchworth, where the plain man went about tearing his hair in the hopeless

407.—ROAD TO ROMAN CATHOLIC CHURCH, GRETNA GREEN.

408.—EAST RIGGS, THE ROAD TO THE CHURCH.

endeavour to find here and there a cottage the design of which showed the most rudimentary elements of common-sense. Here all was plain, practical, straightforward, of pleasant and reasonable proportion, and mercifully devoid of ornament or prettiness. A satisfying feeling of variety was achieved, not so much in an artificial attempt to get variety in the individual houses as by a happy scheme of plan and by the retention, wherever possible, of trees that existed on the site, and by seizing on any feature or contour that suggested a reasonable motive.

" The admirer of the Kate Greenaway type of garden city house doubtless found the Gretna variety too reminiscent of

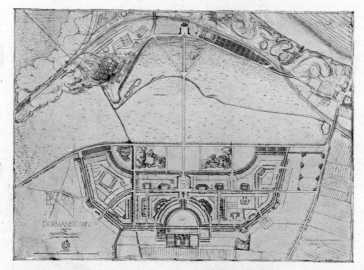

409.—DORMANSTOWN : LAY-OUT OF SITE.

what Morris called the ' brick box with the slate lid ' ; but these houses had to be rattled up at a tremendous pace, and a plain roof in which there are neither dormers nor gables is obviously cheaper and more rapidly constructed and slated than one that is cut up by features.

" The interesting character of the new Roman Catholic Church is shown in Fig. 407. Designed by Mr. C. E. Simmons, it is a fresh and expressive piece of architecture and illustrates how, if a man has a feeling for rhythm and proportion and fitness, and is able to handle his materials, quite excellent results can be achieved by the knowing use of ordinary brick and plain white plaster."

*Adshead, Ramsey and Abercrombie.*

410.—DORMANSTOWN : SIMPLICITY WITH REFINEMENT.

411.—DORMANSTOWN : A GOOD SWEEP ON A CURVED ROAD.

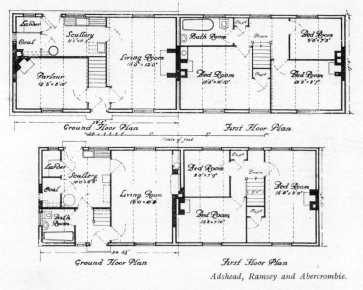

*Adshead, Ramsey and Abercrombie.*

412.—DORMANSTOWN : PLANS OF TWO PAIRS, PARLOUR AND NON-PARLOUR.

413.—DORMANSTOWN : PART OF A BLOCK OF FOUR.

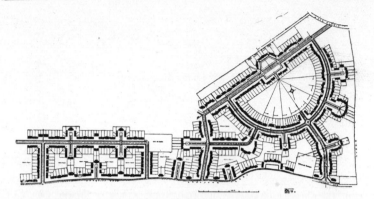

414.—BLOCK PLAN OF STANMORE ESTATE.

*Fifty-three acres have been built on at the rate of ten to the acre.*

Several visits to Gretna gave me the same sense of pleasure that caused Sir Robert Lorimer to write so appreciatively. By the spring of 1919 the whirl of activity which impressed the visitor during the war had ceased. Those who realized the extraordinary value to the working community of such admirable housing conditions have grown more and more depressed at the failure of all attempts to utilize Gretna for some industry of peace, so that it might, as a living organization, inspire the design of

415.—STUART CRESCENT, STANMORE, WINCHESTER.

416.—STANMORE, WINCHESTER : A BLOCK OF FOUR COTTAGES.

417.—PRINCESS PLACE, STANMORE, WINCHESTER.

many an industrial village yet to be built for the service of, rather than the destruction of, mankind.

Among the best of the war housing schemes on a large scale was Dormanstown, an industrial village for the employees of Messrs. Dorman, Long & Co. Begun in 1916 to the designs of Messrs. Adshead, Ramsey and Abercrombie, it was laid out on

418.—PAULET PLACE, STANMORE ESTATE.

sound town-planning lines and given that air of distinction which comes from the employment of refined lines and well-considered

*Curti Green, A.R.A.*

419.—KING'S AVENUE, STANMORE, WINCHESTER.

proportions in work so simple that the foolish suppose it leaves no scope to the artist.  On the contrary, the artist has his real opportunity when seemliness has to be secured with the absolute minimum of expenditure. Dormanstown began in brick, but shortage impelled a search for alternatives, and a steel-framed cottage was devised.

Within the steel framework was fixed a reinforced concrete cavity wall, out of which has developed Messrs. Dorman Long's method described in an earlier chapter.

The plans (Fig. 412) of a typical pair of houses show generous accommodation and an upstairs bathroom.

The great Stanmore housing scheme at Winchester, with its lay-out by Mr. William Dunn and its cottages by Mr. Curtis Green, A.R.A., is one of the beneficent results of the Addison programme. The features of the layout include small gardens for each house with convenient allotments adjoining each group. This is far more practical than a stereotyped size of garden forced alike on the keen gardener and the tenant who finds the ground only a burden and a source of weeds and untidiness. The curved roads and the successive breaks in the alinement of the various blocks of houses prevent any sense of monotony without straining at a continued picturesqueness.

The accommodation of the houses is very properly varied to suit all

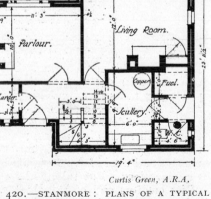

*Curtis Green, A.R.A.*

420.—STANMORE : PLANS OF A TYPICAL PAIR OF COTTAGES.

sizes of families, from two-bedroom cottages without parlour, to parlour cottages with four bedrooms. The simple brickwork is admirable, and the ugly black coke-breeze mortar joints in some of it are not to be laid to the door of Mr. Curtis Green, but were forced on him " by authority." Every house has a bathroom, fed with hot water—if upstairs, from a circulating boiler ; if downstairs, from a copper. A good point to be observed was the raising of the copper on a brick base, so that the hot water runs into the bath by simple gravitation.

A great feature is the lack of " back additions " : they are often necessary in rural cottages, so as to get an E.C. grouped with a wood-shed, but in more urban surroundings they are generally a confession of unskilful planning. In nearly every case on the

421.—MILNER PLACE : STANMORE ESTATE, WINCHESTER.

Stanmore estate a back porch or lobby is provided to cover the doors of the scullery, the W.C., and the fuel store (*see* plan in Fig. 420). This enables the scullery door to be left open in bad weather and gives a place where boot-cleaning and other dirt-producing tasks can conveniently be done. A small criticism may be made of the absence of door hoods or other protection at the front doors. Waiting in the rain for a tardy response to the bell must give trying moments, and though a porch of the bathing-box type is needless and costly, door hoods are inexpensive and would have mitigated a slight sense of baldness in the elevations. But taking the estate as a whole it is worthy of its creators and of Winchester.

In contrast with the classical severity both of the lay-out of such schemes as Dormanstown, and of the architecture of the cottages, is the picturesque housing scheme devised at the Durlocks, Folkestone, by Messrs. Culpin and Bowers for Sir Philip Sassoon, begun in February, 1920, and finished the same

year.  Prices were then ranging about £1,000 for an ordinary
five-roomed cottage, but the Durlocks scheme was so well devised
that the cottages there cost only £750, still a prodigious price.

*Curtis Green, A.R.A.*

422.—A TYPICAL PAIR OF COTTAGES : STANMORE, WINCHESTER.

On a site abnormally sloping the grouping was worked out in a
very interesting way, with pairs and blocks of four.  The cooking
is done in the large living-room, which is fitted with a " Regis-

z

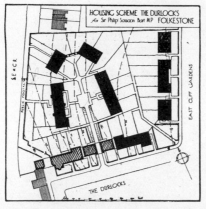

423.—SITE PLAN OF DURLOCKS SCHEME.

troven " stove, that serves the dual purpose of an open fire and a closed stove with boiler for hot-water supply.

In the larger cottage (in the middle of the plan reproduced in Fig. 427) the bathroom is separate from the scullery and contains the W.C. In the smaller the bathroom is part of the scullery, but divided from it by a pair of doors, which gives an equal privacy in practice. In both cases hot bath water is got from the copper installed at one end of the bath, which thus serves also for rinsing on washing days.

A liberal, but not essential, provision is a covered space which serves as an outer lobby to scullery and coal-cellar.

Many building programmes on private estates begin well, but

*Ewart Culpin & Bowers.*

424.—COTTAGES FITTED TO THE SLOPE AT THE DURLOCKS.

425.—GENERAL VIEW OF THE DURLOCKS HOUSING SCHEME, FOLKESTONE.

go wrong because they are carried out at haphazard ; a pair of cottages here, a group of four there, without relation to each

*Ewart Culpin & Bowers.*

426.—AN ARCHWAY IN THE DURLOCKS SCHEME.

other or to the existing buildings, such as a church and schools, which ought to be focal points.

If we regard the village and suburb planning schemes shown in this chapter as examples of what has been, and therefore can be, done with housing enterprises of very different size and scope, what lessons are to be drawn from them as to the future of town-planning? It is obvious that such conceptions are not likely to be lying dormant in the consciousness of borough surveyors. If our public architecture is to be worthy of the nation, it will only be by employing the greatest ability available.

Some day people will realize that the beauty of the streets amid which their life is passed is one of their intimate concerns. Perhaps, indeed, they may go so far as to fulfil the whimsical

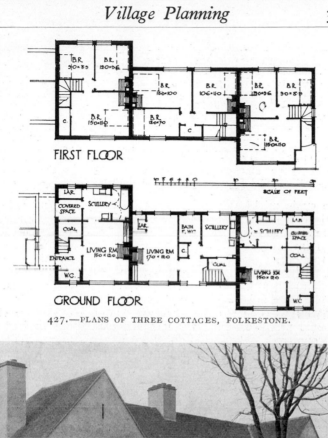

FIRST FLOOR

GROUND FLOOR

427.—PLANS OF THREE COTTAGES, FOLKESTONE.

428.—AT FOLKESTONE.

prophecy which Mr. Wells gave us in the *New Utopia*. This is what he came upon in Lucerne :

" We discover an odd little election is in progress. This is the selection . . . of the ugliest local building. The old little urban and local governing bodies . . . survive to discharge a number of curious minor functions, and not the least among these is the sort of æsthetic ostracism. Every year every minor local governing body pulls down a building selected by the local plébiscite, and the greater Government pays a slight compensation to the owner. . . . The idea would strike us at first as simply whimsical, but in practice it appears to work as a cheap and practical device for the æsthetic education of builders, engineers, business men, opulent persons, and the general body of the public."

The cynic might say, with regard to this engaging policy, that the field of choice for destruction in actual modern England is so large as to baffle the wisest and most æsthetic democracy, even if invested with such delightful powers, and we should have to agree. That is a difficulty on which Mr. Wells did not dwell, for he was then in Utopia, where ugly buildings were the exception rather than the rule. His views on the present state of public taste are sufficiently clear from his closing sentence : " But when we come to consider its application to our own world, we should perceive it was the most Utopian thing we had so far encountered." It should not, however, be Utopian to insist that we shall create our new villages and suburbs without such ugly buildings as called for demolition in the *New Utopia*.

# CHAPTER XVII

## SOME HOUSES AT WELWYN GARDEN CITY

Idealism and Economic Common Sense—The Model for Satellite
Cities—Details of House-planning—Concrete Houses—Public
Utility Society Finance

THE experience gained at Letchworth, the first Garden
City, enabled the promoters of Welwyn Garden City to
avoid the pitfalls inevitable in pioneer enterprises. It is obvious
that the first people to develop a scheme so novel and difficult
must make mistakes, but they were few at Letchworth, which
has at last justified itself financially, as it did from the first
socially. Architecturally, Welwyn has no features of the experimental sort seen at Letchworth, and benefits from the fact that,
when it began, contrived picturesqueness had gone out of
fashion. Economy as well as current fashion have been on
the side of a greater severity of mass and line. This is not the
place to go into the social and administrative aspects of the
Garden City movement. Suffice it to say that Welwyn, under
the chairmanship of Sir Theodore Chambers, is developing
services to the community which are worthy of careful study.

*L. De Soissons.*

429.—WELWYN : HANDSIDE CLOSE.

343

Sir Theodore and his colleagues have based their adventurous idealism on a foundation of sound economics. It used to be said that garden cities were the homes of cranks. Welwyn Garden City has reacted in this matter and is almost aggressively commonsensical.

The Welwyn directors are uninterested in phrases and do not chop logic about social theories. The system is in some respects

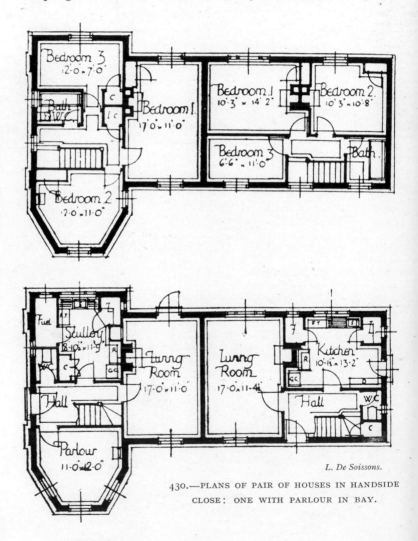

L. De Soissons.

430.—PLANS OF PAIR OF HOUSES IN HANDSIDE CLOSE: ONE WITH PARLOUR IN BAY.

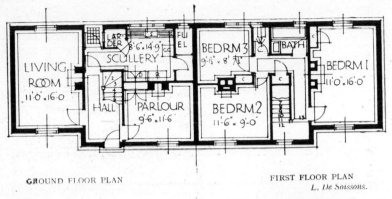

GROUND FLOOR PLAN

FIRST FLOOR PLAN
*L. De Soissons.*

431.—WELWYN : PLANS OF PAIR AT END OF HANDSIDE CLOSE.

acutely socialistic, but there is no democratic control. The administration is almost feudal, but so controlled by its self-imposed altruism, that it is the citizens of Welwyn as a body, and they alone, who will benefit by the values now being developed so rapidly and so shrewdly. When the Nation and the Government have the wit to see that the problem of London can only be decently and intelligently solved by the creation of a ring of satellite towns, the model for their creation will inevitably be found at Welwyn Garden City. My concern, however, is rather with the architectural aspect of the place and the character of the citizens' homes. Mr. Louis de Soissons is the City Architect and has done much of the work, but other architects have been employed and there is no sameness of aspect. Handside Close is one of the many attractive groups of quite small houses—they can reasonably be called cottages—which achieve their dignity by simplicity of mass and outline, with just those variations which emphasize scale and banish dullness. An example of this is the treatment of the two pairs of cottages flanking the pair which fills the end of the hollow square (Fig. 429). The farther house in each pair has a boldly projecting octagonal bay, which gives the needed variety. But it has the practical purpose of linking a parlour house (there are also living-room, working kitchen and three bedrooms) with a non-parlour cottage, and so widening the choice of available accommodation. Note from the plans that the living-rooms in both types are through-lighted, as is the best bedroom in the parlour type. The same good features of planning are shown in the pair at the end of the close (Fig. 431). The ample effect of the street planning is well seen in the next picture (Fig. 432), and I

432.   STREET EFFECT :   WELWYN GARDEN CITY.

H. G. Cherry, Supervising Architect.
L. De Soissons, Architect of Houses.

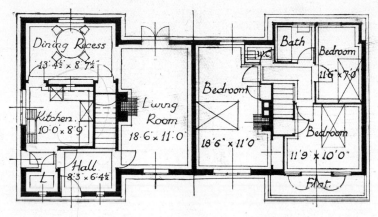

433.—PLAN OF A PAIR OF COTTAGES BELOW.

L. De Soissons.

434.—WELWYN : PAIR OF COTTAGES WITH SQUARE PROJECTING BAYS.

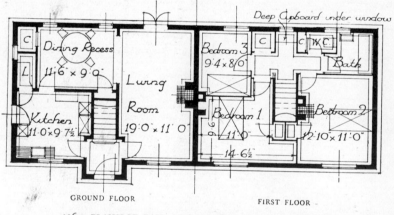

L. De Soissons.

435.—WELWYN : PAIR OF COTTAGES WITH MANSARD ROOF.

Deep Cupboard under window

Dining Recess
11·6" × 9·0"

C

L

Kitchen
11·0 × 9·7½

Living
Room
19·0 × 11·0

Bedroom 3
9·4 × 8·0

C

C  W C

Bath

Bedroom 1
11·0

14·6½

Bedroom 2
12·10 × 11·0

GROUND FLOOR

FIRST FLOOR

436.—PLANS OF PAIR OF COTTAGES WITH DINING RECESS.

include a detail photograph (Fig. 434) of a practical and attractive
type of mansard-roofed cottages with square projecting bays,
which contribute much to the good effect of the street.   The

Hennell and James.

437.—WELWYN : BLOCK OF FOUR.

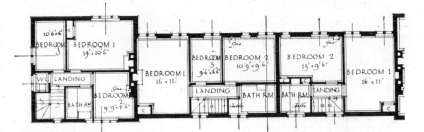

FIRST·FLOOR·PLAN·

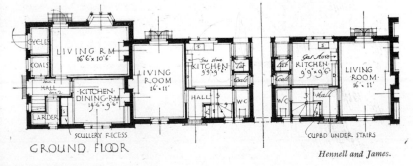

GROUND FLOOR

Hennell and James.

438.—WELWYN : PLANS OF LEFT-HAND THREE OF THE BLOCK OF FOUR.

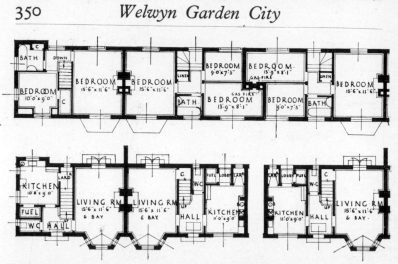

439.—WELWYN : PLANS OF THREE OF GROUP OF FOUR WITH BAY WINDOWS.

*Hennell and James.*

440.—WELWYN : A GROUP OF FOUR IN A QUADRANGLE.

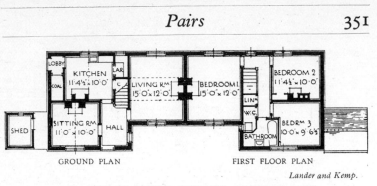

GROUND PLAN                     FIRST FLOOR PLAN

*Lander and Kemp.*

441.—PAIR OF GABLED COTTAGES, HANDSIDE LANE.

*Lander and Kemp.*

442.—WELWYN : GABLED COTTAGES IN HANDSIDE LANE.

plan of this type (Fig. 433) again reproduces the through-lighting of living-room and chief bedroom, but the arrangements for meals are different. A dining-room recess opens off the living-room, with one door to the hall passage and another, for service, to the kitchen. The plan shown in Fig. 436 is an interesting variant of the last, but on a smaller scale and with through-lighting in the living-room only. Mr. de Soissons appreciates the value of the mansard roof for inexpensive construction, and with a scarcity of bricks ; he uses it again in this simple pair. I come now to two groups designed by Messrs. Hennell

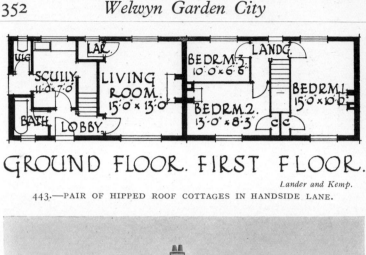

GROUND FLOOR.   FIRST FLOOR.

*Lander and Kemp.*

443.—PAIR OF HIPPED ROOF COTTAGES IN HANDSIDE LANE.

*Lander and Kemp.*

444.—WELWYN : HIPPED ROOF PAIR IN HANDSIDE LANE.

and James. They adopted the gable and dormer as the characteristic features of their houses, but used the former in large simple units at the ends of the groups and provided good stretches of unbroken roof-line to connect the gabled ends. In each group a central through-passage was provided in the middle, to be seen in the plans, which show in each case three houses of the four. In both groups the presumption is that no maid is kept and there is a compactly arranged kitchen-dining-room (*see* plan, Fig. 438) and a large living-room. The planning of the middle two of the four is ingeniously devised in one of the

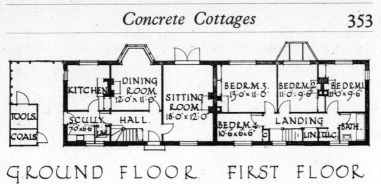

GROUND FLOOR. FIRST FLOOR

*Lander and Kemp.*

445.—PAIR OF COTTAGES, BRIDGE ROAD, WELWYN.

blocks (Fig. 438), so that the area occupied below by the through-passage dividing the houses is used above to give a third bedroom in one of the houses, the outer two having, also, three bedrooms each. In the other block (Fig. 439), with the attractive little octagonal bays, the bedrooms in the middle two are planned interlocking, so that each house has the same accommodation, but in this block the outer two of the four have only two bedrooms. These points are small in themselves, but of use as showing how infinite is the variety of planning that is possible and how necessary that the skill of architects should be exercised in providing accommodation that will suit the small shades of different people's ideas of living.

Other interesting Welwyn houses are those designed by Messrs. Lander and Kemp, six-roomed (Figs. 441 and 442) and five-roomed (Figs. 443 and 444). The remaining plan of these architects (Fig. 445) shows a pair with rather more accommodation specially devised to suit a north aspect.

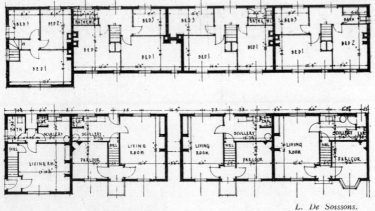

*L. De Soissons.*

446.—PLANS OF CONCRETE COTTAGES.

A A

447.—CONCRETE COTTAGES AT WELWYN.

Welwyn, like every other centre where building is active, has been obliged to explore methods of construction alternative to brick. Their latest device is specially interesting. By giving especial pains to the preparation of a flint aggregate for concrete, the City's building department is building houses with 8 in. solid walls, 5 in. outside of flint concrete and 3 in. inside of breeze concrete. They are satisfied that what seems a risky business, the omission of a cavity, has succeeded in giving a perfectly weatherproof wall. So am I, for I have never seen a better aggregate, but it is necessary to warn builders of solid concrete walls that unless they allow expansion joints, cracks will inevitably develop. These are not likely to endanger the structure, but they look very bad. The walls at Welwyn are put up between special steel shuttering, which yields a good surface, and reinforcement is provided where required. Mr.

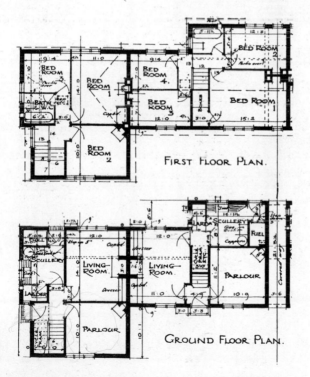

*C. M. Crickmer.*

448.—PLANS OF TWO COTTAGES OF GROUP OF FOUR, IN HANDSIDE LANE, WELWYN.

de Soissons has given the groups a very attractive shape (Fig. 447). The little glazed bays are novel and very practical in conjunction with the method of wall-building. Despite the simplicity of the elevation, it is not bald, but has its own touch of distinction. The importance of the construction is that the cottages, despite their adequate accommodation, shown in the plans (Fig. 446), cost on an average, parlour and non-parlour, about £525 each, and land, roads and sewers account for about £50 per house, with a nominal ground rent of ten shillings a year. This makes a feasible financial scheme for the Welwyn Public Utility Society which is building them. Of the total sum required the Local Authority advances ninety per cent., repayable over a period of forty years. The Government subsidy is £75 a cottage. It is therefore possible, by issuing six per cent. loan stock for the comparatively small balance of capital required for each house, to let them at an average rent of 16s. 6d. per week, including rates. So satisfactory a result is only got by first-rate organization in building, as well as shrewdly considered economies in design, and by carrying through a good number at one time. Not the least attractive part of the scheme is that the loan capital required is only about £50 a house, and so sound is its financial basis that the Garden City Company is able to guarantee the six per cent. payable on the housing bonds. One valuable point on rent must be noted ; it is differential. From the basic rent of any one type of cottage, sixpence a week is deducted for each child under sixteen, and one shilling a week is added for any lodger.

All these developments are well worth studying on the spot.

# CHAPTER XVIII

## POST-WAR HOUSING BY THE L.C.C.

THREE GREAT LONDON HOUSING ESTATES—A WORD ABOUT SPECULA-
TIVE BUILDERS—THE BRICK PROBLEM AGAIN—AND MR. TOPHAM
FORREST'S FUTURE RECOURSE TO TIMBER

WE may lament the practical disappearance of the large-scale
speculative builder from the London suburbs during the
last ten years on the ground that he did somehow house the
people, but the throwing of the task on to the broad shoulders of the rate-payer, in the guise of the London County Council, has led to the creation of some fine dormitories, notably Becontree, Bellingham, and Roehampton, none of them yet finished. In the year I write, 1926, the speculative builder has begun to join in the task, and it is fair to say that he has learnt something since pre-war days. The frontages of his terraces are still meagre, but he is not so obsessed by the bay window, by the trimmings meanly carved in Bath stone, and the flutter of cheap white-painted woodwork which gave an incurably flimsy look to his handiwork.

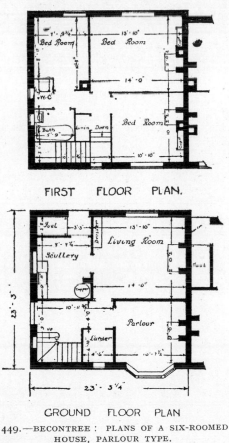

FIRST FLOOR PLAN.

GROUND FLOOR PLAN

449.—BECONTREE : PLANS OF A SIX-ROOMED
HOUSE, PARLOUR TYPE.

357

450.—BECONTREE : GENERAL VIEW UP MAYESBROOK ROAD.

451.—BECONTREE : VIEW TOWARDS ANGLE GREEN FROM BURNSIDE ROAD.

It is probable that the examples of municipal housing, and not least that of the London County Council under the leadership of their superintending architect, Mr. Topham Forrest, have had much to do with this levelling up of taste.

432.—LAY-OUT OF BELLINGHAM ESTATE.

It would be a happy thing if Mr. Topham Forrest were invested with the powers of an ædile, to forbid the new type of jerry-building which now afflicts the outer suburbs, the very small bungalow with roof of pink asbestos slate and a general air of rabbit hutchery. The magic of these is, of course, in the fact that with the aid of building societies, and sometimes a little financial faith provided by the builder, the man of slight capital, say £50 to £100, and small income, can in the course of twenty years become the owner of his home. The development by the L.C.C. of a big estate for sale in a similar way, not for letting,

453.—ROEHAMPTON : THE PLEASANCE.

would be thought a socialistic device to compete with the speculative builder and put him out of business, but what a difference it would make to the architectural amenities of Outer London. But I must return to the achievement of the L.C.C. At Becontree, beyond the East End, and near Barking, was an area of 3,000 acres, which had to be taken from market-garden lands. The proposals included 18,000 houses with their needful complement of shops, churches, schools, fire stations, and so forth. When finished, Becontree will house five times as many people as Salisbury. The shortage of labour and materials has slowed down the programme, and I doubt not the transport problem

454.—ROEHAMPTON : FROM SWINBURNE ROAD TO HUNTINGFIELD ROAD.

has contributed to the delay, but the work goes forward on 400 acres, and Figs. 450 and 451 and the plans in Fig. 449 show how it is shaping.

The houses are on wide frontages, have no back additions, and many are provided with parlours.

The Bellingham estate at Lewisham, similarly laid out on sound town-planning lines (Fig. 452), is a smaller but still large proposition. There are 2,090 houses and flats on 175 out of the total 250 acres, and all this meant seven miles of roads and twelve of sewers. The Roehampton estate is nearing the provision of its full quota of 1,115 dwellings, some of them two- and three-room maisonettes, others four-, five- and six-room cottages.

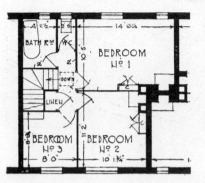

FIRST FLOOR PLAN.

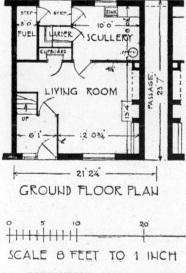

GROUND FLOOR PLAN

SCALE 8 FEET TO 1 INCH

455.—ROEHAMPTON : PLANS OF A FIVE-ROOMED HOUSE, NON-PARLOUR TYPE.

The liberal number of developed trees have yielded some charming street pictures. The rents of these new L.C.C. houses can be gathered from the figure of 21s. a week, including rates and taxes, for a five-roomed cottage, i.e. living-room, scullery, three bedrooms and bathroom. It is a big figure, but even so the rents do not cover the cost of the scheme by a long way, and the ratepayer or taxpayer, or both, have to give a hand.

Particular attention must be drawn to the charming quality of the Roehampton houses, which suggest that Sir Christopher Wren has looked that way. Mr. Topham Forrest's recent visit to the United States and his very interesting report, which shows how what he saw has coloured his view

456.—ROEHAMPTON : HUNTINGFIELD ROAD.

457.—ROEHAMPTON : IN HUNTINGFIELD ROAD.

*Topham Forrest.*

458.—L.C.C. HOUSES AT DULWICH.

of London's problem, have resulted in a leaning towards timber houses as perhaps the best, certainly one of the most feasible, ways of defeating the brick problem. If he is successful with timber as with brick he will have put all housing experts much in his debt. At present many of them are frankly scared at the idea of timber for town housing, and give it a grudging assent even for rural districts. But it may be hoped that the L.C.C. will not wilt at the problems connected with the monolithic concrete house, for the excellent reason that they provide work for a larger proportion of unskilled labour than any other type of construction.

Another admirable housing estate of the L.C.C. is at Dulwich. Fig. 458 shows a quadrangular scheme off Sunray Avenue which is delightful in its modesty and reserve.

# CHAPTER XIX

## HOUSING AT HAMMERSMITH

A Panel of Architects—Open Forecourts *v.* Hedged Gardens—
Square Houses—Playgrounds—Linoleum and Dry-rot

SUCCESS in laying out a housing scheme on a big scale is not easily come by. If but one architect is employed he is overweighted with work, and there will tend to be a considerable amount of repetition not only of elevation but also of plan. If the estate is cut up into several areas, under several architects, it is apt to be scrappy. The ideal way is to have a team, with one of them as Chairman, but no more than *primus inter pares.* That is what the Hammersmith Borough Council wisely decided to do in 1919 with a great site on the edge of the new Western

FIRST FLOOR PLAN

GROUND PLAN
*H. T. Hare and Bertram Lisle, Architects.*

459.—HOUSE PLANS AT END OF AN OCTAGON.

*Hare and Lisle.*

460.—PEONY GARDENS, HAMMERSMITH.

*Hare and Lisle.*

461.—VIOLA SQUARE, HAMMERSMITH.

Avenue, which will ultimately be one of London's main approaches.

The late Henry T. Hare, then President of the R.I.B.A., was asked to undertake the task with three others to be nomin-

*Hare and Lisle, Architects.*

462.—SHOPS AT HAMMERSMITH.

ated by himself. He did so; and chose Mr. J. Ernest Franck, Mr. Matthew J. Dawson and Mr. Streatfeild, whose partner is Mr. Atwell. This panel of four acted as one firm, so far as fees and responsibility were concerned, and they divided the work between them thus : Mr. Hare as Chairman did the negotiations with the Ministry of Health and the Borough Council. Mr. Matthew Dawson did the lay-out, in close consultation, of course, with his colleagues. Mr. Franck conducted the correspondence and kept the general accounts. On the lamented death of Mr. Hare in January, 1921, his partner, Mr. Bertram Lisle, was appointed in his stead, and Mr. Streatfeild became Chairman of the panel. Each of the four took over all the buildings on certain roads and squares, so that general harmony should be preserved in the smaller units of the lay-out, while yet a character of variety was achieved throughout the scheme as a whole. Each architect was responsible for the supervision of the blocks he had designed, but the estimates were obtained and certificates for payment granted by the Panel as a whole. The whole scheme covered 122 acres, and since 1920 50 acres have been developed and 600 houses built.

The Panel system has worked admirably, and there can be no doubt that the Borough Council scored by having at its disposal the experience of four skilled professional advisers instead of one. The corporate mind of such a team is something more valuable than the separate efforts of the four men, for they act and react on each other. Of course, it gives them an added burden of work in meeting often for consultation, in circulating copies of correspondence and so forth, but the results justify it. I have no doubt that Hammersmith proves the wisdom of the team method and that the scheme would have been less successful if it had been designed and carried out by a single architect.

The essence of successful working is in the loyalty of the members of the Panel to each other, and above all to their Chairman. If each did not stick to his appointed share in the common task there would be confusion, and if there were mutual criticism, except frankly and in private conference, the whole value of the Panel idea would disappear in disaster. But the Hammersmith Scheme bears the mark of that unity which comes of friendship and mutual loyalty.

*Hare and Lisle.*

463.—HAMMERSMITH PLANS.

With regard to the lay-out, this will only be complete when the White City is developed for building ; but attention must be drawn to some features of it.

There are no houses at the corners of roads. This not only gives a valuable sense of spaciousness, but affords an effect of openness at the backs of the houses, and enables motors to approach the cross-roads in safety. Wherever possible, open playgrounds for children are provided at the ends of the gardens —a valuable arrangement, as it prevents children being driven to play in the road, and open archways through the blocks need not be provided to give access to the backs of houses.

Certain general rules were laid down for the planning of the houses. Their backs have been kept without breaks, so that the street fronts should have the architectural interest of projections. Everywhere the coal-shed is reached under cover.

*Matthew J. Dawson.*

464.—SQUARE IN CLEMATIS STREET, HAMMERSMITH.

In all but the smaller and cheaper types, the bathroom is upstairs and served from the kitchen range, and the W.C. is separate *and upstairs*. This avoids the troublesome arrangement of

## HOUSE UNITS·

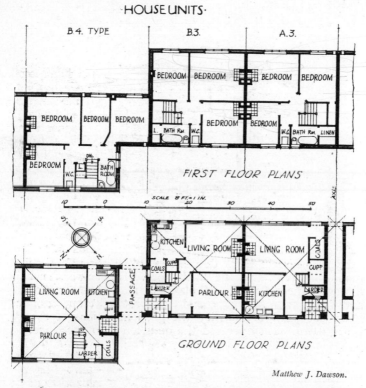

B.4. TYPE    B.3.    A.3.

BEDROOM   BEDROOM   BEDROOM   BEDROOM

BEDROOM   BEDROOM   BEDROOM

BEDROOM   BEDROOM

L. | BATH RM | W.C.   W.C. | BATH RM | LINEN

BEDROOM
W.C. | BATH ROOM | DN.

*FIRST FLOOR PLANS*

SCALE 8 FT.=1 IN.

KITCHEN   LIVING ROOM   LIVING ROOM   COALS

COALS | CUPP   CUPP

LIVING ROOM | KITCHEN   LARDER   PARLOUR | KITCHEN   LARDER

PARLOUR   LARDER   COALS

*GROUND FLOOR PLANS*

Matthew J. Dawson.

465.—HAMMERSMITH : PLANS OF SQUARE TYPE OF HOUSE.

Matthew J. Dawson.

466.—ORCHID STREET.

Matthew J. Dawson.

467.—IN NORBROKE STREET : CONCRETE AND BRICK.

carrying bedroom slops downstairs, often through the living-
room to a W.C. near the back door.    In non-parlour houses,
however, the exigencies of planning make upstairs bathroom
and W.C. practically impossible, at least quite uneconomic.

On one point of amenity the good intentions of the Panel
broke down.    They pressed the omission of enclosed front gar-

Matthew J. Dawson.

468.—FOXGLOVE STREET : A BACK VIEW.

*Streatfeild and Atwell.*

469.—YEW TREE SQUARE, EAMXERSMITH.

dens and the substitution of grass forecourts between house and pavement. This is common practice in America and has been adopted at Welwyn Garden City with admirable effect. But the tenants would have none of it. Their sense of privacy was

*Streatfeild and Atwell.*

470.—CLEMATIS STREET, HAMMERSMITH.

outraged, and their Englishman's home only became their castle when the Borough Council agreed to privet hedges enclosing the forecourts, much to the sorrow of the architects. But in all the wider roads a broad band of grass was provided between footway and roadway. This prevents children suddenly stepping off the path under the wheels of passing motors and saves pedestrians from being splashed with mud.

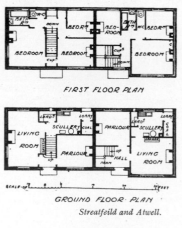

FIRST FLOOR PLAN

GROUND FLOOR PLAN

*Streatfeild and Atwell.*

471.—TYPICAL PLANS.

On details of construction a few points are worth recording. Stoves that combine the qualities of sitting-room fireplaces and kitchen ranges are fixed in kitchens and gas cookers in sculleries. The former proved satisfactory for hot water to the bath, but only when the pipes to the cylinder were kept short. Projecting hinges of all upper windows enable the glass to be cleaned from inside. The danger of dry rot in wooden floors, which is so real where linoleum is used, drove the Panel to employ red granolithic paving in all living-rooms and kitchens. Tenants are

*Streatfeild and Atwell.*

472.—A CORNER OF YEW TREE SQUARE, HAMMERSMITH.

apt to object to this, but at Hammersmith did not complain.

Among Mr. Matthew Dawson's contributions is the charming square shown in Fig. 464. The triple arches are an attractive feature : the larger central one leads through to the backs, and the other two give porches to the entrance doors. Fig. 468 is to be studied with this because it gives a typical back, equal in seemliness of design to the front and guiltless of any " back addition." These houses, in Foxglove Street, are of stock brick

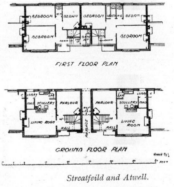

*FIRST FLOOR PLAN*

*GROUND FLOOR PLAN*

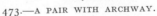

*Streatfeild and Atwell.*

473.—A PAIR WITH ARCHWAY.

with arrises and arches in red brick, and with pantiled roofs. The tiles are laid Norfolk fashion with the undersides only bedded in lime mortar. It should be noted that Mr. Dawson has avoided valleys and other roof-breaks. These houses and those of Fig. 466 are to the unit plan (Fig. 465), and all avoid external woodwork, the windows being standard metal casements. Norbroke Street (Fig. 467) has a markedly different character, arising out of a change of materials. The centre houses of the group are of concrete, with projecting pavilion houses of brick

474.—TAMARISK SQUARE, HAMMERSMITH.

*Ernest J. Franck.*

Ernest J. Franck.

475.—PANSY GARDENS, HAMMERSMITH.

at intervals of every five houses. In the end houses concrete floors carry the projecting gables, and the concrete blocks in the upper part of the gables were faced with a cast diaper pattern and colour-washed. A further changefulness was given by using pantiles on the main roofs and plain tiles on the pavilion gables and the "gab-lettes." The door hoods are of plain tiles and the entrance doors painted in different colours.

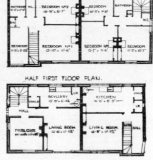

HALF FIRST FLOOR PLAN.

E. J. Franck.

476.—HALF PLANS OF GROUP OF PAIR, PANSY GARDENS.

Lack of space forbids my ex-amining in detail the planning of all the houses, so I make a few notes on Mr. Dawson's only. He decided on two main types, the long-fronted house (30 ft.) and the square type (20 ft.). The latter was developed princi-pally, as it gave greater economy and more latitude in grouping. It affords better proportioned rooms, is more compact and economical in planning and has less external walling. With this type it is easier to avoid breaks in external walls, and to design roofs appropriate to pantiling. The standard house was 23 ft. square on plan, with parlour and three bedrooms. Houses with four bedrooms were contrived by placing the extra room over the through-archway provided in blocks of four, and so

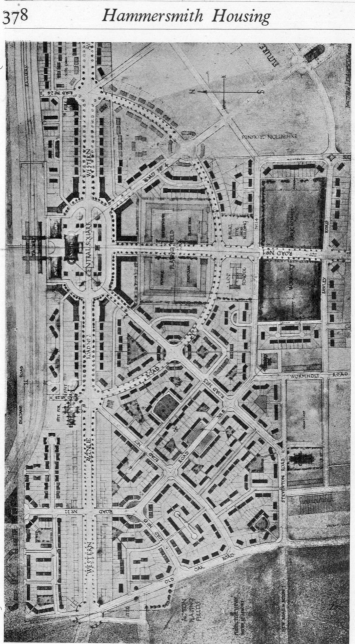

477.—PLAN OF THE HAMMERSMITH HOUSING SCHEME.

*Ernest J. Franck.*

478.—HEMLOCK ROAD, HAMMERSMITH.

saving extra space and foundations on the ground floor. The fireplaces were grouped on party walls, which resulted in good solid chimney stacks penetrating the ridges at regular intervals.

To sum up, the Hammersmith Scheme shows the advantage of team-work in a high degree ; but, needless to say, so marked a success would not have been achieved unless each member of the team had pulled his weight.

# CHAPTER XX

## DUCHY OF CORNWALL HOUSING AT KENNINGTON

The King and Prince of Wales as Housing Reformers—Simplicity and Dignity of the late Eighteenth-Century Tradition— Cottages and Flats by Professor Adshead and Mr. Ramsey.

ALTHOUGH the main purpose of this book is to illustrate multifarious types of cottages for the country and for suburbs, I include some notes on the very urban scheme of the

479.—DUCHY OF CORNWALL ESTATE : BLOCK OF FLATS, CHESTER STREET, KENNINGTON.

380

480.—COTTAGES ON THE NORTH AND WEST SIDES OF NEW SQUARE OFF COURTENAY STREET.

*Adshead & Ramsey.*

Kennington estate, London, because it shows many points of interest. Many of our most attractive villages and little towns owe their charm to the classical lines and modelling of very modest dwellings, and there is no reason why this spirit should not be recaptured in modern housing schemes.

When the King was himself Prince of Wales, he inaugurated a far-reaching scheme of improvement for the great estate at Kennington which is part of the property of the Duchy of

481.—THE LATE EIGHTEENTH-CENTURY TRADITION.

Cornwall. He has always taken, not a perfunctory, but a real and practical interest in all reasonable projects of social reform, in which housing takes so prominent a place. The Kennington property was occupied by working-class tenants and the houses left a great deal to be desired. The Prince, as he then was, decided not merely to patch here and rebuild there, but to create *de novo* an area of buildings which should be worthy of their ownership and establish a dignified standard for the rebuilding of town dwellings. As the problem was not only concerned with the provision of the best sort of domestic architecture,

482.—LOOKING DOWN COURTENAY STREET.

but also with the replanning of a district, there was a peculiar fitness in the choice of Professor Adshead as architect for the scheme. He is one of the major prophets of to-day in town-planning matters, and has exercised a large influence on the rising generation of architects by his educational work. To him and his partner, Mr. Ramsey, warm praise must be given for approaching the Kennington problem in so large a spirit. The present Prince of Wales, on succeeding to the Duchy of Cornwall, showed no less enthusiasm in the fulfilment of his high duties. Not only as one of the great landlords of London, but as one of the largest holders of agricultural land in the west of England, His Royal Highness has been zealous to develop the properties of the Duchy for the benefit of the tenantry and, in the case of rural districts, for the increase of the productivity of the land. This policy has been finely carried out by the Council of the Duchy, and by its able secretary, Sir Walter Peacock, K.C.V.O.

Figs. 479 to 483 show the admirable simplicity and dignity of the buildings at Kennington. For many years there was a feeling that town architecture ought to be remodelled on rural lines—that we should adopt a jumble of picturesque breaks and gables in place of the air of urbane sobriety, long parapets and balanced fenestration which we inherited from the eighteenth century. This ill-considered fancy has been responsible for the freakishness of modern suburbs, with their restless welter of materials and colours. At Kennington the thread of the older classical tradition has been picked up again, and the buildings are cast in a sober mould which is seen to be not only truly urban in character, but urbane in the right sense of the word. The architects have adopted the Adam manner for such patches of decoration as they have employed, well and sparingly, to give relief to the plain masses of brickwork. The old and crowded tenements have given place to a new scheme of streets and quadrangles, laid out on spacious lines, but without that striving after high ground-rental values which drives the ordinary builder to extend his crowding upwards by creating blocks of flats of six or seven storeys.

Flats have been provided, but the buildings are mainly of two or three storeys. The new square off Courtenay Street is a delightful creation, with its simple trellised porches and the lower windows fitted with glazing bars that make the pointed upper panes " gothical " in the fashion beloved about 1780.

Some of the blocks (e.g. in Chester Street) have modest classical porches with stone columns, and the balconies are fitted with iron railings in delicate patterns of diamond and fret which Cottingham did much to bring into popularity more than a century ago.

483.—FLATS IN UPPER KENNINGTON LANE AT THE ENTRANCE TO COURTENAY STREET.

C C

The estate is not only a fine symbol of the profound public spirit of the King and of his Heir Apparent, but also a pattern for the development of town estates on healthy, ordered, artistic lines. It is time to be done with the nonsensical idea that classical treatment is "un-English." Robert Adam, in whose steps the architects of the Duchy Estate have walked, based his art on classical models indeed, but translated them into the vernacular with so just a sense of national character and needs that the result is as rightly British as anything can be. It must be borne in mind, however, that urban housing by landlords, less well able to consider the dignities than was the Duchy of Cornwall, cannot ordinarily take so charming a shape as Kennington. We may also expect that the influence of foreign countries will have its effect here in buildings which rely not so much on æsthetic tradition as on the austere efficiency that comes from the logical use of new materials and methods. We must look to the twentieth century to yield new traditions for the future, not merely to re-create old ones. But, leaving aside æsthetic considerations, it is to be hoped that the striking success of the Duchy Estate will be pondered well by those who have to do with the re-modelling of our urban areas, so that, when a serious start is made with the problem of slum-clearance, the town planning of the immediate future may produce not parodies of villages but an ordered architectural expression of the best city life.

# LIST OF ARCHITECTS' NAMES AND ADDRESSES

*The following are the names and addresses of architects whose work is illustrated in this book :*

ABERCROMBIE, M.A., Prof. L. R., University of Liverpool, Liverpool.
ADSHEAD AND RAMSEY, 46, Gt. Russell Street, W.C.
ASHBEE, M.A., C. R., Godden Green, nr. Sevenoaks.
AYRTON, O. MAXWELL, 3, Verulam Buildings, Gray's Inn, W.C.
BARKER, A., County Land Agent, Kent C.C.
BARNSLEY, SYDNEY H., Sapperton, Glos.
BENNETT AND BIDWELL, Letchworth, Herts.
BLOMFIELD, M.A., R.A., Sir REGINALD, 1, New Court Temple, E.C.
BOLTON, F.S.A., ARTHUR T., Soane Museum, Lincoln's Inn Fields, W.C.
BRIERLEY, F.S.A., WALTER H., 13, Lendel, York.
BUNNEY, M.B.E., MICHAEL, 33, Henrietta Street, Strand, W.C.
CAMPBELL, A. HORSBURGH, Director of Housing, Edinburgh.
CHAPMAN, HENRY ASCOUGH, Ministry of Health, Whitehall, S.W.
CHERRY, HAROLD G., High Welwyn, Herts.
CLOUGH, A. H., Castletop, Burley, Brockenhurst, Hants.
COLLINS, ARTHUR H., Collins & Collins, 37, South Audley Street, W.
CRANE, LIONEL F., 94, Church Street, Kensington, W.8.
CRICKMER, C. M., 1, Lincoln's Inn Fields, W.C.
CULPIN, EWART G., Culpin & Bowers, 27A, Bush Lane, E.C.4.
DALE, THOS. LAWRENCE, " Allington," Woodstock Road, Oxford.
DAWSON, MATTHEW J., 9, New Square, Lincoln's Inn, W.C.
DENING, R.W.A., CHAS. F. W., Gaunt House, Orchard Street, Bristol.
DUNN, WM., c/o W. Curtis Green, A.R.A., 5, Pickering Place, St. James's Street, S.W.
ETCHELLS, FREDERICK E., 1A, Kensington Place, W.8.
EVILL, NORMAN, 67, George Street, Portman Square, W.1.
FALKNER, HAROLD, 24, West Street, Farnham, Surrey.
FAREY, CYRIL A., 19, Bedford Square, W.C.1.
FIELD, HORACE, 5, Gower Street, W.C.1.
FORBES AND TATE, 97, Jermyn Street, S.W.
FORREST, F.R.S.E., F.G.S., G. TOPHAM, New County Hall, S.E.1.
FORSYTH AND MAULE, 12, Stratford Place, W.1.
FRANCIS, ERIC C., St. Tewdric, nr. Chepstow.
FRANCK, JAMES E., 1, New Court, Lincoln's Inn, W.C.
FYFE, J. SIMPSON, Wyggeston House, Highcross Street, Leicester.
GILL, MACDONALD, 1 Harc Court, Temple, E.C.

GOODHART-RENDEL, H. S., 60, Tufton Street, Westminster, S.
GREEN, JOHN W., 79, Burngreave Road, Sheffield.
GREEN, A.R.A., W. CURTIS, 5, Pickering Place, St. James's Street, S.W.
W. CARBY HALL AND DAWSON, 42 and 43, Prudential Buildings, Park Row, Leeds.
HAMP, STANLEY H., 126, Wigmore Street, W.1.
W. ALEXANDER HARVEY AND WICKS, 5, Bennett's Hill, Birmingham.
HENDRY, H. DUNCAN, Hendry and Schooling, 43, Doughty Street, W.C.1.
HENNELL AND JAMES, 97, Jermyn Street, S.W.
HIGNETT, CECIL H., Croft Lane, Norton, Letchworth, Herts.
HOBBISS, HOLLAND W., 33, Newhall Street, Birmingham.
HORDER, F.S.A., P. MORLEY, 5, Arlington Street, Piccadilly, S.W.1.
HOTCHKISS, J. M., County Land Agent, Staffordshire C.C.
HOUFTON, PERCY, Chesterfield.
JARVIS AND RICHARDS, 60, Tufton Street, W.1.
KAY, C. J., Bank Chambers, Horsham.
KIEFFER AND FLEMING, 83, Pall Mall, S.W.
KITCHEN, G. H., Compton End, Winchester.
LANDER AND KEMP, Bridge Road, Welwyn Garden City.
LAWSON, WILFRID, Newcastle.
LIPSCOMB, W. T.
LISLE, BERTRAM E., 2, Gray's Inn Square, W.C.1.
LODGE, O.B.E., Capt. THOS. ARTHUR, Rythe Lawn, Thames Ditton.
LONGDEN, R. THRELWALL, St. Edward Street, Leek, Staffs.
LORIMER, A.R.A., Sir ROBERT A., 54, Melville Street, Edinburgh.
LUCAS, T. GEOFFRY, 19, Bedford Square, W.C.
LUTYENS, R.A., Sir EDWIN L., 17, Queen Anne's Gate, Westminster, S.W.
MARTIN, LEONARD, Seymour House, Waterloo Place, Pall Mall, S.W.
MATHEWS, RIDLEY AND PEARCE, 3, Paul's Bakehouse Court, Godliman Street, St. Paul's Churchyard, E.C.4.
MAULE, D.S.O., M.C., Major H. P. G., 12, Stratford Place, W.1.
MAY, C. QUAIFE, c/o E. J. May, 9, New Square, Lincoln's Inn, W.C.2.
MITCHELL, ARNOLD, 17, Hanover Square, W.1.
MOORE, ARTHUR H., 11, Dowgate Hill, Cannon Street, E.C.
NORTH, B.A., HERBERT L., Llanfairfechan, North Wales.
NUNWEEK, ARTHUR, Town Hall Chambers, 87, Fargate, Sheffield.
PARKER, J.P., R. BARRY, Norton Way, Letchworth, Herts.
PARKER, W. J., 97, Jermyn Street, S.W.1.
PEPLER, F.S.I., G. L., Ministry of Health, Whitehall, S.W.
POLEY, EDWIN W., Temple House, Temple Avenue, E.C.4.
POWELL, E. TURNER, 23A, Ebury Street, Eaton Square, S.W.1.
RAWLENCE AND SQUAREY, County Land Agents, Glos.
RICARDO, HALSEY R., 13, Bedford Square, W.C.1.
ROBERTS, Major A. B. L., 126, Wigmore Street, W.1.
ROBERTSON AND SWAN, Edinburgh.
ROYDS, ALAN F., 2, Gray's Inn Square, W.C.1.

Scott, Baillie, Messrs. Scott and Beresford, 8, Gray's Inn Square, W.C.1.
Simmons, Chas. E., Palace Chambers, Bridge Street, Westminster, S.W.1.
Skipper, George J., 7, London Street, Norwich.
Smith, A. Dunbar, 6, Queen Square, Bloomsbury, W.C.
Smith, M. Maberley, Harpenden Wood, Henley.
Starkey, A. P., Dunsmore, South Hill Avenue, Harrow.
Streatfeild and Atwell, 24, Old Buildings, Lincoln's Inn, W.C.
Stuart, John, 79, Duke Street, Chelmsford.
Tipping, M.A., F.S.A., H. Avray, 11, Dorset Square, N.W.
Unsworth and Triggs, 38, Sackville Street, Piccadilly, W.1.
Unwin, Dr. Raymond, Ministry of Health, Whitehall, S.W.
Verity, Francis T., 7, Sackville Street, Piccadilly, W.1.
Warren, F.S.A., Edward P., 20, Bedford Square, W.C.
Watson, Paxton, 125, Pall Mall, S.W.
Weir, William M., 17, Victoria Street, S.W.1.
Welch, Herbert, 7, New Square, Lincoln's Inn, W.C.2.
Willcocks and Greenaway, 11, Friar Street, Reading.
Williams-Ellis, Clough, 226, Ebury Street, S.W.1.

# INDEX

NOTE.—The LARGE numerals indicate ILLUSTRATIONS of the subject indexed, and refer not to the figure numbers, but to the PAGES on which illustrations will be found. The SMALL numbers INDICATE REFERENCES IN THE TEXT.

Printed in Great Britain by
Butler & Tanner Ltd.,
Frome and London